Neo-natio

Neo-nationalism and Universities

Populists, Autocrats, and the Future of Higher Education

JOHN AUBREY DOUGLASS

WITH CONTRIBUTING CHAPTERS BY
Brendan O'Malley
Wilhelm Krull and Thomas Brunotte
Marijk van der Wende
Karin Fischer
Bryan E. Penprase
Igor Chirikov and Igor Fedyukin
Elizabeth Balbachevsky and
José Augusto Guilhon Albuquerque

JOHNS HOPKINS UNIVERSITY PRESS | *Baltimore*

Johns Hopkins University Press
2715 North Charles Street
Baltimore, Maryland 21218-4363
www.press.jhu.edu

Library of Congress Cataloging-in-Publication Data
Names: Douglass, John Aubrey, author.
Title: Neo-nationalism and universities : populists, autocrats, and the future
of higher education / John Aubrey Douglass.
Description: Baltimore, Maryland : Johns Hopkins University Press, 2021. |
Includes bibliographical references and index.
Identifiers: LCCN 2020052737 | ISBN 9781421441863 (paperback) |
ISBN 9781421441870 (ebook) | ISBN 9781421443201 (ebook open access)
Subjects: LCSH: Nationalism and education—Case studies. |
Higher education and state—Case studies. |
Education, Higher—Political aspects—Case studies.
Classification: LCC LC71 .D68 2021 | DDC 379—dc23
LC record available at https://lccn.loc.gov/2020052737

A catalog record for this book is available from the British Library.

Special discounts are available for bulk purchases of this book. For more information,
please contact Special Sales at specialsales@jh.edu.

Johns Hopkins University Press uses environmentally friendly book materials, including
recycled text paper that is composed of at least 30 percent post-consumer waste,
whenever possible.

CONTENTS

Neo-nationalism is a term that describes the rise, and in some cases revival, of extreme right-wing movements in key areas of the world, often characterized by anti-immigrant and xenophobic rhetoric; economic protectionism; constraints on civil liberties; attacks on critics, including journalists and academics; denial of science related to climate change and the environment; and the emergence and empowerment of demagogues and autocrats.

As in past right-wing movements, economic dislocation and status anxiety play an important part in fueling political support for modern-day adoptions of nationalism. But today's breed of right-wing populism has the addition of three accelerators: (1) the postmodern pace of globalization and technological change that generates economic uncertainty for many, (2) the pace of immigration and demographic change, and (3) the ubiquitous use of social media and technologies that bypass traditional forms of media and that allow for increased surveillance and targeting of political opponents. And it appears that the COVID-19 pandemic has emboldened many nation-states, and their autocratic-leaning leaders, to further restrict free speech and mobility, and to bolster self-supporting conspiracy theories.

Geopolitical events play a role in this story. The unstable political environment in the Middle East and northern Africa led to a surge of political and economic refugees; the aftermath of the 9/11 terrorist attacks on New York's World Trade Center raised tensions between nations and generated increased visa restrictions; and the onset of the Great Recession brought increased economic disparity and, in some nations, the pursuit of severe austerity policies that hurt the most economically vulnerable.

This collection of essays offers the first significant examination of the rise of neo-nationalism and its impact on the missions, activities, behaviors, and productivity of major leading national universities. This book also presents the first major comparative exploration of the role of national politics and norms in shaping the role of universities in nation-states, and vice versa, and it discusses the circumstances and ways in which universities are societal leaders or followers.

In the modern world, universities are institutions that promote both national development *and* global integration—codependent pursuits, particularly for research universities. Yet in a number of important national examples, the contemporary political environment poses a major challenge to the societal role of universities.

In China, Hong Kong, Russia, Hungary, and Turkey, for example, there are increased attacks on civil liberties and free speech, and academics are being fired or jailed. In Brazil, universities are viewed by the Bolsonaro government as hubs of sedition. In the United Kingdom and the United States, anti-immigrant rhetoric and visa restrictions have consequences for the mobility of academic talent. The elongated and often confusing negotiations and final late December 2020 Brexit agreement with the European Union, just days before the deadline, brings into question the fate of Britain's close research links with the EU and the prospect of a severely altered flow of international students and talent to the UK. Academic research that runs counter to neo-national ideologies or the economic interests of a ruling oligarchy are often portrayed as simply politically biased opinions and "fake news."

Three themes emerged in organizing this book. One is that, historically, universities played an important role in nation building and in shaping or being shaped by various forms of nationalism, and they continue to do so. Geography, and nation-states, still matter in understanding the organization, behavior, and status of universities. Indeed, as discussed in chapter 1, universities can be conceptualized largely as extensions of the nation-state. In this view, the national political environment and governments, past and present, are the most powerful influence on the mission, role, organization, and effectiveness of universities and the higher education system to which they belong—more influential than internally derived academic cultures or globalization and international norms of university management. As I note in the first chapter, universities are subordinate to and usually a participant in the national political ecosystem; they are rarely outside of it, even if many still cherish the concept of the ivory tower and seek to protect their autonomy. Hence, their internal worlds, as well as their international networking opportunities, are largely determined by prevailing political norms and are exemplified in the extreme by the controls exerted by neo-nationalist and autocratic governments.

A second and related theme is that neo-nationalism has different meanings and consequences for universities in different parts of the world, depending on their historical role, their academic culture, and the current political context in which they must operate. For example, while the neo-nationalist policies in the United Kingdom and United States are strongly anti-immigrant, with an impact on international student enrollment, China and Russia, each with its own form of revivalist nationalism, are actively recruiting students from abroad—albeit from selected parts of the world as part of a conscious geopolitical effort at influence and power. In the case of China and Russia, after a period of liberalization, there is now a decided shift toward the repressive practices of the past that is intended to eliminate criticism of the ruling regime, often abetted by university administrators.

The third theme is that the isolationist, anti-globalist leanings of neo-nationalist governments have a significant impact on universities, which are inherently globally engaged institutions. The impact is not only felt in illiberal democracies. In Europe, for example, restrictions on civil liberties, including the persecution of academics, affects the global flow of talent mobility. One version of this story is the flight, or attempted flight, of students and faculty from repressive governments, such as those of Turkey, Hungary, and Poland. The United Kingdom and the United States provide another example: in the wake of Brexit and during Donald J. Trump's presidency, both countries placed new restrictions on international faculty and graduate students attempting to obtain visas to study and pursue research. Trump instituted a ban on students from a group of largely Muslim-populated countries, and his administration's concerns with academic espionage led to new barriers to collaborative research with international colleagues.

To decipher and describe the complexity of neo-nationalism and its impact on universities, the chapters in this book are organized as a series of national and pan-national case studies that reflect a range of neo-nationalist movements: the United Kingdom and Brexit; Trumpian neo-nationalism in the United States and its legacy; Turkey under Recep Tayyip Erdoğan; China under Xi Jinping; Hong Kong and Singapore; Vladimir Putin's Russia; Jair Bolsonaro's Brazil; a comparative look at Germany, Hungary, and Poland; along with a larger consideration of trends in the European Union and an assessment of the impact of neo-nationalist movements on global academic talent mobility.

The number of case studies could have been expanded to include South Africa with a leftist form of populism, to Narendra Modi's Hindu nationalism, to more extreme examples, such as the Philippines under Rodrigo Duterte; Venezuela under Nicolás Maduro, where nationalism is used to suppress political opposition; Iran under the autocratic rule of a theocracy; Egypt under a military dictator; or even North Korea.

The case studies chosen, however, provide enough of a window onto the varied realities of neo-nationalist movements, broadly defined, that are affecting universities today. I also consider this book to be exploratory, as neo-nationalism is both a complex and a fluid topic— one that is best initially studied by focusing on a selected group of nation-states and regions. The content is also influenced by whom I could recruit to seriously study a spectrum of nationalist movements. To be frank, it would be difficult to find an expert on China or Turkey from those countries because of their records of reprisals against criticism.

In approaching each case study, contributing authors, all with considerable knowledge in the subject of their chapter, were asked to consider five policy realms:

Academic Freedom and Civil Liberties: How and to what degree are national governments restricting or influencing freedom of speech and teaching and learning within universities?

Autonomy and University Governance: To what degree are governments seeking control of and restrictions on universities?

Talent Mobility and Immigration: What emerging national policies are influencing the inflow and outflow of academic and student talent?

Learning and Knowledge Production: How are current or potential restrictions, sanctions, and government controls influencing knowledge production and societal reflection?

International Engagement: How do nationalistic government priorities shape and possibly restrict the ability of universities to engage with the international community?

These are complex questions, and contributors often focus on only one or two of these policy realms.

This book was conceived prior to the COVID-19 outbreak that significantly altered global and national commerce, exacerbated socioeconomic inequality, and created significant uncertainty about how universities will operate. At the time of writing this preface, it appears that universities, and schools in general, will be more reliant on online course instruction and less on in-person classroom experiences—a trend already in the making. Talent mobility is also altered, at least in the short run, with visa restrictions and personal choices by international students not to travel abroad, or to avoid hotspots where COVID-19 is more prevalent, often corresponding with nation-states that failed to effectively constrain the virus. Faculty mobility is part of that story: fewer international hires, fewer travel options. The pandemic also has altered research activity, from new constraints on international collaborations to how labs are operated.

The full impact of the COVID-19 pandemic, in the short and long term, cannot be fully assessed in this book. One can hope, and perhaps assume, that new therapies and the rollout of effective vaccines will mean a return to a new form of normalcy, in society at large and for universities. One can also hope that the financial impact of the pandemic will eventually be mitigated, despite serious short-term implications for the funding of national systems of higher education. Chapter authors were asked to update their contributions as best they could to assess how COVID-19 is affecting their national case studies.

My introductory chapter is meant as a way for the reader to gain a larger theoretical framework for understanding the spectrum of neo-nationalist movements in which universities operate, ranging from various forms of populism as a political movement, to the formation of illiberal democracies, and finally as vehicles for retaining and enhancing authoritarian power—or what could be termed state-led nationalism. The chapter begins by presenting a brief discussion of the modern concept of nationalism, followed by observations regarding the historical role of universities in nation building. It then explores a model for analyzing the role and impact of neo-national movements and government policies, and discusses the question of when universities are leaders or followers: When are they agents of social and economic change or agents reinforcing and supporting an existing social and political order? Depending on the national context, universities can also hold an intermediate position, sometimes resisting the worst aspects of nationalism through a kind of inertia, waiting for a later time to emerge as a social leader.

There are admittedly challenges to writing about neo-nationalism and universities. As noted, it is a fluid topic, subject to rapidly changing world and local events, including the pandemic. At the time of completing this book, there are indicators of ebbing of neo-nationalist movements in some parts of the world—in Italy, in Austria—where nationalist, anti-immigrant political parties recently experienced electoral losses. With the election of Joseph R. Biden Jr., the United States seems to have turned a corner; many of Trump's errant higher education policies, including repeated attempts to eviscerate the federal budget for research and financial aid, will prove ephemeral. And with the belated Brexit agreement with the European Union in late 2020, some form of clarity for universities, for good and bad, may follow the long period of uncertainty in the United Kingdom.

Then again, China and Russia, Turkey and Hungary recently increased constraints on civil liberties. In each of these case studies, progress toward a more open society was reversed, often marked by a return to autocratic practices of the past, but modernized. China, for example, is quickly developing artificial intelligence and other technologies to surveil the behaviors and to constantly assess the loyalty of its 1.4 billion people, academics among them. The Communist Party is exerting greater control over the management of Chinese universities and is prioritizing patriotism over academic independence. COVID-19 has further strengthened Xi's resolve to exert control over civil liberties, often jailing critics. At the same time, the student-led demonstrations in Hong Kong appear to be faltering under a new wave of crushing repression. In the midst of the pandemic, Beijing passed a national security law in July 2020 establishing new powers to crack down on dissidents, including university students and faculty in Hong Kong.

On the other side of the world, substantial numbers of Turkish academics were fired from their jobs under flimsy charges of sedition. They were barred from further employment, had their passports confiscated, and remain in a state of limbo with no sign of a resolution. Brexit is also becoming a reality, with the full extent of its consequences to be seen. The United Kingdom may be in the process of dissolution, for one. But more to the point, ending membership in the European Union will mean that British universities will be cut off from some, but apparently not all, EU research funding; they will face new barriers to collaborative research and attracting international talent; and their funding models, highly dependent on fee-paying international students, will come into question.

The global trajectory of neo-nationalism is hard to determine. One might surmise, however, that an anticipated downturn in the world's economy, with recessions or depressions in developed as well as developing economies, might exacerbate extreme nationalist movements. Perhaps more certain is that the scars of the most extreme examples of neo-nationalism on the role and operation of universities—such as in China with the jailing of Uighur academics, and in Turkey with the mass firing of academics—will remain for decades. There is the human toll as well at the toll on the culture and behaviors of universities, including the ideal of independence in teaching and research that is the hallmark of the best universities.

Another casualty of the era is the validity of science and expertise, in academia and elsewhere, manifest most importantly in the denial of climate change on ideological grounds and assertions that the COVID-19 virus was a hoax. Neo-nationalist discourse tends to consider academic research—and facts—hopelessly politically biased and, hence, part of the fake news machine of the opposition. Today's factual relativism adds to the degradation of public institutions, creating obstacles to the identification of real societal and environmental challenges, and the search for solutions.

What can universities do to combat the worst aspects of neo-nationalist movements within their own national contexts? This returns us to the concept of when universities are societal leaders and when they are followers. Student-led protests in Hong Kong are reminiscent of other major periods of student protest, often with complicated and unexpected results. Universities can be conduits for pushing society toward substantial change—like student protests in support of the civil rights movement in the United States—but they can also result in further oppression: the Tiananmen Square uprising led arguably to an even more conservative Communist Party leadership in China, paving the way for Xi's rise to power. Academic research can lead to breakthroughs that improve human health and well-being in a nation; it can also contribute to the development of a surveillance state or provide basic research that supports what President Dwight D. Eisenhower called the military-industrial complex in the United States.

The larger reality is that universities, as noted, are part and parcel of the national context in which they operate. They are most effective in instituting change when they have the political and public support to pursue their mission of teaching, research, and public service relatively independently. Under severe autocratic regimes and illiberal democracies, universities have little room to be a force for progressive change.

A number of the chapters do discuss how universities can pursue greater interaction with society with the goal of increasing their value to the societies that sustain them and to help mitigate reactionary political movements. This includes demonstrating to a larger public the value of having international students and staff at universities and the positive impact, economic and otherwise, they have on local communities, as well as necessity of collaborative research with international colleagues in finding solutions to global challenges, from climate change to preventing future pandemics. There is also a need for universities, and academics specifically, to be better communicators regarding their research findings. Indeed, most universities are not doing enough to engage with the national and regional stakeholders that give them life and meaning, or to convey the importance of international exchanges or the role of their universities as agents of progress.

Arguably, the pursuit of many universities to improve their international rankings, largely based on a narrowly defined band of research productivity, distracted them from their larger purpose and influence within their own national and regional context. Government policies and funding fed into a ranking frenzy that devalues, for example, research and public service activities that improve the life and environment of local communities. There is much room for innovation. Universities should generally pursue strategies to expand their societal impact and their links with key stakeholders.

Universities can be agents of change. But one must again recognize the limitations universities and their students and faculty have in shaping national cultures that embrace radical right-wing, nationalist movements or that operate under autocratic governments. They need the help not only of the global academic community and the array of nongovernmental organizations that, for example, monitor and condemn blatant violations of academic freedom. They need the support of government leaders and the political pressure that can come only from major democracies.

These same political leaders additionally need to espouse at home the value of international engagement, generally but also in specific reference to universities; they also need to support through government policies and money the promotion of international research collaborations and exchange programs, as well as champion the importance of science and academic research. The COVID-19 pandemic, and the rapid and successful search for therapies and vaccines, should elevate in the public mind, and the minds of national leaders, the value of shared data and research findings, scientific expertise, and international academic cooperation. Combatting the worst aspects of neo-nationalist rhetoric requires not only an alternative and persuasive narrative, but a collective and international effort.

This publication was made possible by a generous grant from Carnegie Corporation of New York. Funding allowed me to organize a conference on the book's theme in November 2017 that provided an initial scan of neo-nationalist movements throughout the world and how universities were coping with often significant attacks on the autonomy of institutions and on academic freedom. The conference helped to identify an initial cohort of chapter contributors. I also want to thank Greg Britton, Kyle Howard Kretzer, and their colleagues at Johns Hopkins University Press, and copy editor Carrie Watterson, for helping to guide the transformation of the initially submitted manuscript into this book.

JOHN AUBREY DOUGLASS
University of California, Berkeley

Neo-nationalism and Universities

1

Neo-nationalism and Universities in Historical Perspective

JOHN AUBREY DOUGLASS

UNIVERSITIES ARE EXTENSIONS of the societies that give them life and meaning. Beginning in earnest in the early 1800s, the modern university emerged as part and parcel of the modern nation-state. Today, the forces of globalization tug and pull at the reality of universities as national enterprises, but it remains clear that nation-states still matter in shaping and directing domestic institutions and economic policy. All globalism is, in reality, manifest at the national, regional, and local level.[1] The onset of the COVID-19 pandemic, while a global event, actually reinforced the power and importance of the nation-state.

But what is nationalism? What role has it played in the development of universities and in their historical and contemporary roles in the societies they are intended to serve? The following provides a brief discussion of the modern concept of nationalism followed by observations on the historical role of universities in nation building.

Concepts of Nationalism

Nationalism is found in nation-states with distinctly different political cultures: from the authoritarian forms of government in Soviet Russia and China to republics such as the United States and France. It can manifest as conservative efforts to preserve a dominant culture, often defined by ethnicity, language, and religion, within a country; or as a reason and justification for territorial expansion, as in the case of Nazi Germany; or for the breakup of nations such as Yugoslavia. It can also positively contribute to national identity and the building of public institutions and a more inclusive society.

Writing in the 1960s, one of the earliest theorists on nationalism, Ernest Gellner, viewed the rise of nationalism as an organizational and "sociological pathway to a more urban, more industrial world in need of a more formal role for government in the promotion and regulation of economic development." Before the rise of the modern state, the feudal rulers who controlled a specific geographic area usually did not impose cultural homogeneity, as it limited their empires, small and large. The old order began to give way to rapid societal and economic changes on the eve of the Industrial Revolution. Loyalty to a monarchical and usually brutal authority, for example, shifted as societies became more complicated and power more dispersed. In many cases, including the United States, France, Italy, and Germany, the transition was driven by the rise of an economic middle class that demanded a redistribution of political authority and new concepts of republican government.[2] England followed a similar path but retained a monarchy with diminishing authority. Gellner and others saw the rise of formal, publicly funded national education systems as fundamental to the rise of nations and in turn nationalism.

For our analysis, it is important to recognize the difference between the arrival of nation-states as formal organizations and bureaucracies and the emergence of the concept of nationalism—essentially, a sense of belonging to a nation-state formed around a shared sense of values, history, cultural identities, and often language.[3]

One school of thought emphasizes the importance of symbols, myths, values, and traditions—what is termed as *ethnosymbolism*, first articulated by John A. Armstrong in his book *Nations before Nationalism*, published in 1982. Armstrong focused on human identity and argued that "groups tend to define themselves not by reference to their own characteristics but by exclusion, that is, by comparison to 'strangers.'"[4] Other scholars observe different strands of nationalism, depending on variables including concepts and policies related to citizenship, political traditions, and the unified or varied values of its citizens (and noncitizens). Pluralistic societies, such as the United States, provide, in theory, for a multiethnic society, with room to accommodate different senses of nationalism—the product being one of the first nation-states with no state-sanctioned religion and with a population composed largely of succeeding waves of immigrants.

Beyond these generic and somewhat benign theories on nationalism, and to truly understand it as a social and political movement, one needs to also account for the role of contextual factors and the role of institutions and political actors. *Nationalism* unto itself is not a pejorative term.[5] But in terms of twentieth-century world politics, it has tended to equate with extremist populist movements on both the left and the right.[6]

Germany provides an example of different phases of nationalism. Once a group of distinct regions and peoples, it evolved into independent states, including Prussia, Bavaria, Saxony, and Austria. Shared variations of the German language, increased trade, urbanization, a desire for military power in the wake of the Napoleonic Wars, and social upheaval fed the desire for national unity, although with different visions of what that should mean. Not until 1871 was Germany formed as a single nation under a kaiser. With its network of leading universities (Berlin, Heidelberg, Freiburg, and Göttingen) and its industrial and military might, Germany became the dominant power in Europe.

Ambition and Europe's complex web of alliances led to World War I, defeat, and a long postwar economic collapse for Germany. The rise of Nazism, and Hitler as a nationalistic demagogue, fed on social and political chaos, proclaiming the injustice of the Armistice, blaming Jews and communists for a multitude of societal ills, and decreeing Germany's return to a mythical, and race-based, greatness.

Hitler also justified his initial wave of invasions as claiming or reclaiming land occupied by those who spoke a version of the German language—a nationalistic argument that temporarily blinded much of

Europe to a scheme of territorial expansion that would result in World War II. Nazi Germany provides one of the darkest examples of nationalism: economic decline, a sense of national humiliation, and the scapegoating of a subpopulation (the fear of the other) provided a populist platform for an authoritarian politician, the elimination of civil liberties, and the triumph of militarism.

There are, of course, many other illustrative examples that indicate the complexity of nationalism. In China, a reform nationalist movement led by Sun Yat-sen succeeded in ending dynastic control and promised the idea, if not the reality, of republican government in China. The effort to build a new China led to conflicting views on what that should include and eventually resulted in a revolutionary war led by two different nationalists with opposing views and foreign alliances: Mao Zedong and Chiang Kai-shek.

Nationalism also plays a significant role in the formation of empires (in which a dominant power, for example, exports its educational system) as well as in successful campaigns to end colonial rule. In most cases, universities are subordinate to and a participant in the political ecosystem; they are rarely outside of it, even if many retain the concept of universities as autonomous ivory towers.

Universities and Nation Building

What role have universities, and national higher education systems in general, had in shaping modern forms of nationalism? First, and historically, they have played a critical role in educating future civil servants and political and religious leaders of nations. In the movement from elite to mass higher education, universities became one of the primary tools for creating an educated citizenry and talent pool for labor markets.

Second, universities are usually charged with helping to study, preserve, and enhance national cultures. In a number of notorious cases, this also, as noted, fed theories on race and national superiority that supported nationalist movements, leading to catastrophic events. But that is not the only story. Many nations attempting to emerge from their colonial pasts looked to building their higher education systems to help recover, preserve, and further their traditional cultures, values, and knowledge.

Third, university-generated research, from philosophy to the practical application of the sciences and engineering, promotes economic development and, in turn, national identity and political power. The transition from serving primarily as institutions for teaching or the preservation of knowledge to centers for knowledge production is long, emerging first as a core concept at the University of Berlin. It is in the United States, however, and based on European models, that research in the service of the nation gained purchase and widely defined the purpose of its emerging network of public universities, exemplified by the passage of the Morrill Land-Grant College Act of 1862. As early as the turn of the twentieth century, academic research shaped in a significant way virtually every economic sector of a rapidly growing nation. In the Cold War era and since, universities have been the primary drivers of fundamental research that propelled technological innovation and, in turn, national economic and military competitiveness.

And fourth, universities are global actors that serve the state as a form of soft power (see figure 1.1). The international flow of students and faculty among universities has a long history, although with significant differences among nations. Open societies, like the United States, benefited greatly by providing paths for talented students and researchers from other nations to come to its universities, including the exodus of academic talent from Europe in the decade leading up to World War II. Britain's vast empire imposed educational systems around the globe that reflected those established in England created a colonial and postcolonial network of talent mobility. Students in these colonies came to England to attain a university degree, usually returning to their home nation and expanding Britain's influence throughout the world—a matriculation system with former colonies that remains today. A similar Soviet network of allied nations and satellite states sent their students largely to Moscow; this is also a network that persists in an altered form in the post–Cold War era. France has its network of international students from postcolonial nations,

Figure 1.1. The Historical Role of Universities in Nation Building

largely from central and northern Africa. Paris has the largest population of international students of any city in the world.

There are other ways that universities serve the foreign policy objectives of nation-states. With the emergence of the Cold War, in 1946 the United States established the Fulbright Program with the purpose of improving intercultural relations and competence, as well as diplomacy. American students and faculty would go abroad for a period of study and reflection, and foreigners would come to American colleges and universities for the same. At the heart of the program was an attempt to increase the knowledge of Americans of foreign lands and cultures, and to build international networks: "to bring a little more knowledge, a little more reason," stated J. William Fulbright, "and a little more compassion into world affairs and thereby increase the chance that nations will learn at last to live in peace and friendship."[7]

Altruistic intentions aside, the Fulbright Program was also a Cold War strategic effort to learn more about nations both friend and foe. As the technological and foreign espionage competition with the Soviet Union grew in intensity, universities grew in importance as vehicles for generating knowledge and expertise about foreign nations. In reaction to the launch of Sputnik in 1957, the National Defense Education Act of 1958 provided funding for area studies programs at universities specifically focused on developing greater knowledge of nations within the Soviet sphere of influence and areas that might be prone to social upheaval and communist movements. This included bolstering foreign-language programs. Through such efforts, the US State Department developed candidates for a growing diplomatic corps as well as for intelligence agencies like the CIA.

Today, and in an era of increasing international mobility and communication, universities provide an increasingly important pathway for attracting talent and creating future citizens. Most universities are seeking international collaborations in research and best practices for expanding their national or regional role in spurring economic competitiveness, with a resulting impact on their rankings—seen as an international benchmark of quality and influence. At least for a group of leading universities and their governments, their real and perceived international standing is also about national prestige, with foreign policy as well as budgetary implications.

With sharp declines in funding for universities, Australia and the United Kingdom has relied significantly on foreign student enrollment and fees to sustain their higher education sectors; with declining populations, both Japan and South Korea are seeking more international students to help with their future labor needs and to create international networks. And in a familiar form of soft power, China recently launched a significant expansion of its scholarships for foreign students as part of its One Belt One Road campaign to solidify strategic alliances around the globe.

Historical Examples

The earliest universities link their origins and development to the political and religious organizations that gave them life and sustenance. There are few examples in which advanced centers for learning were somehow independent of authoritarian sanction—whether organized religion, a regional monarch, or both. While there are antecedents in Asia and Africa, it is in Europe that a corporate structure for universities emerged in which, either by papal decree or monarchical sanction, institutions had the right to exist for specific purposes.

In their earliest form, universities like the University of Bologna (1088), the University of Paris (1150), and the University of Oxford (1167) were loose confederations of students and student-hired faculty, operating within accepted norms of the ruling elite as quasi-organizations. These and other early "universities" eventually became, in one form or another, entities of the state—through official sanction to operate or by allocations of money and land, and often both. For example, the University of Bologna was granted a charter (the Authentica habita) in 1158 by Holy Roman Emperor Frederick I for the study of civil and cannon law. The Authentica habita set out the rules, rights, and privileges of not only Bologna but also of future universities established in Italy.

Reflective of dramatic societal and economic change in much of the world, universities, and more generally national systems of education, emerged as a significant building block for nascent nations in the early and mid-1800s. In the midst of the Enlightenment and new concepts of reason and the ideals of republican government that led to the French and American Revolutions, universities were vehicles for forming a national identity.

The disciples of the Enlightenment professed the virtue and indeed superiority of human reason over superstition. Its ideals gave rise to the notion of scientific inquiry, the accumulative process of creating new knowledge, and the idea of natural laws. This in turn elevated the sense that society could be shaped for the better. Under the right circumstances and nurturing, government and communities could sustain the goodness and productivity of its citizens. Most importantly, a new and radical thought emerged: the idea of perpetual progress. An unlimited future awaited an enlightened people. Here were the seeds of new ideas about human capital and the possibility of socioeconomic engineering. The key was to provide the individual with not just freedom but knowledge and opportunity.

The following provides brief historical examples of the role of universities in nation building, including Germany, France, the United States, China, and a few observations regarding postcolonial nations.

The Case of Germany

Before the arrival of the unified German state in 1871, Prussia was one of the first governments to provide for free primary education and the professional training of teachers, and to articulate the idea that mass education, and the cultivation of an individual's talents (*Bildung*), was an essential foundation for Prussia's economic and cultural progress. Influential German philosophers Johann Gottlieb Fichte and Friedrich Ludwig Jahn argued that expanding formal education provided the framework for a unified German state—in part, a nationalist movement formed in response to Prussia's occupation and humiliation by Napoleon Bonaparte's logistically superior army beginning in 1806.

From this milieu surfaced Wilhelm von Humboldt's plan for the University of Berlin that professed the ideal of students broadly educated as future citizens. Humboldt's vision included two powerful concepts: the symbiotic nature of teaching and systematic research (*Wissenschaft*) and the importance of sufficient levels of academic freedom for the teacher and university to advance knowledge and expertise. Established in 1809 and formally opened to faculty and students in 1810, the Friedrich Wilhelm University of Berlin, known simply as the University of Berlin, provided an initial model for the modern university, built upon the concept of empowering and socializing the individual and providing for learning and research relatively free from the dogmas of organized religion and political interference. This was then the foundation for creating a more innovative Prussia, and eventually a German state.

The concept of teaching and learning independently of ideological, economic, political, and religious influences, however, was not an invitation for sedition; universities were to be engines for progressive social and economic development that, because of their relatively high level of independence from organized religion that opposed early forms of scientific inquiry, would then best meet the needs of a state attempting to modernize. Influenced by the Humboldtian model and adopting its reforms, German universities generated some of the greatest minds of the nineteenth and twentieth centuries that included, perhaps ironically, two who sought to destroy capitalism and ameliorate what they perceived as the plight of the industrial classes: both Friedrich Engels and Karl Marx attended Humboldt's university, at different times, both later finding refuge in England.

Universities played a part in the eventual unification of Germany in 1871. But their role took a different turn with the onset of World War I and the eventual rise of the Nazi political movement, as exemplified by the fate of Humboldt's university. The Humboldtian model essentially encouraged the concept of the academy, and its self-anointed exclusively male elite cadre of faculty, as necessarily distant from the larger socioeconomic issues facing Germany. And indeed, academics—what Fritz Ringer called the German Mandarins—became hostile to the social processes of industrialization and democratization. German universities, which once played a central in unifying Germany, came to represent the vestiges of the old regime, distant from the needs of society and the tragedies of war and the Great Depression.[8]

By 1933 all German universities were under full political attack by the rising tide of National Socialism. That year Joseph Goebbels spoke in the main square of Berlin's famed university following the burning of some 20,000 books from the university's library. The Law for the Restoration of the Professional Civil Service, passed just two months after Hitler's ascendency as führer, resulted in the firing of 250 Jewish professors and the dismissal and often deportation of countless students and other academics.

In the wake of World War II, the University of Berlin now sat in the Russian-occupied sector of the city. The Russians began their own purge of faculty and staff, appointed ideologically correct academics, and reshaped the curriculum in accordance with Marxist principles. In turn, a substantial group of students and faculty fled to the western sector of Berlin, where they founded the Free University of Berlin. The University of Berlin and the Free University of Berlin became symbols of divergent political environments and governments, one a harsh autocracy, and the other an emerging democracy. After the reunification of Germany in 1989, both remained in the city as separate institutions.

France and Education

France provides another important yet different example of universities as essential for nation building and national identity. The first *écoles normales supérieures* for the training of teachers and government officials were established during the French Revolution, eventually emerging as the pathway for a new class of public servants and elites. Established in 1794, the École Polytechnique also has its origin in the era of the revolution, as a military academy that included the first formal engineering education and that, in turn, fed Napoleon's pursuit of an empire throughout Europe. The École Polytechnique's motto: *Pour la Patrie, les Sciences et la Gloire* (For the nation, science, and glory). Similarly, the École normale supérieure was established in 1798 to provide education and research on the values of the Enlightenment, ultimately evolving into the primary elite institution for training civil servants and future academics.

Napoleon recognized the importance of education, along with legal reforms, for building a highly centralized national government thought essential for ending the decades of postrevolutionary turmoil that characterized France. Napoleon initiated a series of reforms, including the establishment of public *lycées* that eventually provided the path to a

Of all our institutions, public education is the most important. Everything depends on it, the present and the future. It is essential that the morals and political ideas of the generation which is now growing up should no longer be dependent upon the news of the day or the circumstances of the moment. Above all we must secure unity: we must be able to cast a whole generation in the same mold.

Emperor Napoleon, message to the Council of State, 1807

future system of state-sanctioned universities that effectively reduced the educational role of Catholic religious orders—once the dominant provider at the primary level. In the new *lycées*, students were taught the sciences along with modern and classical languages; religious topics no longer dominated the curriculum.

In the wake of the first *grandes écoles*, Emperor Napoleon merged an existing network of French institutions that called themselves universities into a new Imperial University, managed centrally under a ministry, with a uniform mission and eventually curriculum and with its number of students dictated from Paris. Napoleon's demand for centralization and control by the state remains an organizing principal of French higher education, modified in the 1890s to again allow for a plurality of universities in principal but not in fact and only recently modified to include greater autonomy by the neoliberal predilections of recent presidents.[9]

A New Nation: The United States of America

No other nation embraced education for nation building more than the United States. Its full force would not emerge until the mid-1800s, in the midst of a bloody civil war. Yet the transformative value of education, and the notion of a national university, was sown in the earliest years of the new republic.

In the years after the American Revolution, a consensus developed among key political actors that a necessary element for ensuring progress, and a functioning democracy, was an increasingly educated citizenry. Influenced by Germany and France, and more significantly by new ideas about human nature and talents, Americans embraced a belief in a decisive if selective role of government and public institutions to shape a new American society. This included the model of the free public common school and the ideal of an American public university that together, in the words of Thomas Jefferson, would generate a "natural aristocracy" to lead the nation.[10]

Altruistic and philosophical motivations aside, other more mundane reasons for establishing schools and universities existed. New states were desperate for institutions that could bind their communities together and promote their affluence. Colonial America was a cultural backwater, a fact that many of its inhabitants were painfully aware of. Education and higher learning offered the hope of cultural development and civility. But how to promote education and in what forms became the focal point of debate. Should it be promoted by a federal government, or left to the states, or simply to local initiative and private benefice?[11]

Benjamin Rush, a native of Pennsylvania and former student at the University of Edinburgh, insisted on the creation of a federal university as the appropriate first act of the new Congress. "Should this plan of a federal university or one like it be adopted, then it will begin the golden age of the United States," exclaimed Rush in a 1788 pamphlet published in Philadelphia. America's first four presidents agreed. James Madison argued as much 14 years later. This new "temple of science" could, in due time, provide benefits of civic leadership to "every part of the community; it might diminish sources of jealousy and prejudice," enhance "features of national character," and promote social harmony.

The admonishments of these politically influential leaders, however, resulted in no act by Congress. The debate and divide over the role of the federal government, resulting in the emergence of Alexander Hamilton's Federalist and Jefferson's Democratic-Republican political parties; the advocacy of newly formed states; and the lack funding meant there would be no single national university. No mention was made in the Constitution of a federal role in education, thereby indirectly granting that authority to the states.[12]

There is nothing which can better deserve your patronage than the promotion of science and literature. Knowledge is in every country the surest basis for happiness. Whether this desirable object will be best promoted by affording aids to seminaries of learning already established, or by the institution of a national university, or by any other expedients, will be well worthy of a place in the deliberations of the Legislature.

George Washington, message to Congress, January 8, 1790

In the early years of the American republic, private colleges dominated, usually as residential colleges in the English tradition, linked to specific religious dominations and largely serving their sectarian constituencies. But by the mid-1880s, most states, particularly those in the Midwest and reaching toward the Pacific, established a new breed of public universities, a movement bolstered by federal legislation. In the midst of the Civil War, Congress passed and President Abraham Lincoln signed the Land-Grant College Act in 1862. Like earlier federal efforts to promote education, the new legislation granted federal land, mostly in the vast stretches of the West, to states to manage and sell. The proceeds were to then fund tertiary institutions that met a national purpose: the emergence of a core group of state-chartered public universities distinct in their governance, in their commitment to broad access, in the scope of their academic programs, and in their commitment to regional economic engagement and public service.

In all, there are today a total of 106 land-grant universities in the United States; the vast majority are public institutions but with some notable exceptions, including the Massachusetts Institute of Technology (MIT). These public universities provided a catalyst for socioeconomic mobility and were leaders in developing comprehensive state systems of education—for example, many public universities were at one time responsible for accrediting state high schools. They also quickly became the primary sources of trained engineers and other professionals, and they pursued research that profoundly shaped America's agricultural

> Each State which may take and claim the benefit of this act, to the endowment, support, and maintenance of at least one college where the leading object shall be, without excluding other scientific and classical studies, and including military tactics, to teach such branches of learning as are related to agriculture and the mechanic arts, in such manner as the legislatures of the States may respectively prescribe, in order to promote the liberal and practical education of the industrial classes in the several pursuits and professions in life.
>
> Morrill Land-Grant College Act of 1862

and emerging industries. Combined with the advent of other public tertiary institutions, like California's invention of the community college, these universities gave meaning to the ideal, if they did not attain the complete reality, of America as a land of opportunity, and they served as a pathway to inclusion in a nation that welcomed immigrants.

The Case of China

In China, the ancient Guozijian (sometimes translated as Imperial College) was an institution of learning open to all via an exam system, located in the capital of each succeeding dynasty, and intended to provide civil servants for the emperor. A shift began in the late Qing dynasty with the increased influence of Western ideas following the First Opium War in the 1840s and the subsequent arrival of missionary colleges. The Guozijian structure eventually gave way to a set of imperial universities, beginning in the 1890s with the establishment of what would become Peking University, that then emerged as a vehicle to further the nationalist movement led by Sun Yat-sen, built around Western concepts of an educated citizenry as a pathway to a Chinese form of democracy.

However, as noted previously, competing political philosophies and a momentous political battle between Communist leader Mao Zedong and Sun Yat-sen's errant disciple, nationalist Chiang Kai-shek, drastically changed the fate of China's universities. The Chinese Revolution of 1949 marked a dramatic shift toward the Soviet model of higher education, in which virtually all tertiary institutions, existing and newly established, were to specialize and serve specific economic sectors as part of a centralized planned economy and to focus on teaching and training under a Beijing-determined curriculum.[13]

The higher education sector in China, originally conceptualized as a key instrument for furthering the Communist regime, then became the target of one of the most potent populist movements of the twentieth century: the Cultural Revolution (1967–1976). Universities and their faculties became a symbol of elitism and imagined sedition. Many institutions closed their doors, and a whole generation of faculty was sent to reeducation camps and forced labor in agricultural fields. The number of students enrolled dropped from an estimated 674,400 to 47,800.

The resurgence of China's higher education sector after 1976 is a remarkable story best understood as a clear mandate of nation building, although with historical legacies that we will return to in the following chapter.

Postcolonial Nations

Finally, there are the examples of postcolonial nations and their governments that have viewed higher education as a vehicle for reshaping society and forming a new national identity. In India, the 1966 Education Commission report proposed that Indian universities should adopt a curriculum to foster national consciousness among students and inculcate some understanding of India's cultural heritage—some have argued to the detriment of developing science and engineering capacity.[14]

South Africa, Brazil, and Mexico each have similar stories of reforming existing colonial-era tertiary institutions or creating new universities to address their complex postcolonial social needs and to elevate their national identity. The 1910 charter of the Universidad Nacional Autónoma de México stated as its purpose "to provide higher education to train professionals, researchers, academics and technicians useful to society; organize and conduct research primarily on national conditions and problems, and spread as widely as possible the benefits of culture." The Universidad de Buenos Aires had a similar mission: "the promotion, dissemination and preservation of culture. It serves this purpose in direct and permanent contact with the universal thought and pays particular attention to Argentina's problems."[15]

This short dive into the history of universities demonstrates their centrality to nation building under the direction of sovereign governments. Usually, but not always, universities were viewed by governments, and their political leaders, as collaborative actors in social and economic development. But that positive relationship in many parts of the globe has frayed over many decades. The rising Far-Right nationalist movements and autocratic governments, and their populist leaders, have tended to view universities as real or potential places of sedition. What are the causes of this shift?

Old versus Neo-nationalist Movements

While the characteristics of neo-nationalism (sometimes also called new nationalism) are similar to historical forms of populist nationalism, the circumstances are different and important for understanding the contemporary political environment in which universities operate. Neo-nationalism is a radical form of populism with specific characteristics, including protagonists leveraging the politics of fear to attack and blame perceived enemies, domestic and foreign, wrapped in the mantle of patriotism.[16] These are predilections of previous forms of populism.

But the causes of today's breed of nationalism (and hence the prefix *neo*) are modern: the rapid pace of globalization leading to economic uncertainty for many, the pace of immigration and demographic changes among and within many countries, and the ability of a new generation of populists and demagogues to use technology and social networks to promote themselves and their movements. This last advent allowed right-wing populists to bypass conventional media, build a following, and create a separate political reality for their adherents. The mainstream media, and the filter they offered, are no longer the primary vehicles for politicians and activists to communicate. In the United States, almost all of President Donald J. Trump's significant policy directives were announced in tweets, sandwiched between vindictive comments and aspersions about political opponents; in China and elsewhere, the state not only controls all media outlets; it now has technologies that offer new paths for monitoring and punishing dissent.

Globalization, and specifically the growth of transnational trade, promised cheaper goods and a rise in living standards for many, but it also led to economic stagnation, job losses, and a decline in the wages of lower- and middle-income for others in the United States, the United Kingdom, and elsewhere. Add to this mix a historic and rapid shift in the demography of many nations, marked by significant immigration, mostly to Western economies, caused in part by the search for jobs as well as attempts to escape war, poverty, and dysfunctional societies.

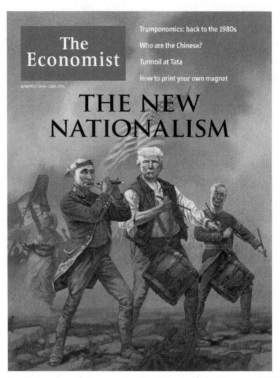

Figure 1.2. Putin, Trump, and Farage on the Cover of the *Economist*, November 19, 2016. Courtesy of The Economist Group Limited

In many parts of the world, largely homogeneous nations and regions (or ones perceived as such) faced the increasing reality of a more diverse population, often with very different cultural and linguistic backgrounds.

Open borders, open markets on an unprecedented scale, and the shock of the Great Recession, all are widely recognized causes of a populist reaction characterized by anti-globalism, nativism, protectionism, and opposition to immigration. In 2016, the *Economist* featured a cover of the bandleaders of nationalism, Vladimir Putin and Nigel Farage, and in the background Marine Le Pen, marching to a drum-pounding Trump in a parody of a famous depiction of American Revolutionary soldiers marching to war: "New nationalists are riding high on promises to close borders and restore societies to a past homogeneity," proclaimed the lead article (figure 1.2).[17]

Today's nationalism is also a means for reinforcing authoritarian rule and solidifying political power. China provides an example where nationalism is leveraged to suppress anti-regime movements and individuals—this after a period of marginal improvements in individual liberties once thought central to China's future economic growth and global competitiveness. Nationalism as a tool for solidifying power is also exemplified in the growth in the number of so-called illiberal democracies: nation-states with populist leaders and governments that increasingly limit civil liberties, justify their power initially through elections whether free or rigged, and usually draw political support through nativist rhetoric and policies.

In the transition from Cold War autocracies, nations without a history or culture built on participatory democracy and civil liberties can slide toward a political environment of corruption and demagoguery; they become lighter versions of the repressive regimes they replaced, often with substantial popular support.[18] Hungarian prime minister Viktor Orbán famously declared in 2014 the end of liberal democracy in Hungary and his intention to build "an illiberal new state based on national values," citing China, Russia, and Turkey as his inspiration and encouraging others to follow.[19] Orbán and other populists feed on a growing alienation from the international order and opposition to the seemingly imposed ideals of liberal democracies: human rights, multiculturalism, free elections, open markets, and, in the case of Europe, the sense of external controls and values of the European Union.

The nonprofit Freedom House, which ranks the political and legal environments of national governments, observed 13 consecutive years of decline in its global measures of freedom. Its 2019 report revealed a significant shift toward repressive policies: "More authoritarian powers are now banning opposition groups or jailing their leaders, dispensing with term limits, and tightening the screws on any independent media that remain. Meanwhile, many countries that democratized after the end of the Cold War have regressed in the face of rampant corruption, antiliberal populist movements, and breakdowns in the rule of law."[20] Although with important variations, this is the case in Hungary, Poland and Turkey, as well as the Philippines, Brazil, Venezuela, Turkmenistan, and the playbook is being revived in Russia and China. One might also point to forms of nationalism that led to the Arab Spring, rooted initially in a call for democracy and economic opportunity in nations with a high number of young people but also, in some instances, resulting in religious conservative governments or simply another autocratic regime as in Egypt.

Yet new forms of nationalism, or revivals of nationalism with new characteristics, are not solely the domain of right-wing politics. Modern nationalism also has a version on the left side of the political divide. In the words of one observer, "The left-wing variant of Neo-Nationalism combines a democratic socialist ideology with a populist discourse, thus expressing the 'voice of the people.' They oppose capitalism on the grounds of inequality and adopt an egalitarian, universalist agenda."[21] In many cases, both Left and Right share anti-globalist views: for example, that the International Monetary Fund (IMF) and multilateral trade agreements are a conspiracy leading to increased levels of inequality.

The COVID-19 pandemic seems to have simply reinforced the isolationist policies of many right-leaning countries, and it has fed extremist views and increased the attraction of conspiracy theories. The virus provided an opportunity to solidify and expand the power of nationalist leaders—as noted previously. The state, in general, or regional and local governments, imposed necessary restrictions on social interaction and mustered resources for medical care. Some nations have done better than others in controlling the virus, ranging from a denial of the reality of the pandemic to the imposition of a form of martial law. In states with strong traditions of civil liberties and democratic elections, there tended to be a middle ground, with social distancing a voluntary act or imposed only as a last resort on businesses and social activities, with citizens either uniting in a common cause or, in the case of the United States, with a significant proportion of the population viewing such restrictions as an infringement on their civil liberties, perhaps a conspiracy by the Left, resulting in belligerence. A pandemic should be an event that unites people in a common cause. Instead, it was used as a political litmus test.

The net result of these most recent events and trends? We have yet to see a significant decline in the number of illiberal democracies or autocratic states, or the demagogues and firebrands that lead them. They are constructed to be self-perpetuating. As a result, universities in these nations are caught up in ever-expanding visa restrictions, in efforts to restrict international research collaborations (in part fed by concerns about intellectual property theft and national security), and in financial difficulties. They are also attacked as bastions of liberal academics and students critical of the state.

In the United States, with the presidential election of Joseph R. Biden Jr., there is hope for a more moderate politics and stronger effort at working with international allies and agencies—a politics that comprehends the realities of climate change and seeks a more collaborative role with the nation's colleges and universities. The United Kingdom may also see the advantages of a more moderate politics as it struggles with the post-Brexit world. But it appears at this time that right-wing populists and autocrats, and their followers, are increasingly powerful political actors; the drift toward illiberal democracies and authoritarian states may simply worsen, at least in the short term. And this will have consequences for the health and vitality of their universities, and in turn for their productivity and role in society as agents of social and economic change.

2

Neo-nationalism and Universities

A Conceptual Model

JOHN AUBREY DOUGLASS

OVER THE PAST two decades, a wave of nationalism has gripped much of the world. Donald J. Trump's surprising 2016 election as president and calls for America First policies; Brexit with its elongated uncertainties; nationalist movements in France, Italy, Germany, Brazil, and India; and the rise of illiberal democracies in Hungary, Poland, and Turkey. Neo-nationalist movements in these and other nations are characterized by some combination of anti-immigrant, nativist, anti-science, anti-globalist, and protectionist sentiments. Like right-wing populist movements in the past, neo-nationalist supporters are often reacting to their own sense of waning political power and perceived decline in social status and economic opportunity. Under autocratic regimes, like those in China and Russia, neo-nationalism has different characteristics: it is a tool to revive older as well as new forms of control and suppression, enabled by new technologies—a form of nationalism redux.

To varying degrees, universities are feeling the brunt of this rise of neo-nationalist movements and governments, usually led by powerful political demagogues. For the purpose of generating populist support and solidifying authority, we have entered an era in which neo-nationalists often attack universities as hubs of dissent, symbols of global elitism, and generators of biased research; academic freedom is being more overtly suppressed, faculty and administrators fired and jailed, and university governance and management altered to ensure greater control by autocratic-leaning politicians.

Universities are at the forefront of both national development and global integration. They will undoubtedly continue to play this dual role. But the political and policy world in which they operate is undergoing a transition. This has an impact not just on universities within autocratic-leaning nations but on global talent mobility and the evolving global ecosystem of universities, where collaboration and exchange are key components in their success and productivity.

With the objective of providing a useful analysis of the interface of neo-nationalism with universities, a number of themes are discussed in this chapter, leading to a hypothesis. As outlined in the previous chapter, one theme is that, historically, universities are essential in nation building and in shaping or being shaped by various forms of nationalism. A second theme is that neo-nationalism has contemporary causes different from those of the past that have different meanings and consequences for universities in different parts of the world, depending on their academic culture and the current political context in which they must operate.

The hypothesis is what I call a *political determinist* view: the national political environment, past and present, is perhaps the most powerful influence on the mission, role, and effectiveness of universities, and the higher education system to which they belong—more than internally derived academic cultures, labor market demands, or the desires of students. Further, the particular national political norms and environment largely, but not completely, determine the internal organization and academic culture of universities and their interface with the larger world. Their level of autonomy, in governance and internal academic management, for example, is to a great extent dependent on the political culture and determinants of national governments.

The emergence of the COVID-19 pandemic in early 2020 appears to simply reinforce the central role of the nation-state, in particular the societal controls of nationalist-leaning governments. The power and authority of national governments, right or left leaning, only increased in response to the pandemic. In many cases, autocratic governments used the crisis to expand their authority, with a direct impact on the operations of universities and the civil liberties of academics and students. China's imposition of its National Security Law passed in July 2020 is a case in point; it provided Beijing a path for an expanded and harsh crackdown on dissidents, including university students and faculty in Hong Kong and elsewhere.[1] Restrictions imposed as a consequence of COVID-19 on social and political gatherings arguably provided an improved environment for Beijing to pass the law and to put a desired end to mass prodemocracy protests. At the same time, China's national response to the virus has boosted nationalism and the claim that its one-party autocratic system of government is superior to Western democracies, specifically a politically chaotic and seemingly weakening United States.

The concept that the political environment is determinative in shaping the mission, organization, and academic culture of universities is not in itself a revelation. Sociologists focus on institutional theory that, in part, sees universities as significantly influenced by their environment and traditions that shape their internal "institutional logics"; economists look at resource dependency that, in the case of higher education, is largely furnished by the state; policy historians chronicle the essential role of governments in chartering and shaping universities to meet political ideals and perceived social and economic problems. In my view, these various analytical approaches are inadequate in themselves in explaining the context and behaviors of universities. They tend to focus on internal universal norms of universities and not on the larger and specific political context driving their organization, mission, and national role.

At the same time, there are weaknesses in the political determinist viewpoint. Political culture and organizations are, after all, the sum of complex social, economic, geographic, and demographic variables over time. There is also a global trend toward organizational convergence in some aspects of university management, including the adoption of "best practices." Yet this political determinist view provides an interesting starting point for assessing the meaning and impact of neo-nationalism, in its varied national forms, on universities and their role in the societies they serve. Political geography still matters.

Hence, in exploring the topic of neo-nationalism and universities, this book is organized as a series of national case studies, including Turkey, Hungary, Russia, China, Hong Kong, Singapore, Brazil, the United Kingdom, and the United States, along with two pan-national essays focused on the European Higher Education Area. We can, in short, test the concept of the pivotal role of the state, historically and currently, relative to other influences on academe. These case studies also provide a rudimentary assessment of the meaning and impact of the worst pandemic since the so-called Spanish flu around the time of World War I. Has COVID-19 accelerated trends in each case study, or is there some other complex outcome?

One can only speculate about the full impact of the pandemic. We do know that the virus required university leaders and academic staff to pursue a major transition to teaching online, addressing probable declines in revenue, implementing hiring freezes and layoffs, and attempting to plan for what lies ahead. In fundamental ways, the teaching, research, and public service activities of universities will be altered. But how will COVID-19 alter the relationship of universities with their national governments? Will it result, in some national cases, in more restrictions on free speech? More disputes and manipulation of science to serve the interests of nationalist leaders and governments? Time will tell.

The following discusses the different national varieties of neo-nationalist movements and governments and how they impact universities. I then briefly explore the question of when universities are leaders or followers in the national context—agents of social and economic change or for reinforcing and supporting an existing social and political order.

A Neo-national Spectrum

Neo-nationalism is primarily a right-wing political movement with, as noted, varying consequences for universities and national systems of higher education. To provide a contemporary view of this movement, the following provides a framework for understanding the spectrum of neo-nationalist environments in which universities operate, ranging from various forms of *populism* as *political movements*, to the formation of *illiberal democracies*, and finally nationalism as a vehicle for retaining and enhancing *authoritarian power*—or what could be termed *state-led nationalism*. Universities have different roles in their societies depending on where a country stands on this spectrum.

Figure 2.1 offers an illustration of this spectrum, with the understanding that there are significant variations. For example, some illiberal democracies border on being authoritarian regimes, characterized by securing nearly indefinite presidential terms, repressing or controlling media outlets, eroding the independence of the judiciary, pawning off state resources to an oligarchy, and persecuting opponents while keeping the semblance of open elections. The distance between each point on the spectrum is simply an attempt to indicate the significant political separation between, for example, nationalist-leaning governments and illiberal democracies.

Where nationalism is driven by populism, it tends to be a grassroots movement, often fed by demagogues who promise to preserve or reclaim an eroding or seemingly lost national cultural and political identity. The golden age myth remains a powerful political tool. In this spirit, neo-nationalist movements are found in the United States, the United Kingdom, France, and the Netherlands, as well as in emerging illiberal democracies, such as Hungary and Poland, that are tearing at the communal concept of the European Union.

What are some of the examples of neo-nationalist movements and their impact on universities? In the United States, Trumpian populism led to a nationalist-leaning federal government that seemed, at times,

| Nascent Populist Movements | Populist Political Parties | Nationalist-Leaning Governments | Illiberal Democracies | Authoritarian Regimes |

Figure 2.1. A Spectrum of Neo-nationalism

to be on the road to an illiberal democracy. Trump attempted to delegitimize the 2020 presidential election of Joseph R. Biden Jr., giving up power reluctantly, and showing that his cult of personality built around neo-nationalist themes will likely remain a potent political force. In what had all the elements of a coup attempt, in the waning days of his presidency, Trump successfully encouraged his angry supporters to storm the nation's capital to halt the ceremonial final count of Biden's victory; even in America, the concept of democratically elected presidents seemed to teeter on the edge of a significant redefinition.

During his presidency, Trump never voiced a coherent policy agenda for higher education besides deregulating for-profit institutions. "Make America Great Again" (MAGA) was the larger agenda, with serious implications for universities. In the first week of his presidency, Trump voiced his hostility toward higher education institutions: he sought media attention by claiming that the University of California, Berkeley, campus was intolerant of conservative speakers and views after a clash of pro- and anti-Trump demonstrators. As part of a larger set of anti-immigrant MAGA policies, the Trump administration pursued restrictions on visas for academics, students and professors alike, and reversed Barack Obama's policies that allowed undocumented youth to enroll in college. The acidic political environment created by Trump eroded the interest of international talent to enter America's universities and private sector. And Trump pursued anti-science policies, repeatedly proposing dramatic funding cuts for the National Science Foundation and the National Institutes of Health, denying the existence of climate change, and initially claiming COVID-19 was a hoax.[2]

Brazil offers another example of a neo-nationalist politician attacking universities. In his successful populist campaign for the presidency, the former military officer Jair Bolsonaro promised to crack down on academic freedom and to curtail the "leftist proselytizing" at universities. He also vowed to abolish affirmative action policies of the former government and to cut funding for Brazil's universities in favor of vocational education—all evidently attractive policies for a significant percentage of the voting public. Since his election, a decided pall settled over the nation's federal and state universities that conjures memories of Brazil's harsh dictatorships. One example: with Bolsonaro's blessing and early in his presidency, police forced the cancellation of a talk entitled "Fighting Fascism" at the Federal University of Grande Dourados and undertook office raids of leftist academics.[3] "There is a climate of tension and of fear," said professor of education Adriana D'Agostini at the Santa Catarina Federal University.[4]

In many cases, nationalism is a tool of the power elite, a way to leverage and shape popular sentiment, and often to limit or control any form of opposition. In Turkey, the solidification of national power by President Recep Tayyip Erdoğan following the July 2016 coup attempt is having a profound impact on civil society, and on Turkish academics. Since the failed coup, under the rubric of their alleged ties with cleric-in-exile Fethullah Gülen, some 8,500 faculty and 1,350 staff members at universities in Turkey were fired.[5] At least 553 university employees and students were taken into custody or named in warrants on suspicion of using an encrypted messaging app to organize anti-government protests, branded as "terrorists" and "coup plotters."[6] Dismissal bars faculty from future government employment and requires them to apply for a new passport. "A climate of fear now prevails in universities, where academics fear making any kind of comment in the classroom about government or politics," noted one Turkish academic who fled the country.[7] But attempts at suppression reach across Turkish borders. Erdoğan's government announced plans to charge Turkish academics living in Germany who signed a petition against military operations against Kurdish militants with cooperating with terrorists.

Hungary's prime minister Viktor Orbán and his government sought the abolishment of the Central European University as part of a nationalist impulse to expunge foreign influences, including CEU founder and American philanthropist George Soros. With a supermajority in the parliament, Orbán's Fidesz party asserted control over the media, religious groups, and the courts and targeted critics, including academics.

In Russia, Putin-style nationalism led to partial reversals of programs once intended to bring academics from outside of the old Soviet bloc back to the Russian Federation and included arbitrary crackdowns on dissidents, leading some important scholars to leave the country.[8] For academics in Russia, there is an increasing awareness of instability, all in the name of sustaining the current order in the Kremlin—a revival of the Soviet era with new and modern characteristics.[9]

In China, one of Xi Jinping's early policy statements was an edict to avoid Western values in the nation's universities, ordering them to "adhere to the correct political orientation" and accept firm party leadership.[10] Prior to this statement, Xi's central government issued Document No. 9 in 2012 outlining a campaign against "seven unmentionables" in Chinese society, including "Western constitutional democracy," human rights, media independence, promoting "universal values" in an attempt to weaken the theoretical foundations of the Communist Party leadership, judicial independence, pro-market liberalism, and "nihilist" criticism of the party's past. In these and other policy directives, Xi sent a clear warning to Chinese academics that the rules had changed after a period of greater civil liberties. Any criticism of the party or national policies is now suspect. "What you are seeing," stated one observer of China at the time, "is a reassertion of ideological control because they feel that colleges and schools are the hotbeds for ideas that potentially could be problematic; ideas of constitutionalism, ideas of liberalism."[11]

Academics always posed a possible challenge to the Communist Party's desire for conformity and loyalty. Mao decimated China's relatively small network of universities by forcing a whole generation of faculty and students into collective farms, in part because of this fear of nonconformism among academics. When China did begin to open up its economy and sought greater interaction with the world, universities in the capital did become a home to a nascent democracy movement. In 1989, student protests in Tiananmen Square focused on demands for greater civil liberties, and they were brutally crushed by government soldiers.

Fast-forward to 2020: student protests in Hong Kong are a reminder of universities as a possible threat to party control. As noted, the COVID-19 pandemic appeared to provide a reason for Beijing to legally restrict prodemocracy protests and then to pass a law that provides almost unlimited authority to jail perceived and real dissidents, seemingly marking the approaching end of the "one China, two systems" promise.

At the same time, the growth in enrollment and academic standing of many of China's leading national universities is a major goal for Beijing. But this now includes increased party control of universities via their governing boards and administrative leadership, renewed pressure for conformity among academics, and increased efforts to control the voice of anyone who dares to speak out, within or outside of China. Xi's government wishes to suppress dissent and criticism of his regime throughout the world. Chinese students are the single largest cohort of international students in the United States, Australia, Canada, and elsewhere. At least before the COVID-19 pandemic, one in three international students in the United States was from China. In both Australia and the United States, government-sponsored Chinese student associations have exerted pressure on academics criticizing China's political order.

For a period leading into 2020, nationalist momentum in Western nations appeared to have ebbed, or at least became more muted. European elections resulted not in Marine Le Pen but Emmanuel Macron as president of France, and Angela Merkel remained Germany's chancellor, although with a larger contingent of anti-immigrant nationalists in the Bundestag. The US Congress repeatedly denied the Trump administration's budget plans to severely cut funding for academic research and student financial aid. And Trump lost the 2020 presidential election.

Perhaps the current wave of neo-nationalism is only a passing phase—a temporary halt and, in some countries and regions, a short-term regression from the inevitable march of globalization and the once-powerful movement toward democratic forms of government. Perhaps Xi's warning to universities is simply an example of two steps forward, one step back: exerting political control to expunge enemies and limit talk of sedition, before again moving toward a more open society. Similarly, Erdoğan's crackdown may be an effort at political stabilization that could set the stage later for reopening Turkish society and perhaps even then restart the country's bid to enter the European Union.

Unfortunately, this more optimistic scenario seems doubtful, in part because nationalism in its more extreme forms has found more strength during the pandemic, not less. Right-wing populists and autocrats retain popular support and are increasingly effective in controlling the media and social networks, monitoring and suppressing criticism, and shaping a nationalist narrative. In many cases, technology is not so much a tool for expanding free speech and networks promoting greater civil liberties, but a means of enhancing the ability of authoritarian-leaning leaders and governments to identify and track their potential and real opposition.

Modeling the Impact on Universities

Since neo-nationalism comes in many different forms and with different meanings and consequences for universities, how might we analyze the range of consequences for universities? Using the spectrum of neo-nationalism offered previously, figure 2.2 provides a model that aligns the contemporary characteristics of neo-nationalist movements and governments with policy variables that impact universities. These are categorized as nascent populist movements, nationalist-leaning governments, illiberal democracies, and authoritarian regimes that, in various forms, use nationalism to solidify their political power.

The different forms of neo-nationalism and policy implications generally build upon one another as you move left to right. Hence, illiberal

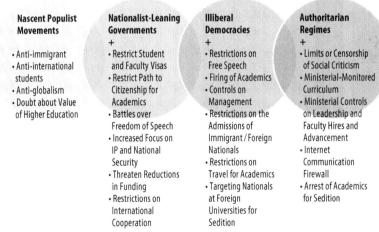

Nascent Populist Movements	Nationalist-Leaning Governments +	Illiberal Democracies +	Authoritarian Regimes +
• Anti-immigrant • Anti-international students • Anti-globalism • Doubt about Value of Higher Education	• Restrict Student and Faculty Visas • Restrict Path to Citizenship for Academics • Battles over Freedom of Speech • Increased Focus on IP and National Security • Threaten Reductions in Funding • Restrictions on International Cooperation	• Restrictions on Free Speech • Firing of Academics • Controls on Management • Restrictions on the Admissions of Immigrant / Foreign Nationals • Restrictions on Travel for Academics • Targeting Nationals at Foreign Universities for Sedition	• Limits or Censorship of Social Criticism • Ministerial-Monitored Curriculum • Ministerial Controls on Leadership and Faculty Hires and Advancement • Internet Communication Firewall • Arrest of Academics for Sedition

Figure 2.2. Neo-national Spectrum and Impact on Universities

democracies characterized by restrictions on free speech, controls on university management (such as the selection of rectors and presidents), and sometimes the firing of academics also include many of the characteristics of nationalist-leaning governments. The model is not intended to imply that there is an inevitable progression from, for example, an illiberal democracy to an authoritarian regime—although that has, in some instances, been the case and is a significant fear for many.

There are nuances and differences among nations with neo-nationalist movements that this simple dichotomy cannot properly reflect. For example, how many nations are truly authoritarian regimes? North Korea would probably be the best example of a true autocracy. China might be viewed as between an authoritarian regime and an illiberal democracy regarding its policies and control over its higher education institutions as well as how it picks its government leadership and asserts economic and social controls over its population. There are multiple indicators of a drift rightward. China has fired and detained academics, as well as civil rights lawyers, and systematically sent a large portion of the minority population of Uighurs into what can best be called labor camps.

After a period of greater academic freedom, President Xi, as noted, has pursued anti-Western rhetoric, placed greater restrictions on access to information generated outside of China, tracked the behavior of its citizens via new technologies, increased warnings against sedition, and made high-profile arrests. For example, China's invention of a Social Credit System uses big data on individuals, businesses, and government officials to track and evaluate their fealty to the Communist Party and to Xi.

When China first began to open to the world, former president Deng Xiaoping stated the dictum, "Hide your strength, bide your time." Now Xi's Chinese Dream includes a nationalist claim that the country is now ready to assert its economic and geopolitical power—to assert its rightful place and to expunge the scars of past Western economic dominance. While the Chinese Dream is intended as a message of empowerment, it has been accompanied by a crackdown on dissidents and the arrest of political rivals of the president. Some hoped the decline in civil liberties was simply part of Xi's initial effort to consolidate power and that the trajectory of greater freedoms would resume later. But that appears not to be the case, with significant influence on the future of China's universities and co-opting the behaviors of students and faculty.

The rhetorical code of China's party leaders is always complicated. There is a push-and-pull quality to China's rising tide of universities—a push by successive ministerial edicts to engage with universities globally, via academic collaborations and partial adoption of management practices that mark the world's best universities. The One Belt One Road policy is a multiregional socioeconomic initiative and a form of Chinese soft-power colonialism that also includes encouraging Chinese universities to engage strategically with academics throughout the world. The pull is Xi's macro-goal of the Chinese Dream that increasingly includes the suppression of any oppositional voices and an anti-corruption campaign that seems a mix of attacking a real problem and power consolidation.

Hungary also seems to bridge the variables listed under illiberal democracies and nationalist-leaning governments. At this time, it does not include significant restrictive government policies on free speech or on the travel of academics. However, the Hungarian government has ordered the ending of academic programs in gender studies and seems bent on placing controls on academic research, including barring research on immigrant populations. In September 2018, the European Parliament condemned Orbán's government for its attacks on the Central European University that forced it to move Vienna, along with a range of civil society violations: from corruption and data protection to assaults on the rights of Roma and Jews. It is safe to say that observers are concerned that Hungary is moving increasingly rightward and that more formal and overt policies to suppress academic freedom will follow.

In the effort to formulate a historic stimulus bill to counter the economic downturn due to the COVID-19 pandemic, Hungary and Poland held the entire EU community hostage, refusing to agree unless language was removed regarding the civil rights demanded of all members.

The budget bill required unanimity among the members. In late 2020, the other EU members equivocated. Orbán's government then received stimulus funding and the National Assembly proceeded to pass legislation that reduced individual freedoms and revised election laws that further favor the Fidesz party.[12]

In the drift to the right, and toward greater control of universities, a pattern emerges: in Hungary, Turkey, Russia, Hong Kong, and elsewhere, neo-nationalist leaders have pursued ways to alter the governance of universities with the objective of directly or indirectly choosing rectors or presidents and other key academic administrators; ministries also seek to influence or control faculty hiring and advancement, find ways to punish dissent, and deny funding for research in areas such as climate change or gender studies thought counter to conservative values and their messaging. This is usually accompanied by increased control and ownership of the judiciary, as well as the media, along with laws that hinder free elections and that also expand the ability of neo-national governments to issue lucrative contracts to supporters in the private sector. Hence, universities are one part of the formula for right-wing leaders to solidify their power.

Followers or Leaders?

In assessing the current and future role of universities in the nation-states in which they function, it is useful to ask, When are universities societal leaders, and when are they followers—reinforcing the existing political order? Returning to the political determinist analysis offered earlier, it seems that national political history and contemporary context are the dominant factors shaping the leadership or follower role of universities.

We often think of contemporary universities, and their students and faculty, as catalysts of societal progress—the Free Speech and civil rights movements, Vietnam War protests, the anti-apartheid movement, Tiananmen Square, and more recently the prodemocracy demonstrations in Hong Kong. Universities can be, and have been, the locus for not only educating enlightened future leaders but also for opposing oppression and dictators. But universities have also proved over their history to be tools for serving the privileged and reinforcing the class divisions of a society.

The global movement toward mass higher education held the promise of universities as agents of socioeconomic mobility and societal rebirth. There are places where universities pushed the boundaries of knowledge and generated societal disruption. But in others they have also been factories for errant theories that reinforce the worst of nationalist tendencies. Universities are unique environments for educating and mentoring free thinkers, entrepreneurs, and citizens with, for example, a devotion to social change, or for creating conformists—or both.

How might we assess whether universities are followers or leaders in their societies? Here I propose a number of variables when considering this question for higher education institutions in a particular country, and the role of a particular university. The first relates to the institution as a vehicle for socioeconomic mobility, which is vital in countries with moderate to very high levels of income inequality—in other words, nearly all nations. This mobility is meant to be inclusive, providing access for a broad range of ethnic and racial groups and genders, within a nation or region.

The second variable is the role of universities in regional and national, and global, research related to social problems like poverty, health, and pollution. This includes basic research on, for example, disease and water quality or social science–based studies on school districts and urban planning, with the expectation of generating practical solutions.

The third and fourth variables are a university's impact on technological innovation and economic development, along with educating a talented labor force and educated citizenry that includes entrepreneurs and those devoted to government and nonprofit employment. We can add to this educating students to be global citizens, in part understanding that it is increasingly important for employability and in part because the process of globalization ties all of us to common ideas and problems, such as global warming.

The public service role of universities is a fifth variable, including the engagement of students and faculty with and in support of largely public institutions and services, such as local schools, hospitals, and local and national governments. University-run hospitals provide perhaps the best example of the intersection of teaching, research, and public service. This role can also include university-run art museums, performance facilities, libraries, and other facilities and forms of engagement with local communities.

A sixth variable relates to the preservation and study of the art, history, and culture of a university's nation or region. This has been one of the central roles of universities, including faculty-led research and writing, but also the collection and organization of archives and, related to public service, university- or community-operated historical museums. The overt effort of past and current authoritarian leaders and governments to control the historical narrative poses challenges for this vital role of universities.

A seventh variable relates to a university's global engagement. This can include research collaborations with foreign universities and their faculty and students, but more importantly it relates to the exchange of academic talent. The number of international students who are enrolled as regular students at the undergraduate and graduate level—as opposed to short-term programs that are often segregated from the main campus curriculum—is one marker of international engagement. Another is the number of foreign nationals on the faculty or engaged in other capacities, like research. To some degree, the presence of foreign nationals strengthens the global perspective of the home campus and can, depending on national policies, add significant diversity of talent to local, regional, and national labor pools. Global collaborative research can, in fact, function as global communities that transcend national political identities. The COVID-19 virus is a great example of universities generating the foundational science and a collaborative global science community that generated therapies and vaccines and facilitating their distribution.

Finally, the eighth variable is the vital role of universities, and their students and faculty, as informed and constructive critics of society.

Critical analysis of the social and political problems of society is, arguably, one of the most important roles for a university and its academic community. Conceptually, academic freedom relates to the right of faculty to voice sometimes controversial research findings or views that broadly relate to their academic field or discipline. But is also includes the right of faculty and students to voice, for instance, criticism of government policies or the behaviors of politicians as citizens.

There are conundrums in assessing a university's leader versus follower role: for example, university research has an association with national security that offers conflicting uses by national governments. On the one hand, universities are positively engaged in efforts to improve cybersecurity for the purpose of protecting the economic life of the nation and the personal security of its citizens; on the other hand, academic science is currently bolstering spying and surveillance capabilities of national governments that are Orwellian—China's widespread use of facial recognition technology to monitor the behavior of its citizens is a case in point.

My view is that universities can be evaluated according to their leadership or follower role. But this requires some sort of weighting to help understand a university's full impact on the society it serves. Only a few universities in the world may claim that they are truly and exclusively global enterprises, with no national or regional constituency. Hence, national and regional service and impact is the paradigm for understanding the leadership or follower title.

Educating a talented labor force and contributing to technological innovation and economic development in a nation or region are all base activities that, in some form, all universities are engaged in, no matter the political context. Similarly, the preservation and study of art, history, and culture has a basic role for every university—although, as noted, autocratic governments often seek to control and subvert the narrative of a nation's history to support their own, often golden age, nationalist myth narrative.

More aspirational is the objective of promoting socioeconomic mobility—a more complex role that depends on the demographics and politics of a nation-state. And among the highest leadership roles: the concept of universities as social change agents, including research related to social problems, public service, and, in my view, most importantly, critical analysis of society.

Hence, in figure 2.3 the eight variables are tiered (one being important base or lower-order forms of societal leadership, and four being the highest order), understanding that this model is simply a conceptual sketch and not meant to fully gauge the extent of university activities. It is designed to assist in the assessment of the leadership role of universities in their particular nation or region.

Note that I do not use or refer to global rankings of universities or the infatuation of many ministries with its close relative, the world-class university (WCU) model. The most influential global rankings focus on research production and related markers of prestige, like Nobel prizes. Doing well in rankings, and in particular citation analysis that favors the sciences and journals published in English, or the number of patents generated (which can be an imperfect marker of economic impact), can be important and desirable only as a narrow indicator of prestige and influence.

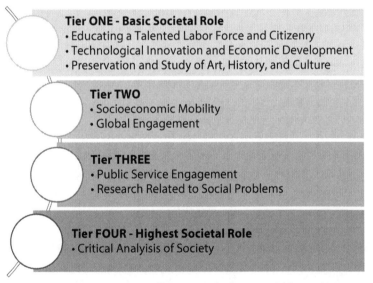

Figure 2.3. Universities as Followers or Leaders: Variables and Tiers

But the ranking and WCU infatuation arguably generates a larger detrimental influence on the leadership role of institutions—devaluing teaching and student learning and driving academic work toward research production goals focused on subjects attractive to journals but not necessarily toward regional social problems.[13] In a conference on the theme of this book, Christine Musselin at Sciences Po worried that the singular concern of many universities with various global rankings was driving them to neglect one of their most important roles in society: developing educated citizens who, in turn, might be a foil for extreme forms of nationalism, whether right or left wing.[14]

I again return to my earlier hypothesis: The past and current national political environment is perhaps the most powerful influence on the mission, role, and effectiveness of universities and the higher education system to which they belong. The national political environment, arguably, has a determining influence on whether universities are leaders or followers—or something in between.

Nation-states with a history of authoritarian rule have sustained higher education systems to reinforce the social structure and political position of the government. In this environment, universities do not have significant autonomy or develop an academic culture openly critical of political leaders. Few have any significant statement or policy related to academic freedom; academic freedom is defined exclusively by the state. Many universities, and hence academics, are also focused on the sciences and engineering, and may consider discussion of significant social and even many scientific problems (e.g., chronic pollution) that reflect poorly on the existing political regime not simply dangerous but unnecessary and probably ineffectual.

Universities and academics functioning in societies with a stronger liberal tradition (e.g., free elections, recognized civil rights, relatively low levels of corruption) have a stronger likelihood of being engaged in critical analysis of society and instilling these values in their teaching, research, and public service activities. Universities also provide a public space for social and political movements that can be progressive or regressive, and sometime extremely disruptive of the institution itself. Examples include the student riots in Paris in the 1960s, the civil rights movement and protests on US campuses, and the recent right-wing speakers at places like Berkeley that generated violence from extreme left-wing groups.

Again, depending on the national context, there is great nuance in how universities actually operate. We might conjecture that many reside in an intermediate sector: exuding elements of being followers and leaders. Further, universities that operate in repressive political environments may foster potent political protests demanding greater civil liberties, often led by students, with a variety of outcomes. In South Africa, portions of the academic community fomented opposition to apartheid that, in turn, generated support from students and faculty, and governments, throughout the world, contributing to a global trend of divestment from businesses in South Africa and political pressure that contributed to the end of apartheid. But in China, student-led demonstrations in April and May 1989 led to a military massacre and more repressive policies imposed by the Chinese government. Hong Kong may, unfortunately, suffer a similar fate.

There are at least two external variables for considering the leader versus follower role of universities. For one, budgets matter. Nation-states with robust and growing economies can invest in and provide the means for universities to be more productive in teaching and research, in public engagement and in their global reach. Economies in decline, or that are developing, often mean significant financial constraints on the services and innovations a university can engage in as societal followers or leaders. And two, universities are part of larger national systems of higher education with differentiated missions within the sector. Often, nation-states historically designated one or more institutions, often in national and regional capitals, as favored in prestige and funding. Often they are allowed to operate outside the ministerial norms for other universities. Most are older institutions, providers of education to a social and political elite. These institutions also have greater flexibility, even within more autocratic nations, to act as leaders.

Canary in the Coal Mine?

Are universities leaders or followers or intermediators in China? In Russia? How about in South Africa and Brazil and Chile? In the United Kingdom in the years leading to Brexit? Or in America during or after Trump's presidency? What is the relationship between the longevity of a university and its role as leader or follower; for example, are universities established for centuries more likely to be leaders or followers, and what have been the conditions for their longevity?

Any careful consideration of these questions requires reflection on the historical role of universities in nation building—political geography still matters.[15] It is also important to stress that the various forms of nationalism we see today are not, of course, entirely new. In Russia, but more so in China, a nationalist revival can be viewed as a historical continuum where all universities, and the economy more generally, remain under one-party governmental control, and where autocratic leaders make the rules. In yet another variation, in Hungary or Poland, recovery from Soviet domination was followed by post–Cold War freedoms but also economic uncertainties, followed by neo-nationalist movements.

Neo-nationalism, and its role in and impact on universities, is also in a process of evolution and devolution. Its power and strength are related to a set of global and national variables, including economic transitions, demographic shifts, new technologies, and broader social factors, including political movements related to race and religion—witness the shift toward Islamic fundamentalism in nations such as Indonesia. This book is an attempt at a snapshot of today's interaction of national politics and policy with universities that may help us peer a bit into the future.

And this leads me to a final exploratory question: Are universities, and more specifically their follower or leadership roles, good indicators for understanding the political nature and trajectory of nations? I think they are and for the following reasons.

Universities are unique social organizations within nation-states. Universities, for example, provide a clear window into the extent of civil liberties allowed in a nation-state. The composition of their student bodies reflects the socioeconomic stratification of society. Their utilitarian role as the primary source of skilled labor and often as a significant player in applied research, provides insights into the composition and future of economic development. Their governance and management structure, including level of autonomy and legal authority to manage their affairs, offers a glimpse into the relationship of a government with other public and private organizations and businesses. The extent of their global engagement—their ability to attract and retain international talent (students, faculty, and staff), their participation in collaborative research across borders, or the freedom of academics to travel—offers a glimpse into political priorities and the fears and opportunities perceived by national leaders and governments.

Global events, like the COVID-19 pandemic, create a more complicated picture of the future. But it seems that the pandemic only reinforces the concept that universities are a barometer of the socioeconomic health of nation-states. Universities, in effect, are a proverbial canary in the coal mine.

3

The Mystery of Brexit

Tumult and Fatigue in British Higher Education

BRENDAN O'MALLEY

THE UNITED KINGDOM embraced a particular form of neo-nationalism, focused largely on regaining control over immigration and gaining greater sovereignty over trade and similar economic issues by leaving the European Union. The 2016 vote to do so created huge uncertainty in three areas of policy making and university operations: first, research funding and international collaborations facilitated by the EU Horizon 2020 program, in which UK universities play a leading role; second, the UK market for international students and its ability to retain and attract top academic talent; and third, UK participation in the EU Erasmus+ study and exchange scheme for students and staff.

Brexit in any form brings into question the financial viability and future research productivity of Britain's universities, yet no serious proposals were made by pro-Brexit political parties to address them. This reflects the general approach of the Brexit movement, which ignored many of the predicted consequences of the dramatic break from the European Union. But more specifically, little attention was paid to the future of the UK network of universities, and the components and health of its knowledge-based economic sector.

The Brexit movement included populist rhetoric on immigration, exploiting the chaos of the refugee crisis in Europe and the ignorance of voters regarding the United Kingdom's role in Europe; it played on a popular resentment of being told by the European Commission what to do; and it painted a wildly optimistic view of how easy it would be to succeed on its own after leaving an economic bloc six times its size in terms of GDP. And as in the United States, facts and expert opinion, including from the academic community, about the likely negative impact of Brexit were portrayed as politically biased. The majority of expert opinion warned of serious economic consequences if Britain voted to leave. But academic expertise was politically weaponized, as epitomized by Leave leader Michael Gove's claim that the British public had "had enough of experts," as well as the conspiratorial "Project Fear." Academics and universities were viewed as part of the "conspiracy by the elite" to stop the British people from "taking back control." Brexit proponents skillfully used social media for propaganda purposes with fake and misleading news.

The post-Brexit world poses a major threat to the health of the UK university sector. Although some Brexit leaders argued they were seeking divergence from Europe in order to increase links with the rest of the world, the movement largely professed isolationist goals antithetical to the mission of universities. With the deadline for a final Brexit deal with European Union only days away, in December 2020 an agreement was reached that included the UK pulling out of the EU's Erasmus+ program yet allowed UK researchers to participate in most of the Horizon Europe research program with a few exceptions.

This chapter discusses the role of neo-nationalism in the lead-up to the referendum, the long period of uncertainty it presented for UK universities, and the potential impacts on universities under the Tory government led by Boris Johnson. In the general election in December 2019, Johnson ran on the campaign theme of "Getting Brexit Done." But as in the past, pro-Brexit leaders failed to articulate what it would mean for Britain's economy and institutions. The post-Brexit world will likely require a reorganization at the ministerial level of funding mechanisms for research and new policies and programs for promoting international collaborations and for attracting and retaining international talent.

Populism versus Internationalism

Neo-nationalism is in part a populist reaction to the economic and social forces of globalization. Across the United States and Europe, including the United Kingdom, populist politicians—from Donald J. Trump in the United States, to Boris Johnson and Nigel Farage in the United Kingdom, to Viktor Orbán in Hungary—advocated closing or restricting the flow of refugees and migrants, attacked the institutions of multilateralism, and blamed globalization for destabilizing their communities and threatening their culture and national identity.[1]

The Brexit movement has many of the characteristics of other neo-national movements, but it includes the added complications of disengaging from the European Union. In the United Kingdom, people in many parts of the country felt left behind, pained by years of austerity, and powerless in the face of forces beyond their control, which, they believed, created uncertainty over the future of their industries, key services, and way of life. They balked at global companies being able to shift jobs from country to country, ripping the heart out of local communities, while avoiding paying their fair share of taxes; they felt anger at a world that seemed to care more about the freedoms of migrants and government benefits for asylum seekers than their own deprivation; and they saw universities and experts who preached against Brexit as part of that other world of economic success in which they did not share.

Many Leave supporters also yearned for the days of empire when Britain forged its own destiny, unencumbered by the complexities of having to seek a common policy with European allies. No matter that the empire was long gone, having been set on a path of decline beginning with World War I, severely weakened by World War II and mostly dismantled by the end of the 1960s. Leave leaders argued for a different version of a global Britain, with more freedom to trade with the rest of the world on its own terms, rather than terms agreed on behalf of a large group of countries with differing interests. Their aim was divergence from Europeanness as a way to return to a lost golden age and notions of British exceptionalism.

At the same time, anti-globalists on the left in the United Kingdom opposed the European Union because they saw it as anti-democratic, against the protection of jobs through state bailouts of important ailing industries, and a vehicle for employers to seek cheap labor from different parts of Europe. Few voters had much of an understanding of or political love for the complex relationship with European partners forged over decades, initially as the Common Market, then the European Economic Community, and now the single market of the European Union. There has always been a significant minority of UK voters who don't see why their government should share power in this way. Without the political yoke of control by Europe, they believed, as Nigel Farage and other Brexit campaign leaders portrayed, Britain would be able to "just get trade deals done" on better terms than with the European Union.

These sentiments were amplified by a steady stream of false or exaggerated stories predominantly in the right-wing media. Some of the most notorious examples were written by the former mayor of London, Leave campaign leader, and journalist Boris Johnson. He made his name as a Brussels correspondent writing entirely false claims that the European Commission was trying to standardize the size of condoms, stop Brits from selling pink sausages, and planned to recruit sniffer dogs to ensure all Euro-manure stays the same.[2] Other journalists joined in the sport of lampooning the commission. The common theme was outrage at the way the European Commission was imposing rules on the United Kingdom, undermining its way of life and traditions with a cavalcade of red tape.[3]

Membership in the European Union is anathema to neo-nationalists because it involves a power-sharing arrangement where member state leaders make decisions by majority vote or unanimously that all member states are required to enforce. Many see this as an unacceptable encroachment on national sovereignty rather than an opportunity to influence what happens across Europe. In addition, being in the single market requires accepting the free movement of goods, services, capital, and labor. This allows people from one member state to travel freely to and live in another member state, thus ostensibly removing control over intra-EU immigration, which was one of the most powerful drivers of support for the Brexit campaign.

One of the goals of the free movement of labor is to encourage partnerships, collaborations, and a common European identity between and across member states. Universities across Europe facilitated and benefited from this open-market approach to talent mobility. Universities are bastions of internationalism and multilateralism. In turn, they generate knowledge and promote economic development, national identity, and political power, while also developing knowledge and skills that promote European development, European identity, and European soft power.

Within the policy realm of higher education, this is being carried out overtly by the European Higher Education Area (EHEA), which covers 48 countries and thus extends across and beyond the European Union, and inside the EU via its research programs, Erasmus+, and most recently the European Universities Initiative. The EHEA is intended to encourage the mobility of talent, the alignment of degrees, the promotion of science, and the forging of a European identity. Leveraging EU funding, the European Universities Initiative involves bottom-up networks of universities across the European Union enabling students to obtain a degree by combining studies in several EU countries. The goal is to increase the international competitiveness of European universities and encourage students and academics to work together to address common issues facing Europe. The networks are "transnational alliances that will become the universities of the future, promoting European values and identity, and revolutionising the quality and competitiveness of European higher education," the European Commission stated.[4]

Of course, science and knowledge respect no borders; they are inherently transnational activities. Researchers across Europe and beyond are exchanging ideas and collaborating with partners in other countries to tackle grand challenges or global problems they cannot tackle on their own. High-impact science requires this type of cooperation, using staff from different countries, enabling the rapid circulation of ideas and talent. Research is more highly cited when it is internationally coauthored.[5]

Because these institutions leveraged and benefited greatly from EU initiatives, leaving the European Union posed particularly stark challenges for UK universities. A significant share of UK research productivity is tied to the European Union. For example, 12.8 percent of awards distributed by the EU's Horizon 2020 went to UK researchers—the second-highest proportion of all EU member states, only after Germany. In 2019, three of the United Kingdom's top-performing universities, Cambridge, Oxford, and University College London (UCL), were the three most successful recipients of Horizon 2020 funding in all of Europe; two other UK institutions featured in the top 10. And more than 40 UK universities were dependent on EU funding for more than 20 percent of their research income.[6]

Another potentially significant impact of Brexit: the high number of students and staff from EU countries studying, researching, or teaching at UK universities. EU students account for one-third of all international students in UK universities and bring in £2.4 billion a year to the UK economy through fees and living expenditures (minus the cost of loan support).[7] In the academic year 2016–2017, after the referendum, the number of applications from EU students dropped by 7 percent.[8] According to Higher Education Statistics Agency data, in the same academic year, 17 percent of academic staff in UK universities were from other EU countries. In some regions, up to half of academic staff in some departments were EU nationals, particularly in economics and modern languages. In Northern Ireland, a quarter of all faculty were EU nationals, while in the West Midlands almost one in two modern languages academics were EU nationals.[9]

As noted previously, also at risk was the Erasmus+ program, which funds the mobility and exchange of students and academics across Europe. Erasmus+ promotes the internationalization of the student experience and is vital to the diversity of UK campuses.[10] It also plays an important role in supporting the development of European language skills and in strengthening students' and academics' sense of European identity. According to Universities UK chief executive Alistair Jarvis, research shows that studying abroad boosts academic performance and helps students from a range of backgrounds develop the skills and global networks they need to secure jobs in a successful globally trading nation.[11] The British Council reported that more than 40,000 people from the United Kingdom went abroad under Erasmus+ during 2015–2016 to study, train, volunteer, or gain professional experience, while 13,800 European staff and nearly 50,000 European students trained in the United Kingdom, which was the third–most popular destination for students.[12]

The Referendum Campaign

The three pillars of internationalization for UK Universities—participation in Horizon 2020 and its successor program, Horizon Europe, which will spend €95.5 billion over the next seven years; participation in Erasmus+; and the freedom of EU academics and students to work and study in the United Kingdom and vice versa—came under threat when Conservative prime minister David Cameron announced on February 20, 2016, a referendum on whether Britain should remain in the European Union. This fulfilled a pledge he had made in the 2013 general election to give the British people the "simple choice" between staying or leaving. Cameron's decision was driven by fear of losing votes to the UK Independence Party (UKIP), led by right-wing populist Nigel Farage. UKIP appealed to hard-right conservatives and threatened to deny the Conservative Party a majority.

Cameron won the 2015 election with slim a 12-seat majority, leaving him reliant on the votes of hardline euro-skeptics on the right of his party. He then sought concessions from the European Union in advance of the referendum to help sway the vote but was only partially successful.[13] In February 2016 he announced that a referendum would be held on June 23 of that year. This led to a polarizing political campaign that included extensive use of social media, false statements, and incitement of hate crimes and violence. This was epitomized by the frenzied murder of one pro-Remain Labour MP. Jo Cox was shot in the head and stabbed 15 times by a far-right extremist.

The Leave campaign's central message was "Let's take back control," and its promoters made two key pledges.[14] The first, displayed on the side of the red campaign bus: "Give our NHS the £350m the EU takes every week." But this was a false promise. In reality, after accounting for EU funding support for UK farmers, aid for socially disadvantaged regions, and research by UK universities and businesses, the net weekly cost to the United Kingdom was £161m, less than half the figure emblazoned on the bus. Of the £115m of EU funds returned to the United Kingdom each week, 18.3 percent was being spent on research and development.[15]

The second pledge was a straightforward promise: a vote to leave would significantly reduce the flow of immigration, which had risen to 330,000 per year. Cameron had previously promised to get the figure down to tens of thousands and failed. The Leave campaign fearfully claimed that 5 million more migrants could enter Britain by 2030 if Turkey and four other applicants joined the EU under a false claim that Turkey, with a population of nearly 80 million, was poised to join. Yet Turkey had reached agreement with the EU on only 1 out of 25 chapters since becoming a candidate for membership in 1999.

Anti-immigrant sentiment was bolstered by extensive media reports of a mass exodus of refugees from Syria fleeing toward Europe, combined with frequent footage of desperate African migrants risking drowning to land in Greece and Italy. Europe had not seen anything like it since the conflict in Kosovo and before that the Second World War. The chaos seen on television screens scared millions of people and reduced confidence in the European Union, whose members were divided over how to deal with the situation. The Leave campaign and its supporters generated a barrage of anti-immigrant propaganda and fear through skillful use of social media: "They are not giving me my medicine because all the foreigners have taken it," read one post. A Leave billboard poster, paraded by Nigel Farage, showed a line of refugees and the headline "Breaking Point, the EU Has Failed Us All," with additional text saying, "We must take back control of our borders: Leave the European Union."

Some Remain campaigners also made inaccurate predictions and claims. Former chancellor George Osborne falsely predicted that an emergency budget would be needed immediately after the vote. A claim by Labour's Alan Johnson that two-thirds of UK jobs in manufacturing depended on demand from Europe was wildly off, the true figure being around 17 percent.[16]

The warnings of economic damage seemed inconsequential for Leave supporters. Many had experienced economic hardship as a result of the government's austerity program and were from communities that felt "left behind." But instead of blaming the Conservative government—which had directly increased their economic woes with cuts in social benefits—they blamed the technocrats in Brussels.[17] Responding to the warnings of academics and others, Michael Gove was reported to compare economists warning about Brexit to scientists wheeled out by the Nazis to discredit Albert Einstein.[18]

Voter participation in the Brexit referendum was high, at 72.2 percent. More than 30 million people voted, and the result was a narrow majority in favor of Leave. A 2 percent swing would have changed the outcome. The passage of the Brexit referendum left the UK higher education community reeling. Nine in 10 academics and students overwhelmingly supported Remain, as did university cities. With some 17 percent of university staff and 5 percent of students coming from the European Union, most university leaders looked on with horror at the thought of the unsettling and unwelcoming impact the vote would have on existing and prospective EU staff and students.

The referendum did not specify what type of Brexit would be sought or what the future relationship with the European Union would be, creating great uncertainty. How could future students commit to coming to or even staying in the United Kingdom if they did not know how or when tuition fees would rise? Likewise, how could existing staff make long-term decisions, such as whether to buy a house, without knowing whether they would be allowed to stay on? Why would EU academics move to the United Kingdom without certainty about their future status?

Far from settling the European question, the referendum campaign triggered three and a half years of political turmoil as MPs remained bitterly divided on the terms of departure and whether the United Kingdom should threaten to exit without a deal. Cameron's successor, Theresa May, called a general election, offering "strong and stable government," only for the electorate to take away her majority, making her task more difficult. Under Article 50 in European law, the United Kingdom had to leave the European Union on March 31, 2019. But Parliament rejected the withdrawal agreement May reached with EU leaders while also voting against a no-deal exit. May had no choice but to seek an extension of the deadline to October 31, 2019. The breach of the Conservatives' promise to leave by March 31 sealed her fate. In the European parliamentary elections, the Conservatives came in a humiliating fifth with 9 percent of the vote, and she resigned the party leadership the next day.

The Threat to Higher Education

May's successor, Boris Johnson, subsequently called a general election in late 2019. It resulted in a substantial majority for the Conservative Party based largely on "Getting Brexit Done." But his campaign and policy agenda provided few clues regarding how universities would fare under a no-deal or hard Brexit. The following provides an analysis of three ways a "clean break" from the European Union—which means Brexit without a trade deal—would have affected UK higher education and its research enterprise, and how universities were preparing for a post-EU relationship.

The Threat to Research

In November 2019, Universities UK president Julia Buckingham warned that Brexit posed a serious threat to British research capacity. Universities had developed an extensive network of researchers and projects on the Continent over the past 30 years. "It is no exaggeration to say that

Brexit is a major threat to the United Kingdom's research base and that Brexit is at the top, or very near the top, of most university's risk registers," she said. Buckingham stated that her own university got around a third of its research grant income from Europe, and 15 percent of its academic staff and 18 percent of its postdoctoral researchers come from EU countries.[19] Manchester University–based Sir Andre Geim, who won the Nobel Prize for his work on graphene, said, "In science, a no-deal Brexit would be like a severe drought for an orchard. You can't expect to have a harvest after watering it again next year. All the trees are already dead."

In January 2018, the minister in charge of universities told the House of Lords EU Home Affairs Sub-Committee that the government was aware that access to European Research Council and Marie Sklodowska-Curie Actions funding would be lost if the United Kingdom were to leave without a withdrawal deal. The government was considering options for domestic alternatives to these programs, prompting Universities UK to urge the government to set out its contingency plans for replacing lost EU funding for UK research. But no plan was forthcoming from government officials.[20]

The uncertainty started to damage the UK research ecosystem. Researchers voluntarily declined leadership of joint research projects with EU colleagues to avoid jeopardizing their success. British academics were not invited to participate in major projects.[21] A 2019 study by University College London of nine leading research universities—UCL, Sheffield, Nottingham, Manchester, Edinburgh, Birmingham, Oxford, Cambridge, and Imperial College London—showed that participation in Horizon 2020 research projects nearly halved in two years. The number of Horizon projects led by UK researchers at the nine universities dropped from 49 in 2016—the year of the EU referendum—to 20 in 2018.[22]

Without a firm plan or commitment of resources from Johnson, university leaders and researchers hoped the United Kingdom could become an "associate" participant in EU programs: associate participants are non-EU member countries that contribute funding and are eligible for EU research grants. This allows researchers to also collaborate with universities in other parts of the world, such as Asia and South America, in seeking EU funding.

Even if UK universities were to become associate participants, there was uncertainty as to what funding they would be eligible for. Jan Palmowski, secretary-general of the Guild of European Research-Intensive Universities, writing in *Times Higher Education,* said it would be difficult for EU finance ministries to agree to the associate status for UK universities. EU officials worried that including the United Kingdom in the Horizon program might lure the best researchers away from member states. Brexit negotiations also revolved around the fear that the United Kingdom would seek to establish a "Singapore-style" low-tax, low-regulation, low-protections economy. British universities might then focus on global partnerships outside of the European Union, essentially in competition with EU universities.

Without a deal to keep the United Kingdom within the EU research program in some form, UK universities would have faced the sudden disappearance of £1.5 billion (US$2 billion) in research funding. This would include no longer having access to funding from the European Research Council (ERC). In the event of losing EU research funding, Professor Adrian Smith of the Alan Turing Institute and Graeme Reid, chair of science and research policy at University College London, stated in a government-sponsored report that the United Kingdom would need to develop its own ERC-like funding agency. Smith and Reid stated their worry regarding the possible disproportionately negative effect on the social sciences and humanities, which the government deemed a lower priority.[23] And without EU funding, university research would need to then compete with other growing demands for public spending.

The trade and cooperation agreement reached with the EU in very late 2020 did finally include UK participation in the Horizon Europe program, which will spend €95.5 billion over the next seven years: UK researchers will be able to compete for most EU funded projects and the United Kingdom will participate as an associated country, subject to the draft protocols being agreed and adopted. The main cost of the UK's contribution will be calculated based on its gross domestic product as a share of EU GDP. UK researchers will not be able to participate in some

EU programs, however, particularly those related to security but also the European Innovation Council, a new funding agency that focuses on emerging technologies and startups. To participate in Horizon Europe, the United Kingdom will be required to allow for freedom of movement of researchers involved in the program, without discriminating between researchers from the different countries participating. While keeping the UK in the Horizon program, the Brexit agreement also brought an end to the its participation in the Erasmus+ program.

The Threat to EU Students and Staff

The consequences of Johnson's deal or no-deal Brexit gambit on attracting European talent, whether staff or students, is complex. A 2019 survey of universities for Universities UK showed that more than 80 percent of universities were either "very" or "extremely" concerned about the impact of a no-deal Brexit on student and staff recruitment and retention.[24]

One impact with financial implications: new cohorts of EU students going to UK universities will no longer pay the same tuition fee rate as native citizens. They will need to pay the higher rate charged to other international students. The first detailed modeling on what Brexit and other global changes could mean for international student enrollment, published by the Higher Education Policy Institute and Kaplan International in January 2019, estimated that the switch would reduce demand dramatically, but the expected fall in the pound would work in the opposite direction, increasing demand by reducing the price of studying in the United Kingdom for those from other countries. There could be a 57 percent decline in EU student numbers, amounting to a net loss of £40 million (US$52 million) in the first year after considering higher fees from those still studying in the United Kingdom. But the effects would be felt unevenly, with the oldest universities standing to gain financially—Oxford and Cambridge Universities might receive £10 million more in fee income each year on average—while less prestigious universities stand to lose around £100,000 on average.[25]

The United Kingdom's research competitiveness and innovation environment depends to a large extent on its ability to attract and retain the best international talent. The Smith and Reid study noted previously found that research leaders wanted to see a very clear alignment of immigration policy with the needs of the research and innovation community in the United Kingdom. They said no exploration of future arrangements for international collaboration in R&D would be complete without looking at immigration policy and regional development.[26] In fact, Smith told an audience at Imperial College London on October 8, 2019, that to meet the challenge of being left without access to ERC funding would require the government to "totally reverse our insane migration policies" and would require funding to "hunt talent." He said flexible visas were needed to make the UK a "research magnet."

The skills-based immigration plan for 2021 requires EU academics entering the United Kingdom to pay for a visa, take a compulsory English-language test, and pay a £2,000 immigration health surcharge, as well as another fee for registering biometric information. To qualify for a work visa, EU scholars will also need to earn a minimum of £30,000 a year, excluding most junior-level academics. According to Olivia Bridge of the Immigration Advice Service, the combined effect of a no-deal Brexit and a tougher visa regime for academics would seriously damage the reputation and attractiveness of UK higher education.[27]

In response to these fears, in August 2019, Prime Minister Johnson instructed officials to devise a fast-track system to attract leading scientists to work in the United Kingdom, which was made available to scientists, mathematicians, and researchers from February 2020. In addition, in September 2019 he announced a new post-study work visa for international students graduating in the United Kingdom, allowing them to work there for two years after graduation.[28] It appears that he will be more flexible on immigration than his predecessor, Teresa May.

The Threat to Participation in Erasmus+

Similarly, Universities UK has stated a concern regarding the lack of contingency plans for replacing access to Erasmus+, the study and exchange scheme for staff and students. Under Erasmus+, students on both sides of the exchange receive EU-funded monthly allowances on top of tuition fee waivers. As noted, and as part of the Brexit agreement, the United Kingdom will end its participation in Erasmus+, and the Johnson government has pledged to replace it with its own scheme to be named after the British computing pioneer Alan Turing. This will include reaching exchange agreements with "the best universities in the world." However, while the scheme will fund outward mobility at a cost of £100 million in the first year, experts said in January 2020 that it is underfunded and in particular lacks details of funding for inbound students. Reflecting the confusion in the United Kingdom's negotiating position right up to the December 2020 trade and cooperation agreement with the European Union, Johnson had assured Parliament back in January 2020 that there was "no threat to the Erasmus scheme."[29]

Switching to the Turing scheme means that the UK economy will forego £390 million per year in export earnings currently brought through incoming Erasmus+ students' living expenses alone. This is because EU students will lose the right to come to UK universities.[30] Further, the United Kingdom will be missing out on the plan to double the size of Erasmus+ in 2021–27, providing opportunities for 12 million people at a cost of €21 billion (US$25 billion).[31]

As Nick Hillman of the Higher Education Policy Institute observed, finding alternatives to the Erasmus+ study and exchange program for students and academics will not be easy. The government proposed expanding exchange programs with non-EU partners, including Australia, New Zealand, and North America, but they would be more expensive for students, who would not benefit from EU financial support toward the cost of living abroad.[32] He pointed out that Erasmus+ offers "a supportive framework to nurture exchanges, with its own substantial budget enabling a reciprocal flow of students and for the administration of these exchanges." But without such financial support, UK universities will "draw from their own resources, both financial and human, to recreate similar arrangements at a higher cost."[33] Some higher education institutions are creating small informal European networks to enhance research and mobility collaboration. But most cannot afford to simply replace the support from Erasmus+.

The COVID-19 pandemic and its impact on staff and students' decisions or ability to travel to the United Kingdom to study, pursue, research, or teach in higher education will make it difficult in the first few years to fully understand the impact of Brexit. Former universities minister Jo Johnson, brother of the prime minister, has warned that the combined impact of Brexit and COVID-19 on international student recruitment represents an "existential threat" to universities.[34]

Lessons Learned

Prime Minister Johnson stated that any loss in international trade, and in the United Kingdom's research productivity and role in the world, can be mitigated by deeper and wider relationships with other parts of the world—a concept he has called "Global Britain." But there are many reasons to worry.

The world is increasingly competitive in the production of intellectual property and in attracting talent. One indicator: China recently overtook the United Kingdom as the country with the second-highest number (after the United States) of highly cited researchers.[35] The UK's reputation for research and innovation may continue to persuade many of the world's most talented researchers, whether citizens of the European Union or other countries, to come. The quality of its universities will still draw talented students. But a significant break from or reduced participation in EU research programs will result in a period of uncertainty and likely a decline in the funding and productivity of British universities. There is also a prospect that the coherency of the United Kingdom's network of universities will be damaged if, for example, Scotland eventually seeks autonomy and rejoins the European Union.

What is the way forward for universities in the United Kingdom? In their November 2019 report, Smith and Reid focused on the research side of this question. They argued for a substantial increase in government funding to replace the loss of funds from the European Union and initiatives to attract talent, including new streams of funding to cover "quality-related" funding for "spontaneous, organic collaborations" and an "agility fund" to invest in emerging international programs of significant potential benefit to UK research and that "capture opportunities that arise unexpectedly." The more limited role of the United

Kingdom in the Horizon Europe program will not mitigate the need for additional government funding. They also proposed a global talent strategy that includes reforms to immigration policy to retain high-quality faculty and new fellowship and postgraduate programs to attract and retain talented researchers. The selection process could be overseen by a prestigious international faculty of peer reviewers, recruited through national academies in several countries.[36]

Beyond the immediate concerns regarding the post-Brexit world, there is the question of how universities can persuade the British public about the value of higher education and its international activities. The Brexit campaign attacked academia and fueled a rising public distrust of experts, and even of science itself. Universities were portrayed as part of the problem, not the solution. Alice Gast, president of Imperial College, argued that universities are partially to blame for this perception. They failed to connect with society and are viewed by many, including Brexit supporters, as contributors to the globalized economy and technological changes that are leaving large numbers of citizens behind, frustrated and alienated. "We need to create opportunities for those who are part of our universities to work *personally* and *directly* with community residents," she noted, "to share knowledge, to listen to their creative ideas and to work together on projects that have practical applications within the community."[37]

Universities should take responsibility in addressing the causes of nationalism and populism by articulating and showing the value of internationalization, but also of science, by seeking greater engagement with local communities. Research indicates that the amount of contact with immigrants, or rather the lack of it, predicts prejudice toward them.[38] Universities may already be a part of the solution, by bringing significant numbers of international students and academics into their campuses and university towns. This may have a more meaningful impact if universities were to structure contact and collaboration with the wider public, as opposed to just students or only in their city locations, in a meaningful way. International staff and students could, for example, engage with local cultural organizations and events, gain work experience and develop job skills with employers and voluntary organizations locally, and engage with local people in research to address key local challenges.

Universities in the United Kingdom and elsewhere operate in two worlds: a national and regional world, and an international world. They must compete internationally for talent, for collaborations, and for prestige. They are part of a global academic supply chain of interconnected relationships and services. But they must also attend to the needs and demands of their national and regional constituents to prove their value. This seems an obvious statement, but, at least in the case of the United Kingdom, we see a disconnect, if not in reality, then in public perception.[39] The fact that the risks to higher education and research were ignored in a political decision of such historic magnitude, Brexit, suggests universities need to engage more effectively not just with politicians but with the larger public.

Trumpian Nationalism and American Universities

JOHN AUBREY DOUGLASS

DONALD J. TRUMP'S NEO-NATIONALIST policies and rhetoric focused on a consistent set of themes and policies: anti-immigrant, nativist tweets and restrictive visa policies; tax cuts that largely benefited upper-income Americans and corporations; reductions in funding for social services; large increases in military spending; anti-science rhetoric that included denying the reality of climate change and, for a time, calling the COVID-19 pandemic a hoax; aggressively reducing environmental regulations and enforcement; and repeated attempts to dismantle the Affordable Care Act. Under his "America First" anti-globalist banner, Trump also actively disengaged from international agreements and alliances and, through executive orders, invoked protective tariffs that led to trade wars and diplomatic isolation.

Whereas past presidents sought some form of enlightened international engagement, Trump portrayed globalization and open markets, and multilateral agreements, as damaging to US economic and political power. And like other populist leaders, past and present, Trump found political support among those who felt a sense of social and economic decline and displacement, particularly in rural America, with many prone to conspiracy theories propagated through social media.

Trump and his political operatives warned repeatedly of the "deep state"—the concept that the political system in the United States is controlled through collusion and cronyism by an association of technocrats and political elites who oppose Trump on ideological grounds. That narrative continues to live and evolve into fantastic subplots on conservative media platforms.

In the months leading into the 2020 presidential election, and with the rise of the Black Lives Matter movement, Trump promoted himself as the "law and order" president, making dystopian predictions of a radical leftist takeover if Democrat Joseph R. Biden Jr. was elected, sowing doubt about the legitimacy of the election itself, and seeking a pathway to what had many elements of a coup: the overthrow of a democratically elected president. In almost all instances throughout his presidency, Trump's modus operandi promoted political division and denigrated his perceived opposition as well as public institutions. Biden's election should be viewed as only a partial rejection of Trump's politics and antics. The millions of votes for Trump show that the nation's severe political division will remain—a divide between a rural, largely Republican and white conservative America, and a largely Democratic, more demographically diverse, and more liberal urban America. Trump's cult of personality, and the media machine that feeds it, will continue to play a role in national and local politics.

Throughout his presidency, Trump and his administration never articulated a coherent policy regarding higher education. Yet his larger America First agenda had a profound impact on the nation's colleges and universities and its academic research ecosystem. Trump's multiple and evolving efforts to restrict visas, for example, damaged the market for attracting international students and academic talent to the United States. He sought to overturn a Barack Obama–era policy that allowed undocumented students to attend college. Trump repeatedly attempted to slash funding for student financial aid. He proposed massive cuts in federal funding for academic sciences, including the National Science Foundation and the National Institutes of Health. And his secretary of education loosened regulations on for-profit and often predatory colleges and so-called universities.

Coloring all his actions, Trump and his administration viewed colleges and universities, and the scientific community, as part of his political opposition—and not without reason. Universities were the subject of ridicule and threats by a president who announced most major decisions or circulated false accusations in often dozens of tweets in a single day. Trump leveraged the growing perception by conservative voters that universities were bastions of the radical Left, intolerant of conservative views, and, worse, bent on indoctrinating their children. He repeatedly portrayed universities, like the campus in Berkeley, as hypocritical in their devotion to free speech and the quest for knowledge. They were instead politically correct police states and producers of politically biased research and teaching.

The Trump administration also viewed universities as hubs for intellectual property theft, mostly by visiting Chinese academics. Prior to the 2020 presidential election, Trump signed an executive order banning Chinese graduate students and visiting faculty the administration determined were linked to the Chinese military-industrial complex. Espionage is a legitimate concern. But the sweeping restrictions on visas, and accompanying anti-immigrant rhetoric, was seemingly more about political messaging than rational policymaking.

In some form, Trump's attacks on America's higher education community can be interpreted as simply a play to his right-wing supporters—his political base that included in 2016 a large block of voters with no college experience. Reflecting a general decline in the trust in government and public institutions, a 2017 poll found that 58 percent of Republicans thought that "colleges and universities have a negative effect on the way things are going in this country."[1] Ergo, being critical of higher education helped get Trump elected president. His modus operandi: attack and belittle any form of opposition to his leadership, administration, and policies. Trump also found purpose in undoing policies set by the Obama administration, including those related to higher education—in part rooted in personal animosity for the previous president.

Anti-intellectualism and distrust of experts found in America's universities is a theme that runs deep in right-wing populist movements in the United States and elsewhere. Trump leveraged this proclivity. Universities and colleges are, therefore, a part of the so-called deep state. Perhaps most troubling, Trump and his administration repeatedly demonstrated a lack of understanding of the role of universities in the nation's economic competitiveness and their value for promoting socio-economic mobility.

Yet because the federal government has limited powers in shaping state higher education systems, universities were afforded some protections from Trump's attacks and budget priorities. The United States is not similar to other parts of the world like Turkey, Hungary, France, or the United Kingdom. There is no ministry responsible for managing, funding, and regulating universities and colleges, as found in almost all other nations. Federal policies in the United States are largely limited to student financial aid, funding of academic research by semiautonomous federal agencies, and regulating nongovernmental accrediting associations. Funding and coordinating higher education is primarily the responsibility of state governments. This created a narrow playing field for the Trump administration to shape higher education policy. Congress also played a role in limiting his impact, passing budgets that often protected funding for academic science and financial aid.

That being said, Trump's America First nationalism and policies left their mark on universities. For example, even before the onset of the COVID-19 pandemic, there were indicators of a significant decline in the interest of international talent coming to the United States, influenced by the president's anti-immigrant tweets and increasingly restrictive visa policies. The pandemic provided a political excuse for even more restrictive immigration policies—a pattern seen in other nations. Collectively and over time, this generated a sense that the United States is no longer a welcoming nation for foreign students and faculty.

Much of the Trump administration's policies related to higher education may be ephemeral—many will be overturned by executive orders and administration policies of the new president, Joseph Biden. Yet Trump's portrayal of science, and academic research in general, as simply biased opinions, will likely have a long-term impact. The debasing of facts and the value of science, most importantly denying the existence of climate change and dismantling related federal environmental policies, translates into a tragic delay in American leadership on an international issue with sweeping implications for the global economy and for humanity itself. Trump's divisive political rhetoric and policies also further eroded the public perception of America's key institutions, including universities, as trusted sources of information and knowledge, largely for political gain.

The following narrative discusses Trump's political rhetoric and policies and their impact on higher education in America, as well as on the public trust in public institutions and democracy itself. But first I provide a brief discussion of the role of nationalism in the development of universities in the United States and the similarities of Trump's version of nationalism to previous forms of national populism.

Nationalism and US Universities

There are aspects of Trump's rhetoric and policies that are simply extensions of the neoconservative worldview of President Ronald Reagan and earlier conservatives, and the neoliberal policies found in other nations: reducing the role of government in society, including interventions in the economy; a sometimes blind faith in the free market; and budget cuts and accountability regimes for public agencies. The anti-immigrant, nativist, anti-science, anti-expert, anti-globalization policies and rhetoric of Trump and his changing cadre of administrative officials provided an American take on populism and nationalism that has deep historical roots.

As discussed in the introductory chapters of this book, nationalism played an important role in the development of higher education in the United States, in particular the development of its public network of colleges and universities. Nationalism is not, unto itself, an evil or detrimental predilection of nation-states. It can be inclusive, as expressed on the Great Seal of the United States, *e pluribus unum* (out of many one). Or it can be as a source of exclusion and division.

Historically, public tertiary institutions were established to promote economic development and socioeconomic mobility, in part explained by a revolutionary understanding of the value of human capital. Arguably, and with the exception of Germany, the United States made the largest bet on human capital in the world beginning in the mid-1800s by providing funding, via federal land grants, to states to establish public universities. Subsequent state and federal investment, particularly after World War II, created the world's first mass higher education system. This progressive effort, however, must be qualified by the regressive, often populist, use of tertiary institutions as a means of repression and as a tool for building America's massive military-industrial complex. Throughout the nineteenth and into the twentieth century, most private colleges and universities were, for much of their histories, exclusive social and religious enclaves that purposefully kept out "undesirable" groups—women, Jews, Italians, the Irish, Catholics, African Americans, and many others. Some state universities also erected barriers for underrepresented groups to gain admission and enroll. Southern states in particular, but not solely, refused to enroll African American students in their major public universities well into the 1960s.

These and other forms of social exclusion were, in many instances, extensions of populist and nationalist (read: nativist) movements, tied to the politics of an era or of a region. The great public universities that emerged largely in the American Midwest and West tended to be more progressive and inclusive. For instance, they tended to open their doors to women and ethnic minorities, if not always initially, soon afterward. But they too were subject to or extensions of the biases and sometimes regressive populist sentiments of the society that established and sustained them.

So how does Trump's version of neo-nationalism, and his view of and policies related to higher education, fit into this historical landscape? As with previous forms of populism, there are not only the ongoing themes of opposition to immigration, distrust of government and urban elites, status anxiety in a changing economy and social world, and adherence to a golden age myth (e.g., "Make America Great Again"). There is also an anti-science and anti-intellectual rhetoric that, in part, is directed at the academic community.

Historians have studied the cycles of nativism in the United States, repeatedly associating them with new waves of immigrants, an ingrained distrust of politicians, and a perceived or real urban ruling business class. Hence, American history is dotted by populist movements that share many of the components of today's neo-nationalist movements, including a fear of the other, corresponding with geographic economic decline and political alienation.

Although one can go back further in time, the Native American Party was formed in 1855 primarily as an anti-Catholic, anti-immigration political movement—also known by critics as the "Know Nothing" party. Some 40 years later, in the 1890s, another powerful populist political movement emerged that also blamed immigrants and corporate interests (banks and railroad monopolies) for agrarian economic decline. And indeed, monopolies in banking and transportation did drive many farmers to economic ruin. Great wealth was accumulated by so-called robber barons in the midst of growing economic disparity, giving the era the nickname the "Gilded Age." The Jeffersonian concept of the yeoman farmer as the bulwark of American society was rapidly giving way to a new industrial and urban world. Populists captured state legislatures in many midwestern states using the rhetoric of nativism and a golden age myth.

On the other side of the Great Depression and World War II, the heightened postwar tension with the Soviet Union—the geopolitical and emotional battle between communism and capitalism—led to the nationalist, anti-communism movement optimized by the congressional hearings led by Senator Joe McCarthy. McCarthy leveraged the fear of spies bent on overthrowing the US government, and in his broad attack identified America's universities and colleges as vehicles for communist espionage. Any and all were potential suspects, including famous academics such as J. Robert Oppenheimer, who led the Manhattan Project. Federal and state government agencies as well as public university governing boards instituted loyalty oaths. They required employees to attest their allegiance to the United States, forcing debates on the meaning of academic freedom and the firing, in some instances, of academics who refused to sign.

This loyalty oath frenzy emerged at a time when the federal government steadily increased its investment in academic research intended, in large part, to support America's technological and military advantage over the Soviet Union. The launch of Sputnik in 1957 spurred a dramatic increase in federal funding for basic research and for expanding graduate programs in the sciences. The National Aeronautics and Space Administration (NASA) was established soon after, becoming the largest single agency funding university research, not only with the purpose of exploring space but as the primary agency for developing rocket technology needed for the development of intercontinental ballistic missiles (ICBMs).

In the thick of the Cold War, historian Richard Hofstadter was the first to study the right-wing movements of America's past in an effort to understand McCarthyism. He attributed McCarthy's political viability not only to the threat of the Soviet Union but also to "status anxiety" and, for many Americans, a deep distrust of intellectuals and the universities that produced them.[2] He called these adherents "pseudoconservatives" because they claimed to uphold American traditions yet projected their own fears and anxieties, which were grounded in contradictions. The radical Right, as opposed to more mainstream conservatism of, for example, Dwight D. Eisenhower and even the libertarian views of William F. Buckley Jr., represented a "paranoid style" of American policies: anti-immigrant, anti-elite, fearsome of conspiracies, anti-government, anti-reason, and anti-science[3]—sound familiar?

Along with Hofstadter, Daniel Bell and other sociologists, including Nathan Glazer and Seymour Martin Lipset, who coined the phrase "radical Right," initiated the first serious scholarly research on populist right-wing nationalist movements in America. This included the beginning of the slow but sure collapse of the Republican Party into an increasingly reactionary political movement, defined by what it was against: communists, the civil rights movement, desegregation, immigrants, any kind of tax, the establishment of Medicare in 1965, Social Security, and the other elements of an emerging welfare state.[4]

At the core of right-wing thought, as noted, was doubt about the credibility of government and intellectuals. "There is a cult of ignorance in the United States," complained science fiction writer Isaac Asimov, "and there has always been. The strain of anti-intellectualism is a constant thread winding its way through our political and cultural life, nurtured by the false notion that democracy means that my ignorance is just as good as your knowledge."[5]

Setting a Tone: Free Speech at Berkeley

Shortly after Trump's inauguration as president in January 2017, anti- and pro-Trump rallies and protests proliferated in cities and on university campuses across America. His election by the slimmest of margins, winning the electoral college but not the popular vote, and his right-wing tirades via a unique use of social media and conservative news channels, furthered political divisions. This included an appeal to and sympathy for extreme right-wing actors, including white nationalists. Trump and many others in the conservative news media viewed most American universities and colleges as liberal enclaves, intolerant of conservatives. As noted previously, polls even showed that many Republicans questioned sending their children to secular higher education institutions lest they be converted into left-leaning voters and presumably Democrats.

During his campaign for president, Trump did not explicitly target American higher education as a vehicle to further his conservative brand and appeal to his Republican base—a political brand that focused on his personal desires and whims as much as on policy. But the political clashes that occurred after his election on many campuses offered a platform to reinforce conservative fears. At the Berkeley campus of the University of California, College Republicans, a student-led organization, invited alt- right provocateur and former *Breitbart* editor Milo Yiannopoulos to give a speech. Yiannopoulos's modus operandi: to generate conflict and media attention by visiting college campuses to profess distain for political correctness and to espouse anti-immigrant rhetoric. In the weeks before his scheduled appearance at Berkeley, his conservative supporters wore "Make America Great Again" hats and carried him into the lecture hall of another college campus on a litter before he spoke on the topic "feminism is cancer."[6] His contradictions are many—he is a gay man.

The Berkeley visit was the final leg on his tour of college campuses. Berkeley's chancellor, Nicholas Dirks, made it clear that Yiannopoulos's views, tactics, and rhetoric were "profoundly contrary to those of the campus." But Berkeley was bound by "the Constitution, the law and the university's values and Principles of Community." In the interest of free speech and openness to the full spectrum of opinion and perspective, Dirks concluded, Yiannopoulos should be allowed to speak, and the campus would provide security for that purpose.[7]

Before he was scheduled to speak on February 1, protesters gathered that day on Sproul Plaza, the main public square on campus, famous for earlier protests that were part of the Free Speech Movement. There was a rumor that Yiannopoulos planned to name undocumented Berkeley students and report them to Immigration and Customs Enforcement (ICE) in the hope of their deportation. As promised, campus police and reinforcements from the city of Berkeley's police department attempted to manage the crowd. Most protesters were peacefully stating their opposition to Yiannopoulos. But the situation soon devolved. A contingent of some 150 protesters associated with the antifa movement (a self-identified anti-fascist group that included anarchists) wearing masks and black clothing began to throw rocks and commercial-grade fireworks at the police. They lit trash fires, smashed the windows of the Student Union, and accosted innocents with pepper spray and fists. After attempting to disperse the crowd, campus officials were forced to cancel Yiannopoulos's speech.

Even with Yiannopoulos's incendiary objectives, a campus task force that later reviewed Berkeley's policies on speakers concluded that he should have been afforded the opportunity to speak on campus. Yet the spectacle of left-wing extremists suppressing a right-wing extremist turned into a major media event, drawing the attention of right-wing outlets, including Fox News. Trump was only in the second week of his presidency and saw the coverage on the morning show *Fox and Friends*, prompting him to tweet, "If U.C. Berkeley does not allow free speech and practices violence on innocent people with a different point of view—*NO FEDERAL FUNDS?*"[8]

Trump's threat presumably included ending student financial aid and academic research funded by the National Science Foundation and other federal agencies. It was an empty threat, probably made out of ignorance, as the president does not have direct control over legislatively mandated financial aid funding or over the process of funding campus research, allocated primarily through peer review. Yet the objective was less about the reality of his threat than the appearance that left-leaning Berkeley, and its academic culture, suppressed conservative speakers and thinkers.

Berkeley's academic leaders struggled with the outcome of the conflict. Should campus police have had more security in place? Should they have arrested and suppressed the most violent antifa protesters? Should the campus, the home of the Free Speech Movement, have allowed Yiannopoulos to speak despite the tumult? In the aftermath of his cancelled event, a newly formed conservative student organization announced its plan for a series of right-wing speakers on campus. The purpose was to test Berkeley's commitment to free speech and leverage media attention. Yiannopoulos stated his plan to return to Berkeley to host a multiday event self-titled "Milo's Free Speech Week." Campus officials stated that the event would require massive security measures, costing an estimated $1 million—this at a time when the campus faced a sizable operating deficit caused in part by years of decreased state funding.

By March 2017, anti-Trump and pro-Trump groups, including self-identified white nationalists, virtually all from outside the campus community, gathered on campus for a series of generally peaceful protests, separated by large numbers of police. Hundreds of Far-Right protesters, some dressed in goggles, gas masks, and knee pads, rallied in support of a planned future appearance of conservative speaker Ann Coulter in a park nearby.

By August, a "Say No to Marxism" rally planned to be held in the same park was canceled by the organizers but still drew both Trump supporters and protesters. Coulter never showed up for her speech. And Yiannopoulos's "Free Speech Week" was canceled at the last minute by its organizers, who promised a series of high-profile conservative activists but failed to confirm their appearance shortly before the planned event. Yet the university still had to spend hundreds of thousands of dollars for security.[9]

On September 26, fights broke out near Sproul Plaza inside an "empathy tent" intended to encourage dialogue between conservative and liberal groups. Trump supporters, including Kyle "Based Stickman" Chapman and others associated with the conservative organization Patriot Prayer, then marched to People's Park (the location of Vietnam-era protests) and spoke about a war on whites and a "battle for Berkeley."[10]

After September, the intensity of the battles between left- and right-wing groups, and the interest of the media, waned. Berkeley had a new chancellor. Carol T. Christ previously served as president of Smith College and before that had been a longtime faculty member and academic administrator at Berkeley. She sought a path to ensure the right of people like Yiannopoulos to speak on campus. Christ appointed a campus task force to review and modify policies on guest speakers and declared "a free speech year" at Berkeley. Yiannopoulos was invited back to Berkeley, along with other right-wing celebrities—some of whom agreed to come but later backed out and others who came but generated only sparse audiences.

Cutting Higher Education Budgets

The events at Berkeley provided Trump and his allies with an opportunity to gain the media attention they thrived on by attacking the nation's universities as unfettered liberal bastions. But potentially much more consequential for higher education was the new administration's first budget proposal to Congress present in March 2017. It included massive federal cuts to higher education. Trump's form of nationalism simply put a low priority on education in general and higher education in particular. The larger goal was to severely cut government spending on social services and entitlements and to reduce the federal role in American society.[11] This included the objective of eliminating Obamacare—a campaign promise made without any realistic replacement plan. At least part of the rationale was to lay the groundwork for one of Trump's main promised objectives: a massive tax cut.

The initial Trump budget lacked details normal in a proposed federal budget. It was formulated without significant consultation with congressional leaders—Republicans or Democrats—or with federal officials.[12] At that time, Republicans controlled both the House of Representatives (where all budget bills originate) and the Senate. Presidents develop and send their federal budget proposal to the House, which then initiates a negotiation with the Senate, and a revised federal budget proposal eventually comes back to the president to sign. Any realistic budget requires cooperation and coordination between the executive and legislative branches.

Under Trump's first proposed budget, the Department of Education's total operating budget was to be slashed by $9 billion, focused largely on reducing funding support for student financial aid. Secretary of Education Betsy DeVos, a major contributor to conservative causes and to the Trump presidential campaign, outlined the cuts: there would be reductions to federal Pell Grants for low-income students and, at the same time, a shift of $8 billion from the federally subsidized Perkins Loan Program to unsubsidized loans. The plan also proposed cutting funding in half for the Federal Work-Study Program that provided part-time jobs for some 670,000 undergraduate and graduate students. Work-Study provides a significant pathway for students to help pay for their educational expenses and is a source of low-cost employment for universities. In addition, DeVos announced that the Trump administration planned to eliminate a loan forgiveness program for students who enter public service—an Obama administration initiative—and end funding for most college-readiness programs.

But the biggest proposed cuts were directed at academic research. As announced by Office of Management and Budget (OMB) director Mick Mulvaney, a well-known deficit hawk, the White House budget would reduce federal funding for science. The National Science Foundation (NSF) and the National Institutes of Health (NIH) faced cuts of 11 and 18 percent, respectively. The Centers for Disease Control and Prevention, which was at the forefront of battling the Ebola epidemic, the Zika virus, and opioid use, faced a 17 percent cut.

The Trump administration had already set restrictions on federal agencies doing research on climate change and would take further action to reduce clean air standards related to carbon emissions—policies in part linked to the US pullout from the Paris Agreement. Trump also sought to eliminate the National Endowment for the Arts and the National Endowment for the Humanities—both small blips in the federal budget but a symbolic gesture for ultraconservatives. The Environmental Protection Agency was also to lose much of its budget.

Federal funding for basic research via these agencies is the lifeline of America's science and technological innovation. It also forms a vital part of the funding model for the nation's network of research universities. The NIH is the largest federal supporter of research and development in the federal government and sends 80 percent of its funding to universities and research centers throughout the country. At the University of California (UC), for example, with 10 research-intensive campuses, the federal government is the single largest source of funding for research. In 2016, UC alone received more than $1.8 billion from the NIH. At public as well as private universities, like Stanford, federal research funds help defray the cost of operating expenses and support graduate and postdoctoral students.

Funding cuts on the scale desired by Trump and his associates would have created a gaping hole in the funding model of America's universities. While corporate and philanthropic funding for academic research primarily in the sciences had grown over the decades, the federal government remained by far the most significant investor. The initial reaction of America's universities, and their various lobbying groups such as the Association of American Universities (AAU), was shock. The proposed cuts were massive. But also worrying was the Trump administration's ignorance of how crucial federal funding is for the nation's higher education system.

What followed was an effort by higher education leaders to push back against Trump's budget proposal, seeking support from both congressional Democrats and Republicans. Historically, Republicans generally favored academic research in science and technology as a form of corporate welfare, generating innovation and intellectual property that has long fed the private sector. The Trump budget "would effectively cripple our nation's scientific efforts, undermining our economic growth, public health, and national security," stated Mary Sue Coleman, president of the AAU.[13]

The proposed cuts did draw bipartisan criticism by lawmakers. In reaction, and seemingly as an afterthought, Secretary of Health and Human Services Tom Price suggested that all the cuts could simply be achieved by eliminating "indirect costs"—the overhead rate the federal government pays to universities for the infrastructure that supports research, like buildings, staff support, and utilities. Price's suggestion was dismissed by Democrats and Republicans in key committees. It raised further concerns regarding the competency of Price and the Trump administration; they seemed ignorant of how federal funding for research was administered. As part of revolving door of political appointees in the Trump administration, Price later resigned in the wake of a scandal regarding his use of private jets at government expense for his business and personal travel.

Despite Republican control of the House and the Senate, Trump's proposed budget cuts for higher education were renounced as unrealistic by congressional leaders. Most student financial aid programs, including Work-Study, retained funding, and the budget for academic research remained nearly the same as the previous year, with an actual bump of an additional $2 billion for the NIH. In the end, Trump's proposed 2018 higher education budget was a symbolic act rather than a serious policy initiative. Yet it was also an indicator of a chaotic White House, where policy was generated largely by Trump's impulsive priorities and generally lacked any significant strategy beyond an attempt to cut social services across the board.[14] With the priority of the White House focused on passing a large tax cut later in the year and forestalling a government shutdown, Trump signed a federal budget bill that also included large increases in funding for national defense.

Yet it appears no lesson was learned. In the Trump administration's proposed budget for 2019, the White House again presented a budget to Congress that outlined large cuts to the Department of Education, the NSF, the NIH, and other funders of academic research. It was virtually identical to the previous year's draconian budget proposal. Again, the House of Representatives ignored the White House and proceeded to approve a spending bill that increased funding for NIH biomedical research programs and even for the Department of Education, including a modest increase in federal Pell Grants provided for low-income students.

Immigration and Talent Mobility

Where Trump did gain support from congressional Republicans, and much of his Republican base of voters, were plans to limit or change immigration policies in ways that would deeply affect America's universities. Trump had used immigration as a potent campaign issue, one that fed on deep divisions in society and on a poorly designed and understood set of policies on immigration largely formulated in the 1970s. Just days after taking office, citing national security concerns, the president's first executive action was to ban travelers from six majority Muslim countries, including students, faculty, and staff.

On the campaign trail, Trump promised to "build a wall" stretching the full border with Mexico, blamed immigrants from Latin America for bringing crime and straining social services, and warned that immigrants from the Middle East and elsewhere exposed America to terrorism. The executive order to ban all immigrants from Iran, Iraq, Libya, Somalia, Sudan, Syria, and Yemen immediately created a problem for universities with students, staff, and faculty from these nations. University officials advised these students and faculty not to travel home lest they not be able to return. But more importantly, Trump's anti-immigrant rhetoric and plans to develop an "extreme vetting" process for visas generated a sense of a closing border to academic talent as well as to refugees.

Doubling down on his evolving anti-immigrant policies, Trump then set a time line for rescinding the Deferred Action for Childhood Arrivals, or DACA—a program established by the Obama administration that promised the federal government would not deport undocumented immigrants who came to the United States as children and who were employed or enrolled in higher education. Obama had provided this protection under an executive order in June 2012, bypassing Congress in an area of policy, immigration, in which the president has substantial powers. Congress had repeatedly failed to pass legislation for much-needed reform of US immigration policies—a jumble of often contradictory laws and policies. Obama had attempted to negotiate a bill for comprehensive immigration reform with Republican party leaders who, by 2010, controlled both the House and the Senate. However, Republican Senate majority leader Mitch McConnell and his counterpart in the House vowed not to pass any legislation promoted by Obama. DACA was a partial and targeted way around Republican opposition, granting a reprieve to young immigrant "Dreamers." According to polling data, it was a program popular with American voters.

As part of Trump's anti-immigrant campaign and vow to overturn Obama-era policies, the White House announced in September 2017 plans to rescind DACA unless Congress passed legislation to keep it. By the summer of 2018, an estimated 699,350 registered Dreamers were residing in the United States.[15] There was growing fear that Trump would rescind the program and use the federal data to deport most or all Dreamers and their undocumented family members. The Trump administration claimed Obama had acted illegally by not asking for congressional approval—a specious argument since Trump had already made executive orders banning immigrants from largely Muslim countries. Still, with Republicans in the majority, Congress failed to extend DACA. A series of lawsuits then made their way through the federal court system. Eventually, the Supreme Court rejected the Trump administration's authority to end the program, largely based on the premise that it offered no policy basis to do so.[16]

The so-called Muslim ban and initial efforts to end DACA were followed by a promise by Trump and his administration to crack down on students who overstay their visas, and more restrictive rules and oversight of the H1-B visa program for high-skill workers, including the hiring of academic staff. In May 2018, the Trump's State Department announced plans to limit Chinese nationals studying in specified technology fields, such as robotics, aviation, and high-tech manufacturing, to one-year visas along with increased scrutiny by federal officials starting in June. The rationale was the fear of intellectual property espionage.

University leaders and higher education associations condemned all these efforts as fear mongering. Ted Mitchell, president of the American Council on Education, stated, "While apparently aimed at Chinese students in certain STEM fields, this would have a chilling effect on our ability to attract international students from all countries. These students have been critical to research that supports U.S. economic growth and fuels innovation."[17]

Historically, the flow of international students and academic talent is a significant reason for America's research strength and leadership role in technological and other fields. International students and faculty have long had a presence in the nation's colleges and universities to a degree unmatched by other nations. The growth in their numbers over the past four decades is due, in large part, to the quality of US universities and colleges, to the possibility of higher education as path to citizenship, and to the American ethos of an open society welcoming to immigrants. The economic benefits for the United States are many. Immigrants who come to study in the States, for example, account for one-third of all start-ups in Silicon Valley.

With the significant long-term decline in public funding for higher education, attracting international students is an important income source for many colleges and universities. In 2018, the direct economic impact of international students on the United States was some $36.9 billion. Chinese students represented almost a third of all international student enrollment, by far the single largest national source, and they generated more than $12 billion in economic activity.[18] US colleges and universities also rely on attracting talented graduate and postdoctoral students and faculty internationally. The University of Illinois, concerned with the rhetoric and unpredictable policy environment, took out an insurance policy to protect itself from a significant potential drop in revenue due to changing US visa policies and Trump's emerging trade war with China.[19]

The Trump administration, with the support of Republicans in Congress, had quickly framed immigration, including the large number of undocumented immigrants, as a social *and* a national security problem. The president reportedly described most Chinese students in the United States as spies and entertained a proposal from a senior adviser to stop awarding student visas to all Chinese nationals, not just those in STEM fields. The reliance on and value of international talent for universities, and for regional economies, was simply not a concern in relation to the larger anti-immigrant narrative: the increased tensions with China in trade and global influence, and the growing sense of a scientific and technological arms race.

During Trump's run for the presidency and shortly after, the United States declined as a preferred destination for undergraduate and graduate studies. After his 2016 election, there were ubiquitous reports of incidents of foreign students being turned back at the border, delays and denials of visas, and arbitrary decisions by border control agents to detain foreign nationals in airports. Both Trump's rhetoric and policies had an impact. After decades of steady increases in international student applications and enrollment, new enrollment of international students fell by more than 6 percent in the first two years of the Trump administration. And in the fall of 2018, first-time international graduate enrollments declined from the previous year by 1.3 percent, according to the Council of Graduate Schools. In engineering, the drop was 8.3 percent.[20]

Trump-era policies and anti-immigrant rhetoric help to partially explain the downturn. But there are other factors. One is the comparatively high cost of tuition and fees in the United States and a growing concern among potential foreign students regarding gun violence and other social ills that make studying in America appear dangerous. Another, and perhaps most important, factor is the rising quality and reputation of international universities, and hence heightened competition for students.

China, Espionage, and Universities

In the context of a trade war with China and growing concerns of the systematic theft of intellectual property, the international engagement of American universities became a focal point of Trump administration investigations. In early 2018, Federal Bureau of Investigation (FBI) director Christopher Wray suggested that university officials were naive regarding the counterintelligence threats posed by Chinese students and scholars. The "China threat" was real and was "going to take a whole-of-society response," including American universities.[21] At a Senate committee meeting, a Trump official claimed, "Our counterintelligence concern is driven by the fact that China has a publicly stated policy goal of acquiring sensitive information and technology around the world, [including] here in the United States, and that they seek [to] access and recruit global experts regardless of their nationality to meet their science and technology aims."[22]

Are there legitimate concerns of foreign espionage at American universities and colleges, specifically in cutting-edge technology fields? There is evidence that there are, particularly among graduate students and faculty doing collaborative work with Chinese academics and with other foreign nationals, including Russians and Iranians. A series of reports by the US government and international agencies note a concerted effort by the Chinese government to infiltrate universities and technology companies and gain access to valuable intellectual property by recruiting or placing conspirators. China's Thousand Talents Plan, for example, is a strategic effort to recruit largely Chinese foreign nationals in scientific fields to provide illegal forms of technology transfer. Academics recruited to the program typically received a salary and funding for their research from Chinese institutions, such as universities or research institutions. "In exchange for the salary and research funding, which sometimes include what's called a shadow lab in China," charged a congressional report, "members sign legally binding contracts with the Chinese institutions that typically contain provisions that prevent the members from disclosing their participation in the program."[23]

In part because of pressure from the White House and Congress, research universities instituted more rigorous reviews of and controls on research involving foreign nationals, guided by a collective concern for avoiding a high-profile scandal and to respond to changing federal regulations. The NIH also instituted a review of China's foreign talent recruitment program in the United States, concluding that "the Chinese government uses them to obtain confidential grant applications and to establish so-called shadow labs in China, where NIH-funded research can be replicated."[24]

But the scale of the problem was not clear. At the same Senate hearing in which FBI director Wray spoke, Senator Dick Durban (D-Illinois) stated what was generally the opinion of the academic community: "I would say of all the possible ways of compromising the economic integrity and even the national security integrity of the United States, this is a small category."[25] Yet China's influence and infiltration of the academy grew as a salient political issue for the Trump administration and congressional Republicans, and many Democrats.

Another focus of concern was the proliferation of Confucius Institutes, and more generally the acceptance of money and deals with foreign governments by a wide range of academic institutions and programs. Initiated in 2004 and funded by China's Ministry of Education, the number of Confucius Institutes on university campuses grew throughout the world, with the stated purpose of promoting Chinese culture and language. But the money from Beijing came with strings, including the stipulation that all academic staffing, events, and speakers be approved by Chinese officials. By early 2019, there were more than 100 operating at US universities and 500 globally (see chapter 8).

A number of congressional hearings focused on these institutes, including the Senate's Committee on Homeland Security & Governmental Affairs. That committee generated a report stating that the institutes operate with "little-to-no transparency" and that they "should not continue in the United States."[26] Academic freedom was one issue of concern, because the Chinese government appeared to approve only pro-Chinese events and programming. Another concern was the sense that the institutes were a Beijing-controlled pathway for espionage—the committee report even suggested that institute staff might need to register as foreign agents with the State Department.

Some five months after the Senate hearings, 15 institutes were closed by US universities, and more would follow. The often-stated reason was a concern over losing federal funding for foreign language programs, faculty opposition, and sometimes pressure from local lawmakers, both Republican and Democratic.[27] Many universities never established a Confucius Institute, despite overtures from Beijing, precisely because of the concerns voiced in the Senate hearings.

The Confucius Institutes touched on the issue of the growing number of financial and program deals made by major US universities with foreign governments, in part rationalized as the desire to be engaged global actors in major markets, like China, and as a pathway for expanding international academic networks. Another motivation was generating income. Brand-name American universities, mostly private, opened branch campuses under financial agreements with foreign governments. And many research universities, public and private, developed contract arrangements with Chinese companies like Huawei or with governments such as Saudi Arabia for research and other services.

A 2019 federal report estimated undisclosed contracts and grants at six universities over seven years to be worth more than $1.3 billion.[28] Such deals, along with the significant presence of Chinese students and faculty at US universities, added to desire by lawmakers for greater transparency, including reporting on all foreign government income. The political pressure and the anticipation of audits resulted in many universities becoming more vigilant in monitoring their many foreign financial transactions and arrangements.

A 2018 report by the Senate's Permanent Subcommittee on Investigations epitomized the growing fear of China's influence on American universities and efforts at intellectual property theft. "China unfairly uses the American research and expertise it obtains for its own economic and military gain," stated the report published in November 2019 focused on China's Thousand Talents Plan. "In recent years, federal agencies have discovered talent recruitment plan members who downloaded sensitive electronic research files before leaving to return to China, submitted false information when applying for grant funds, and willfully failed to disclose receiving money from the Chinese government on US grant applications."[29]

At the same time, and as noted previously, there was growing concern within US research universities that the problem of intellectual property theft and the focus on Chinese faculty and students was perhaps exaggerated and counterproductive.[30] Tightening visa rules led to hundreds of Chinese and other foreign graduate students and faculty encountering delays or denials of visas or entry into the United States. The Committee of 100, a group of Chinese American leaders in academia, business, government, and the arts, raised concerns regarding increased visa restrictions. They also doubted Director Wray's contention that China posed a "whole-of-society" threat to the United States and his implication that all individuals of Chinese descent are not to be trusted. More than 60 science, engineering, and international education organizations signed a letter to US scientific agencies warning that policies to address national security concerns could end up harming scientific progress. And in a July 2019 letter to Secretary of State Mike Pompeo, Harvard University president Lawrence Bacow called the uncertainty around the application process unnecessarily "unpredictable" and "fear-inducing."[31]

How should American universities have reacted to the pressure coming not only from Washington but from Beijing as well? Under President Xi Jinping's increasingly nationalist policies, the Chinese government's own internal logic often refused Chinese visas for US academics and for anyone with a record of criticizing the party and national government. Universities in the United States and elsewhere were being warned not to cross Beijing. After the University of California, San Diego, invited the Dalai Lama to be its 2017 commencement speaker, the Chinese government canceled state-funded academic exchanges with the campus.

Xi's ascendency posed significant problems for academic freedom, not just in China.[32] A 2019 report on academic freedom in China by

Scholars at Risk, an organization that monitors academic freedom worldwide and helps displaced scholars by arranging for temporary positions at member universities, outlined the "systematic and targeted tactics employed by state and university authorities in mainland China to constrict academic activity and to intimidate, silence, and punish outspoken academics and students." It also documented Beijing's international efforts, including reports of Chinese scholars and students placed under surveillance at universities in the United States and elsewhere, along with "intimidation and coercive legal action, and apparent efforts by Chinese officials and their allies to constrain expression on foreign campuses."[33]

The report warned of universities establishing programs or campuses in China. "For decades now, the Chinese government has invested heavily in academic institutions and programs designed to compete with the world's finest," said Robert Quinn, the executive director of Scholars at Risk. "This positive ambition is undermined, however, by state policies and practices that fail to protect academic freedom. This poses grave personal and professional risks for Chinese scholars and students and serious academic, reputational and financial risks for foreign academic institutions with partnerships with Chinese counterparts, in China or abroad."

International human rights organizations called on universities in the United States and elsewhere to beware of Beijing's nationalist international policies and to seek countermeasures. "Colleges and universities that stand together are better equipped to resist Chinese government harassment and surveillance on campuses, visa denials, and pressures to censor or self-censor," said Sophie Richardson, China director at Human Rights Watch. "President Xi's moves to strangle academic freedom inside China makes it all the more urgent to ensure that students and scholars of and from China can enjoy academic freedom abroad," Richardson said. "Institutions can demonstrate their commitment to peaceful, critical expression by adopting smart, robust protections, and keeping their gates open to all who seek academic freedom."[34]

Anti-science Rhetoric and Policies

The onset of the COVID-19 pandemic, Trump's pattern of denial and politically motivated misinformation, and his mishandling of this major national challenge was simply the culmination of a president who regards facts, and science, as merely a political tool. Less than a year into his presidency, the administration's policies related to science became apparent. Trump ran on a platform that firmly denied global warming and portrayed scientists as politically motivated and untrustworthy—messaging that extended to the higher education community.

In its first proposed budget, as noted, his administration called for large-scale cuts in funding to most federal science agencies. The administration also launched a campaign to roll back policy initiatives and funding intended to control climate change and research that is integral to environmental regulations, like monitoring industrial pollution. A report by the Union of Concerned Scientists stated that "the Trump administration has sidelined science in its handling of critical public health and environmental decision-making," with serious consequences not only for the United States but for the world.[35]

Previous presidential administrations had on occasion used science policy as a political tool. The massive investment in NASA in the 1960s included a purposeful geographic distribution of federal funding for science at universities and private-sector companies. Much of the funding for NASA and other agencies such as DARPA (the Defense Advanced Research Projects Agency) went to basic research with no clear government or commercial use. The purpose was to not only help build the nation's science capacity but also to generate political support in Congress and among the public for the space program and Washington's huge investment in research and development following Sputnik.

Science and technology as a tool of defense policy is a central theme of much of US investment in basic science. In the Reagan era, the false promise of developing space-based lasers capable of shooting down Russian ICBMs played into arms control negotiations. Reagan's White House also had no qualms over suppressing research, delaying the release of an expert congressional report that exposed the technical infeasibility of the administration's "Star Wars" missile defense proposal. Later, the George W. Bush administration banned federal funding for most stem cell research, a political concession to the Republican right-wing anti-abortion movement. The Bush administration, and its Republican base, also denied the existence of human-induced global warming. This came in the early stages of federally funded research on what is one of the great challenges to the global community.

But arguably, Trump and his supporters took the anti-science movement to new heights, tied to a populist policy agenda that viewed science as one more component of the "deep state"—the self-serving government elite and bureaucracy.[36] Fulfilling a campaign promise, the first major reversal in science policy came in June 2017 when Trump pulled the United States out of the 2015 Paris Agreement on climate change mitigation. "The Paris Climate Accord," he said in a statement made in front of the White House, "is simply the latest example of Washington entering into an agreement that disadvantages the United States to the exclusive benefit of other countries, leaving American workers—who I love—and taxpayers to absorb the cost in terms of lost jobs, lower wages, shuttered factories, and vastly diminished economic production."[37]

It was not clear whether Trump and his administration were in total denial of the human causes of climate change. Agriculture Secretary Sonny Perdue voiced skepticism about climate change, believing it to simply be due to normal "weather patterns." But what is clear is that the White House, under the guise of deregulation, pursued a concerted effort to reverse national policies related to reducing greenhouse gases and to hinder federal agencies collecting data and conducting research on climate change, including its economic and social impact.[38]

A 2019 study by the Climate Science Legal Defense Fund, specifically formed to provide legal support for federal scientists, listed hundreds of "government attempts to restrict or prohibit scientific research, education or discussion, or the publication or use of scientific information." These included censoring scientists, particularly on the issue of climate change; restricting participation and presentations at scientific conferences; ending or restricting access to federally collected scientific data; inappropriate interference in scientific grants; ignoring or halting science advisory committees; and simply not appointing individuals to key government positions.[39]

In one of many examples, in late 2017 the Department of the Interior and the Environmental Protection Agency adopted unprecedented protocols for review of grant applications by political appointees—normally a peer review process—with the objective that these federal agencies reflect "the priorities of the current presidential administration." In response, a November 2017 AAUP report, *National Security, the Assault on Science, and Academic Freedom*, stated that although funding priorities change from one administration to the next, what was new was the Trump administration's "open hostility toward science, particularly science that touches on climate change, that examines the impact of fossil fuels on public health, or that entails international collaboration."[40]

In another example, Rod Schoonover, a senior intelligence officer, was scheduled to discuss climate change and its impact on national security before a congressional committee. Upon learning of the content of his planned presentation, the White House prevented his appearance. Schooner then resigned. And in early 2019, the Trump administration withdrew most of the funding for the Landscape Conservation Cooperatives, a program that supported more than 16 research centers focused on the climate crisis, species extinction, and energy security. This was in defiance of instructions from Congress, which had approved $12.5 million of federal funding for the cooperatives.[41]

Bush-era restrictions on federal funding for stem-cell research, while partially relaxed under the Obama administration, still hindered cutting-edge research. The Trump administration ended fetal-tissue research by government scientists and placed restrictions on academic researchers seeking NIH grants. Meanwhile, there was no major investment in research related to foreign influence on US elections, as called for by America's scientific community. An editorial in *Science* stated, "We cannot manage what we do not measure. Without an organized research agenda that informs policy, democracies will remain vulnerable to foreign and domestic attacks."[42]

The administration also made no significant effort to study or implement the potential impact of gun control laws. Reflecting the lobbying power of the National Rifle Association (NRA, the gun ownership advocacy group), in 1996 Congress passed a law preventing federal agencies and grants from studying the societal costs of America's high rate of gun violence.[43] The NRA was the single largest contributor to Trump's 2016 presidential campaign. Despite the dramatic increase in gun violence, particularly the use of military-style weapons, presidential leadership on this issue was nonexistent, lest it upset the NRA and his Republican base of voters that opposed any kind of gun control.

The COVID-19 pandemic only accelerated the Trump administration's efforts to either suppress the findings and view of scientists in the federal government and, even more egregious, to make false claims about the nature and extent of the pandemic. Despite the warnings of scientists within and outside of the federal government, Trump initially proclaimed COVID-19 a hoax perpetrated by his political opposition. Trump also saw benefit in mocking those who wore face masks. He downplayed the pandemic, saying for months it would "magically disappear." Clearly, his major concern was the impact of the virus on the economy and his reelection bid, and he promoted open disregard for the safety measures outlined by his own administration as a form of political protest.

In an open letter, some 1,200 members of the National Academy of Sciences lamented Trump's "denigration of scientific expertise" and sought to "restore science-based policy in government."[44] This came at a time when the Trump administration sought to block funding for further testing of the virus and Trump personally promoted unproven claims of effective therapies. Trump made the Centers for Disease Control and Prevention into a political tool, denigrating what is supposed to be a nonpolitical government entity.

The Ultimate Impact: Facts Denied

Trump's nationalism aligned with populist and neoconservative movements of the past, yet to an unprecedented degree, facilitated by his novel use of social media and a willingness to use the federal government for personal political gain. We might conclude that Trump's hostility toward the higher education community was not so much a heartfelt conviction as simply effective politics intended to please his Republican base. Universities were a useful political symbol of liberal academics obsessed with "political correctness" and the suppression of conservative thought. They were a low budget priority—even though polling indicates significant concern among Americans with the rising cost of a college or university education, therefore ripe for some sort of federal policy answer.

During his run for president in 2016, as noted, Trump's campaign paid little attention to education. Without specifics, his campaign staff floated ideas that seemed motivated by his personal desire to reverse Obama-era reforms more than anything else. His presidential platform included getting government out of direct student lending with the intent of going back exclusively to private banks (where the federal government assumed all the risks and banks gained higher profits), requiring colleges to share the risk of student loans, discouraging borrowing by liberal arts majors,[45] deregulating higher education markets that favored for-profit tertiary enterprises, and reducing the authority of the Department of Education's Office for Civil Rights, which enforces federal anti-discrimination laws. Trump's plans to lessen federal oversight of for-profit institutions emerged in the context of a class action lawsuit against the short-lived Trump University—a case that led to a $25 million settlement for false advertising in what was called a "massive scam."[46]

As his administration moved into its fourth year, Trump continued to portray universities and colleges as symbols of intolerant liberal activism. During his March 2019 speech at the Conservative Political Action Conference, Trump returned to the themes he articulated during the battles over free speech on the Berkeley campus. He would soon issue an executive order to deny federal research funds to colleges and universities that did not support free speech as defined by his administration. To the loud approval of the annual gathering of conservative activists and elected officials, he stated, "If they want our dollars and we give them by the billions, they've got to allow people to speak."[47] Yet, like so much of the Trump administration's announced plans for higher education, not much came from the executive order. Universities and colleges comply with First Amendment guarantees on free speech, and the White House holds limited power to restrict congressionally allocated funding for academic research and financial aid programs—the two most significant areas of federal authority over higher education. Symbolism and rhetoric was the most valued commodity for Trump and his administration.[48]

How to speculate on the longer-term impact of Trump's nationalistic populist policies on America's network of universities and on its scientific community? Essentially, Trump's most radical nationalist impulses had a significant yet not necessarily permanent effect on the nation's higher education system. The repeated proposed budget cuts to academic research and financial aid, as noted, were rebuffed by Congress and by both political parties. Anti-immigrant rhetoric and a labyrinth of visa restrictions that depressed talent mobility are reversible under a Biden administration, depending, in part, on the full ramifications of the COVID-19 pandemic. At the same time, the pandemic-induced decline in the economy, and the slow reaction of Trump and Congress to provide adequate emergency funding to individuals and states, will accelerate the financial woes of universities and colleges, public and private alike. With enrollments and tuition revenue plummeting at many tertiary institutions, some will likely close or be forced to merge with other colleges and universities.

What is less sure is the full impact of the demeaning of science and scholarship—that facts are a matter of debate—and more generally the precipitous decline in trust in public institutions and democracy itself. Even in the waning days of his presidency, as noted previously, Trump promoted false accusations on the legitimacy of the election of Biden and attempted to retain power through extortion and threats, even contemplating a pathway for a coup—the formula of right-wing demagogues and autocrats. The spectacle of his supporters storming the nation's Capitol building, at his encouragement, to obstruct congressional certification of Biden's victory, attests to the damage of Trump's presidency. But perhaps the most meaningful test of the long-term impact of Trumpism: the speed, or lack thereof, of an understanding by a larger public, and many conservative politicians, that climate change is a real threat to America's economy and national security, and to humanity itself.

There also is the need for a wider recognition that the United States remains connected to world events, witness the pandemic, and that science and analysis is vital to coherent policy development—and for a nation to face reality. The pandemic could have led to a significant federal response. It was an opportunity to verify the importance and legitimacy of science and the global scientific community in containing the virus and quickly finding a solution: a vaccine. Under this scenario, the science that proves the realities of climate change might have been further elevated in the public mind. COVID-19 had an immediate and obvious impact requiring national leadership; climate change is a slower existential threat and a heavier lift in gaining wider public support for mitigation.

A substantial portion of the American public believed Trump's repeated claims that scientific inquiry is simply a political exercise and that the academy is hopelessly biased, that his failure to win reelection was the fantastical result of a nationwide conspiracy. It's a narrative that will have longevity among voters and right-wing politicians caught in the powerful web of neo-nationalism. Building back the confidence in and reputation of public institutions, including universities, will be a long-term project. The exchange of a divisive neo-nationalist president for a leader who seeks to unify the nation, values science, and understands the importance of higher education as a means of national development might be the first step toward redemption.

5

Turbulent Times

Intellectual and Institutional Challenges for
Universities in Germany, Hungary, and Poland

WILHELM KRULL AND THOMAS BRUNOTTE

> Very unwelcome truths have emerged from the universities, and very
> unwelcome judgments have been handed down from the bench time
> and again; and these institutions, like other refuges of truth, have
> remained exposed to all the dangers arising from social and political
> power. . . . And it can hardly be denied that, at least in constitutionally
> ruled countries, the political realm has recognized, even in the event
> of conflict, that it has a stake in the existence of men and institutions
> over which it has no power.
>
> Hanna Arendt, 1967

HANNAH ARENDT EXPRESSES the full ambivalence of the complicated
connections between truth and politics, as well as the role universities
can play within these complex relationships.[1] However, she also projects the confidence that universities will play a role of fundamental
importance that cannot be ignored by those who are in power, at least
in constitutionally ruled countries.

In the past decade, the fundamental role universities play in advanced
knowledge societies has been challenged by neo-nationalism. Germany
as well as eastern European countries such as Poland and Hungary are
constitutional states. But even there the rise of neo-nationalism, a worldwide phenomenon (China, India, Russia, the United States, and some
European countries), poses a serious test for universities. Moreover, the
COVID-19 pandemic shows how difficult it is to design health policies

that are based on scientific facts, even in countries with stable democratic systems like Germany.

This chapter discusses the reasons why neo-nationalism has grown in Europe and attempts to address the distinct circumstances faced by universities in Germany, Hungary, and Poland. It also presents ideas for seeking solutions to the vexing problems affecting the freedom and autonomy of science and scholarship.

The Rise of Nationalism in Europe

There is not just one explanation for the rise of nationalism and populism. The causes for this worldwide phenomenon are multifaceted. The following discusses five causes that are frequently discussed in sociological analyses. Some are of a more general nature; others apply to Europe in particular.

Rapid Pace of Change and Responsibility of Elites

Scientific and technological progress has led to a tremendous acceleration of social change. Digitization, new modes of communication, intense networking, enhanced mobility, and rapid innovation are accelerating the processes of change at an unprecedented pace—what Hartmut Rosa calls an accelerating society (*Beschleunigungsgesellschaft*).[2]

In addition, society faces grand challenges like protecting natural resources, combating climate change, managing migration movements, and transforming the working world. All this unsettles people, resulting in a form of status anxiety that runs through the history of populist movements. They are experiencing changes in their environment, in their social bonds, and also in their working life. For example, there are differential experiences and perceptions regarding the impact of an economic transition accelerated by the COVID-19 pandemic. This includes, on the one hand, profits and privileges for a minority, and on the other hand, damages, losses, and failures being imposed on society, costs that are ultimately shared by the taxpayers. Those who feel alienated from larger social and economic changes fear that an elite class is almost solely benefiting from rapid changes in science and technology, the accumulation of capital, and political power; they also believe that these economic and political elites are unable to deal adequately with society's problems or to act in a way that meets the needs of the general public.

An alarming skepticism is becoming rife in much of Europe. This is negatively affecting the public trust in politics, in business, and in academia. This is a challenge that must be faced by the scientific community, individual scientists, and scholars as well as university leaders.

Insufficient Management of the Refugee Crisis

In 2015, Europe experienced a large-scale refugee crisis. Refugees arrived in great numbers, traveling across the Mediterranean Sea or overland through southeast Europe. They included asylum seekers but also others: economic migrants and in some cases even hostile agents, including militant members of Islamic terrorist groups disguised as refugees.

Particularly in Germany, a growing segment of the population believed that the government was no longer able to properly deal with the situation, notwithstanding the fact that, as a consequence of an agreement between the European Union and Turkey in 2018, the number of asylum seekers arriving in the EU and in Germany decreased significantly. Polling data shows that most people in Europe vastly overestimated the increase in the non-EU immigrant population.[3] Adding to the perception of mismanagement, the European Union failed to achieve a joint response to a refugee crisis fueled by war and economic instability in northern Africa and Syria. EU member states had diverging policies in dealing with refugees, asylum seekers, and other migrants. As a consequence, nationalist and populist tendencies gained significant momentum.

In the United Kingdom, the pro-Brexit campaign in 2016 used the rhetoric of "Let's take back control" and focused on greater national control of immigration—from Europe or elsewhere. Subsequent elections in Austria, the Netherlands, France, and Sweden were heavily influenced by right-wing political parties and candidates. There were some signs of moderation, as demonstrated by the election of Alexander Van der Bellen as Austrian president and Emmanuel Macron as

French president. Many European countries were undergoing a fundamental reordering of their party systems: President Macron's La République En Marche movement did not exist five years ago, and Italy became governed by a peculiar coalition of the anti-European League party and the left-wing Five Star Movement.

But in Poland and Hungary, right-wing parties gained political power. In autumn 2017, Hungarian prime minister Victor Orbán declared eastern Europe a "migrant-free zone." After campaigning with a strong anti-immigration focus, in April 2018 his coalition secured two-thirds of the seats in parliament in the general election that provided the basis for changes in Hungary's constitution. In the run-up to the European elections in May 2019, Europe seemed to be in a state of "radical disequilibrium," observed George Soros in 2019.[4] The presidential elections in Poland in June and July 2020 again confirmed a nationalistic candidate, even though the result was extremely close.

Increasing Importance of Social Media and Online Communication

Social media and online communication have significant influence on the nature, quality, and development of public discourse. Anonymity, collecting likes from others, competing for attention, and providing algorithmic content, as well as the use of social bots, all influence the exchange of information and the quality of debates in the virtual realm.

Psychological studies consistently indicate that users prefer information that confirms their views and attitudes—a phenomenon known as "confirmation bias."[5] Information, arguments, or facts put forward by those who do not belong to one's own party or peer group get refuted reflexively—what is referred to as "partisan bias." And the so-called backfire effect bewitches those who defend their view even more obstinately if they feel challenged by deviating information. All these effects can be observed as well in ordinary face-to-face discussions. The internet and social media, however, multiply these phenomena.

Through social media, various communities form global connections and create an immense impact in the virtual realm, even if a group merely represents a moderately sized circle in the real world, known as the *illusionary giant* principle. Collectively, these groups polemicized deviating opinions in other communities with an intensity that borders on hate. As a result, we are, figuratively speaking, experiencing a regression into political interest group politics. In this battle of emotions, hard facts fail to make an impact. People appear to be immune to what others call *research-based evidence* or *scientific truth*. In addition, in the course of the COVID-19 pandemic, conspiracy theories have proliferated.

Social media, however, can also be used to support democratic structures or to better convey one's own concerns through direct communication. Recently, scientists repeatedly succeeded in making their own position heard in public. A good example is the German virologist Christian Drosten, who was accused of providing exaggerated statistical evidence concerning the aggressive spread of COVID-19 by the German yellow press. Drosten, however, managed to defend himself successfully via his Twitter account. In this he was even supported by colleagues who had criticized his work before.

Prevailing Politics of Emotions

Psychological or emotional factors also play a part in the emergence of neo-nationalist movements in Europe. This is exemplified by Dominique Moïsi's insights from his 2010 book *Geopolitics of Emotion*: "The Other will increasingly become part of us in our multicultural societies. The emotional frontiers of the world have become as important as its geographical frontiers."[6] Moïsi, however, also speaks about more fundamental societal emotions; namely, cultures of fear, humiliation, and despair, which significantly influence people's views of the world.

Poland provides an example: it is a nation that has lived through the horrors of World War II and the Holocaust, and then suffered under Soviet control. Its ties to the European Union are comparatively young. Its new sense of freedom is intertwined with the desire to determine its own fate and not to let others—like the Brussels bureaucracy—impose regulations. This finds a strong expression in the Polish slogan: "Teraz, kurwa, my."[7] It is hard to translate this, but it means something like, "Now, damn, it's our turn!" This is the expression of a deeply felt social sentiment that nationalists and populists as well as Poland's ruling political party, Law and Justice (PiS), have leveraged in a fierce battle with the European Union to regain Poland's sovereignty and, as one frequently hears in public debates, its "dignity."

Democracies in Crisis

In their 2018 book *How Democracies Die*, Steven Levitsky and Daniel Ziblatt put forward the thesis that democracies throughout history break down because the tacit norms of *mutual toleration* and *institutional forbearance* erode over time.[8] These norms—which can be summarized as respect for the political legitimacy of the opposition—are unspoken but nevertheless are conventions that tie a democracy together. Once all parties accept that they will not be in power forever—which is a natural precondition for democratic systems—they will see that it is in their own interest to treat political opponents with respect because their opponents, in turn, will one day hold power.

Deriding opponents as criminals, showing contempt for critics in public, spreading conspiracy theories about the opposition, and questioning the legitimacy of contrary voices or votes—all erode functional democracies. In times of crisis or threat to democracies, it is important that the mainstream parties, notwithstanding the fact that they represent opposing political views, are able to overcome their antagonism and cooperate. Being in power is not a license to settle personal scores, exact revenge, or self-deal. Levitsky and Ziblatt hold that the survival of democracies requires that politicians prioritize long-term stability over short-term gain and respect the democratic system in general, even if the amount of respect is not prescribed by written law or a constitution.

Europe provides many examples of right-wing parties generating division. The populist and neo-nationalist Alternative for Germany (AfD) is isolated from the rest of the political spectrum in Germany, but it wields power within the Bundestag. The AfD propagates a hostile policy toward refugees. Ironically, shortly after being founded in 2013, this party was often called a *Professoren-Partei* because many of its active members were established academics at German universities who were skeptical of the euro. In Poland, the Catholic Law and Justice

Party has confronted the secular postcommunist part of society. And in Hungary, the neo-nationalistic Fidesz party aggressively attacked the Hungarian-born philanthropist and investor George Soros, who in the early 1990s established the Central European University as a stronghold of liberal education. Only some of the Nordic countries are seemingly successful in integrating neo-national parties and interest groups into the political system and public debates, thus far.

The following offers individual case studies of neo-nationalist movements in Germany, Hungary, and Poland, and the challenges they pose for universities, including talent mobility and immigration, international engagement of universities, academic freedom and civil liberties, and the role of science and scholarship. With respect to the neo-nationalist spectrum introduced in chapter 2, Germany can be viewed as a country with nascent populist movements and populist parties gaining power in national and regional parliaments. Hungary and Poland, by contrast, are countries with neo-nationalist-leaning governments, both of which were recently reelected, and show clear tendencies toward becoming illiberal democracies.

The Case of Germany

Germany provides an example of the intersection of neo-nationalist movements with universities in the policy areas of international talent mobility, academic freedom, and the distrust of science. Since 2015, the refugee crisis has firmly dominated public debates in Germany. The influx of refugees became a divisive political issue, especially during the 2017 federal election campaign. The main focus of criticism from nationalist and right-wing groups, including the AfD, was Chancellor Angela Merkel's open and sympathetic approach to migrants and refugees, derogatively labeled by her political opponents as *Willkommenskultur* (welcome culture). Largely based on its anti-immigrant campaign, the Alternative for Germany won 12.6 percent of the votes in 2017, resulting in 94 members of parliament.

Controversy at Technische Universität (TU) Dresden provides a window into the complexity of neo-nationalist politics in Germany. TU

Dresden is one of Germany's leading technical universities. Beginning in 2012, it became one of the eleven Universities of Excellence that were singled out in a nationwide competition called the Excellence Initiative. Apart from the special case of Berlin, TU Dresden is the only University of Excellence in East Germany. It is highly dependent on international students and staff. Because of its university, Dresden is one of Germany's scientific hotspots. The city strives for international attention and is eager to attract the best researchers in their respective field.

Unfortunately, Dresden is also the birthplace of the PEGIDA campaign, a neo-nationalist movement fighting against the so-called Islamization of Europe. PEGIDA stands for Patriotische Europäer gegen die Islamisierung des Abendlandes, which can be translated as Patriotic Europeans against the Islamization of the Occident. Every Monday— alluding crudely to the weekly protests that were held every Monday in East Germany before the fall of the Berlin Wall and Germany's subsequent reunification—Dresden has experienced demonstrations by citizens of all social backgrounds in support of this movement.

Even though the number of PEGIDA supporters eventually shrank from 25,000 to 3,000 by 2015, the city's prestige suffered from these demonstrations, with a significant effect on TU Dresden's reputation among international students and staff. In 2015, 12.5 percent of students and 7.8 percent of staff were international. To bolster TU's image as an international center of teaching and research, Rector Hans Müller-Steinhagen had previously formulated the goal of raising the proportion of international students to 20 percent.[9] However, he also acknowledged this would be very difficult to achieve because of Dresden's xenophobic climate. "We suffer from a great loss of reputation," Müller-Steinhagen was quoted as saying in Germany's leading weekly newspaper, *Die Zeit*, in 2015. In the same article, Saxony's then state minister of science and arts Eva-Maria Stange conceded that "damage will not be eliminated fast."[10]

TU Dresden's academic leadership subsequently put great effort into attracting international students and staff. This included opening a Welcome Center offering information, assistance, and guidance to international students and researchers. To demonstrate his desire to attract international partners, Müller-Steinhagen tweeted an image of himself with a sign "I am the Rector of the TU Dresden and one of more than 500,000 Dresdeners, who do not attend PEGIDA demonstrations." Because of these and other efforts, the number of international students held steady at approximately 15 percent of the university's total enrollment.[11]

Academic freedom is guaranteed by the German constitution (*Grundgesetz*). Although this provision of the constitution has not been under serious political threat, there were increased efforts by German academics to articulate the value of academic freedom in an effort to combat propaganda ("fake news") and disinformation disseminated on social media platforms like Facebook and Twitter. "We cannot wait until people come to us," Germany's leading sociologist, Jutta Allmendinger, said on the occasion of the March for Science in Berlin. "We need to bring our findings to them." She continued, "Many people are looking for certainty, for simple truths. This is understandable, and yet we cannot offer absolute truths. But probabilities, and that is already quite a lot."[12]

In 2019, the Alliance of Science Organizations in Germany (Allianz der Wissenschaftsorganisationen), the union of the most important German research organizations, launched a campaign that consisted of a series of events focusing on five aspects of academic freedom: as an individual right, as a prerequisite for the rule of law and democracy, as a responsibility, as a protection against external influence and pressure of legitimation, and as a right under threat worldwide. This events also helped commemorate the 70th anniversary of the German constitution in 2019.

Germany's federal president (*Bundespräsident*) Frank-Walter Steinmeier regularly warned against a new fascination with authoritarianism among neo-nationalist-leaning supporters. In a March 2019 speech given at the American Academy in Berlin, Steinmeier spoke on the intersection of reason and democracy. He referred to Fritz Stern's 1961 book *The Politics of Cultural Despair*, which outlines how Germans in the 1920s and 1930s began to give up on reason and to glorify force, causing the nearly inevitable progression to the horrors of the Nazi regime: "His passionate appeal for a policy of reason was underpinned by a deeply held conviction that democracy and freedom themselves were also at stake with the loss of reason."[13]

In 2018, the Science Barometer, a survey conducted by Science in Dialogue (Wissenschaft im Dialog) in which citizens are asked about their attitudes toward science and scholarship, indicated that the distrust of scientists does not stem from their lack of expertise. Rather, two-thirds said that they "completely" or "tend to" agree with the statement that scientists could not be trusted because they are "strongly dependent on their sponsors and donors," and that their lack of independence was partly motived by financial gain. This corresponds with another result: 60 percent said they were not convinced that "scientists conduct research in the public interest."[14] Moreover, the Barometer revealed that the majority of AfD supporters were particularly skeptical of science; a majority also said they did not think that climate change was caused by human economic activity.[15]

The Case of Hungary

In Hungary, the national conservative and populist Fidesz party under Victor Orbán has been in power since 2010. Campaigning primarily on migration issues and foreign meddling, and provoking a climate hostile to the institutions of the European Union, the success of Fidesz is an alarming example of neo-nationalist populism in Europe. Fidesz has used its supermajority to revise the Hungarian constitution to enhance Orbán's political power. Orbán and his party have been criticized internationally for the government's increased control of the media, manipulation of elections, limitations on academic freedom, and erosion of the autonomy of the Hungarian Constitutional Court. Orbán also took advantage of the COVID-19 pandemic to further expand his political power.

Over the past three years, Orbán orchestrated a series of policies to gain greater political control over the nation's universities and to suppress dissent. This included attacks on the Central European University in Budapest. The CEU is a university founded by the Hungarian-born American investor and philanthropist George Soros, and its stated mission is to "engage in interdisciplinary education, pursue advanced scholarship, and address some of society's most vexing problems."[16] Soros became useful to Orbán as a political enemy—a foreign billionaire attempting to influence Hungary with liberal values and institutions. This included attacks on Soros's Open Society Foundations (OSF). The OSF has the goal of fostering democratic development in central European countries in the aftermath of the collapse of the Eastern bloc to pave the way for liberal and open societies. These values were in conflict with the nationalistic and patriotic ideology propagated by the Fidesz party. The OSF has more financial and personal resources than any other nongovernmental organization (NGO) in central Europe. It maintains a network of foundations, think tanks, and activists that is largely financially dependent on it.

Orbán, who ironically benefitted from an OSF scholarship himself in an earlier period of his career, issued political and juridical measures to make life hard for the CEU. Orbán did not make the mistake of attacking the university directly. Rather, he cleverly sought to make the CEU's existence in Hungary difficult by issuing a general law on the status of foreign-operated universities in Hungary as an amendment to the National Higher Education Law. It was evident that this law was targeted to place restrictions on the CEU: it required foreign universities operating and awarding diplomas in Hungary to be based on an international agreement with the government of the country of origin and required any such university to maintain a campus with a teaching program in its home country. The CEU was the only foreign university in Hungary that did not meet these criteria.

In response, the university signed a cooperation agreement with Bard College, a private liberal arts college in New York and set up a teaching program there. But Orbán refused to sign a contract with the state of New York. As a consequence, the CEU's president and board decided in December 2018 to move to Vienna and to start teaching there beginning in autumn 2019, with the hope of eventually returning to Budapest. For CEU students already enrolled in Budapest, however, teaching continued until the end of their courses, as required by EU law.

Reflecting on the series of events in Hungary, CEU president Michael Ignatieff observed a political weakness: "What we didn't see coming at CEU is that we trained the transition elite, a liberal democratic transition elite, but we trained the elite that lost politically. Post-1989, the transition elite, the liberal democratic elite," he continued, "got pulverized in Hungary's election and a new centre right—conservative, religious, Christian, anti-migration—won. We are now facing all the consequences of having trained an elite that lost."[17]

The 2019 elections to the European Parliament raised the profile of the dispute.[18] Notwithstanding the fact that Orbán was trying to win votes with a radical anti-European campaign, his Fidesz party is part of the European People's Party (EPP), the alliance of conservative parties in the European Parliament. Pressure was exerted by EPP chair Manfred Weber to allow the CEU to remain in Budapest; at the same time Weber offered to help form an alliance with the Technical University Munich in Bavaria. But the CEU's academic leaders eventually chose to permanently move most campus operations to Vienna.

Orbán's hostility toward the university caused enormous damage to the Hungarian higher education system. "Driving CEU out of the country was already a huge blow," stated CEU prorector for Hungarian affairs Zsolt Enyedi in a press release. "If the backbone of the Hungarian academic life is broken, however, we will need to face a problem of a much grander scale."[19]

Attacks on universities and the academic community were not limited to the CEU. The Hungarian Academy of Sciences, one of the main entities for funding academic research, was also a target of Orbán. The purpose of the academy is cultivation of science, dissemination of scientific findings, support of research and development, and representation of Hungarian science domestically and around the world. Its members are made up of academics whom Orbán viewed as part of his political opposition. The ruling Fidesz party cut the academy's budget by two-thirds, giving the funds to the Ministry of Innovation and Technology, a new ministry established after the Hungarian elections in April 2018. In justifying its budget cuts, the Hungarian government-controlled media outlets claimed the academy was disloyal and inefficient.

László Lovász, president of the academy, initially told Minister of Innovation and Technology László Palkovics that the transfer of funds to the ministry was illegal.[20] But by November 2018, under political pressure, Lovász announced that the academy had agreed with the ministry to form a joint evaluation commission to consider reorganizing the academy's financial structure. At the end of December 2018, the academy was again faced with the accomplished fact: the Ministry of Innovation and Technology blocked the funds allocated to it for the year 2019.

In another front on the war on universities, in October 2018 Orbán issued a decree to revoke accreditation and funding for gender studies programs at the two Hungarian universities. "The Government's standpoint is that people are born either male or female, and we do not consider it acceptable for us to talk about socially-constructed genders, rather than biological sexes," a spokesperson put forward to justify this radical step.[21] The ban on issuing degrees in gender studies was enforced unilaterally by the Hungarian government without prior consultation with the Hungarian accreditation agency. As observed by Andrea Pető, a distinguished Hungarian historian, "The government is increasingly trying to gain control over science by publicly discrediting individual researchers, by controlling their budgets, and by failing to fund or shutting down what does not fit into their concept" of the role of universities in an illiberal democracy.[22]

The Case of Poland

Poland provides another troubling case study of right-wing populism in Europe. The neo-nationalist party Law and Justice controlled the national government beginning in 2015. The party garnered international attention for its reform of Poland's Constitutional Court and public service broadcasting—political measures pursued under the slogan "The good change" (*Dobra zmiana*). The reform of the Constitutional Court was a significant break from the values of the European Union because it de facto abolished the tripartite division of power between the court and the government. In January 2016, the European Commission launched a mechanism for protecting the rule of law for Poland. Consequently, in 2018 it opened an infringement procedure because of this highly questionable juridical reform.

That same year, the Polish parliament, Sejm, passed the Law on Higher Education and Science—commonly referred to as the Constitution for Science, or Law 2.0. It imposed a comprehensive reform of higher education, including significant changes in the functioning of universities, their financial framework, and the path for academic careers. Critics contend that the law threatens the autonomy of universities. The rectors' power is increased, leading to further centralization and hierarchization of universities.[23] There is also a fear that the governing boards for public universities will include mostly nonacademics and be dominated by politicians or people who support the current government. Minister Jarosław Gowin claimed exactly the opposite: "[This law] significantly increases the autonomy of universities, opens the path of career advancement for young scientists, increases the level of internationalization of Polish universities and science."[24]

The main concern of academics was that the new law furthers the neoliberalization of Polish academia and has a disproportionate emphasis on the commercial applicability of research. While this criticism might be legitimate, the neo-liberalization of academia does not per se entail an authoritarian or neo-nationalist intervention negatively affecting the autonomy and freedom of universities. One might argue that changes in the authority of university leadership, in particular strengthening the power of the rector and the influence of supervising boards, are prone to political interventions or influences from outside academia, which may be abused by political interest groups. This, however, is not necessarily the case in Poland. If these mechanisms and instruments are used wisely, they could—just like in some other EU member states—improve the universities' strategic capacity and their independence from politics. This, of course, crucially depends on the choice of rectors.

A similar critique applies to the introduction of a competitive framework for Polish colleges and universities. The government intends to single out about a dozen universities that in the future will acquire the prestigious status of research university and will receive additional funding. In turn, critics fear that the remainder of Polish institutions of higher education "will be degraded to the status of some sort of 'professional academy' and reduced to the role of producing technical cadres for the economy."[25] Again, a competitive framework for institutions of higher education does not automatically imply a right-wing political intervention. It may also be an instrument to identify research universities with international appeal and visibility.

Another critical issue is the reorganization of academic subjects and disciplines that was introduced with an accompanying executive decree in order to *polonize* the humanities and to establish an overarching evaluation scheme for Polish academia. In this scheme, subjects and disciplines were assigned to a smaller number of newly created umbrella disciplines. This has provoked the protest of anthropologists and ethnologists because these disciplines were assigned to the research area culture and religion, as a subset of the humanities. The fact that anthropology and ethnology could be categorized as part of the social sciences was ignored by the government. These overreaches by the government were a reason that the International Society of Ethnology and Folklore and the Polish Ethnological Society sent a letter to Minister Gowin expressing their fear that this designation would make the discipline unidentifiable, hinder the appreciation of the work of Polish ethnologists, restrict international collaboration, and isolate the Polish anthropological community. Being reduced from a full academic discipline to a mere study program, anthropology will probably become "'Schrödinger's cat'—at the same time alive and dead."[26]

A Synthesis of the Three Case Studies

European universities are deeply rooted in the tradition of the Enlightenment. Historically, they were transformed from academic institutions under the patronage and influence of nobility or the church into institutions that are chartered, maintained, and developed by their respective government and society. Moreover, they have members (students, professors) who are entitled to regulate and manage their own affairs as long as they follow democratic rules and comply with the laws of the state. As a result, universities in Europe enjoy a comparatively high degree of autonomy from political influence.

Things change, however, if the political climate moves from liberalism to populism, or even transforms into illiberal democracy.[27] If the political realm—contrary to Arendt's optimism discussed at the beginning of this chapter—does not recognize that it should not exercise power over universities, things get problematic.

The three case studies of Germany, Hungary, and Poland show that the influence of neo-nationalist movements on universities are varied. While in Germany the democratic foundation of its universities is not in danger and there is little interference by the state in the autonomy of universities, it is clear that the social climate is changing. In cities such as Dresden—but not only there—it is evident that it is becoming more difficult for internationally active research universities to attract the best talent from abroad. However, those who bear political responsibility, the federal president and the major research organizations, do a great deal to maintain the democratic basis of the universities, to bring science and society closer together, and also to give science communication a more important role.

Things are different in Hungary and Poland. In Hungary, we can observe an open conflict between the nationalistic government and the CEU. The interventions in the Hungarian Academy of Science are clearly politically motivated. And Orbán publicly criticizes programs that conservatives object to, such as gender studies, and has taken steps to curb related teaching and research programs.

In Poland, on the contrary, we witness the nationalistic influence of the Polish government on universities largely conforming to a neoliberal reform agenda. The Polish case is more nuanced because if the state and society are the true owners of the universities—as is the case with most European universities—then it should not be a problem for a democratically elected government to regulate universities within the bounds of the electorate's mandate. This would dovetail with the tradition of the European university based on Enlightenment values. It is different, however, if the state is on the threshold of becoming an illiberal democracy, as is the case in Hungary and Poland. Regulatory frameworks, budget priorities, and higher education reforms guided by political interests are only appropriate if they are established by democratically elected governments in liberal democracies and open societies. This is only partially the case in Hungary and Poland.

The basis for the existence of European universities is, thus, a social contract in which the state and society give universities their freedom and autonomy so that they, in turn, can benefit as much as possible from them. For universities, though, this means that their actions cannot be guided by academic interests alone. Universities must be open to society and its concerns and questions. They must be responsible actors in society and educate concerned citizens, who are not only focused on academic issues but also social, environmental, and global challenges.[28]

This social contract, however, is challenged by nationalistic and populistic movements and governments not only in Europe. A potential mitigation is for the academic community to focus more on the societal challenges and problems posed by globalization, and by scientific and technological innovation, that better addresses the concerns and fears of their constituents.

A Way Ahead: European Universities, Public Engagement, and Science Communication

In turbulent times, it is helpful to remind ourselves of the lines of the German poet Friedrich Hölderlin: "Wo aber Gefahr ist, da wächst / Das Rettende auch" (But where the danger is, there also grows / the saving power). One must not be devastated by the current political climate, or the impact of the pandemic, and overlook the opportunities for European universities. In the following we attempt to sketch three ways to respond to right-wing political movements and nationalist governments in Europe. Each focuses on creating a stronger sense of a European identity.

Establishing a Network of European Universities

In a speech given at the Sorbonne on September 26, 2017, French president Emmanuel Macron presented his thoughts for the future of the European Union. He argued that the "cement that binds the European Union together will always be culture and knowledge" and thus that Europeans "should create European Universities—a network of universities across Europe with programmes that have all their students in study abroad and take classes in at least two languages. These European Universities will also be drivers of educational innovation and the quest for excellence. We should set for ourselves the goal of creating at least 20 of them by 2024. However, we must begin setting up the first of these universities as early as the next academic year, with real European semesters and real European diplomas."[29]

Similarly, on November 14, 2017, the European Commission published a proposal to enhance the existing European Education Area. By 2025, the commission called for the establishment of a European university network and a so-called Sorbonne process to achieve mutual recognition of higher education degrees and study periods abroad. Here are, sketched very briefly, some of the resulting initiatives.

On March 10, 2018, Charles University in the Czech Republic, Heidelberg University in Germany, Sorbonne University in France, and the University of Warsaw in Poland founded the European University Alliance 4EU. And although this collaboration was in the making for two years, and representatives of the universities emphasized that it was therefore not motivated by Macron's or the EU proposal, they also said that they would like to be seen as a pilot for a new type of European university.

Similarly, Eucor–The European Campus, in which the Universities of Basel, Freiburg, Haute-Alsace, and Strasbourg, as well as the Karlsruhe Institute of Technology are involved, was founded in late 2015 to establish "a clearly defined economic and research epicentre without walls and borders and with an international flair."[30] On April 12, 2018, a joint declaration was signed, expressing the intention to develop Eucor further into a European university. Another example: the U4-Network of the Universities of Ghent, Göttingen, Groningen, and Uppsala. Its proponents also expressed a strong interest in being a contender for the envisaged status of a European university (jointly with the Estonian University of Tartu and recently even with a much larger consortium of universities spreading across Europe).

Many existing networks are set up as small clusters of nearby universities that jointly develop programs for master's and doctoral courses as well as research projects and possibly even share infrastructure. But a proposal for a quite different kind of European university was made by the German journalists Manuel Hartung and Matthias Krupa in 2018: they argue for establishing just one rather large university with around 75,000 students. This university would in turn consist of a group of institutes focusing on different subject fields: the future of society, digitalization, and technology and engineering. Hartung and Krupa argued for distributing these institutes among the countries at the periphery of the European Union: Portugal, Estonia, the Czech Republic, Sweden, and the Netherlands—each institute building on existing infrastructure and professional experience.

To succeed, the mission and vision of truly European universities need to be more clearly defined, and they must receive substantial funding from the European Commission as well as the respective member states. But together with some other suggestions for changes to higher education, research, and innovation policies, they collectively provide a path for a more sustainable future of academic life in Europe. Especially in the area of research, international cooperation is the best way of working productively. Here it becomes particularly clear that more can be achieved together. In the words of Chekhov, "There is no national science, just as there is no national multiplication table; what is national is no longer science."

However, one must also bear in mind that countries differ with respect to their universities, research funding structures, and systems of higher education. These differences and peculiarities must be considered. Here it is important to identify particular strengths and to strive to collaborate via symmetric partnerships with mutually beneficial advancement. In particular, care must be taken to ensure that such collaborations do not only involve elites. If universities have the task of training the next generation of leaders in science, business, and society at large, the developmental opportunities of society as a whole must also be included in this mission.

Offering the next generation of European students, and future faculty, a truly European education might help promote perspectives that transcend nationalistic thinking and further promote international cooperation. The idea is not to propagate a new form of internationalism or European supranationalism, but to bring heterogeneous perspectives, diverse academic cultures, and different ways of life into a mutual dialogue and an inspiring exchange of ideas. Increased networking among universities will also lead to more international research and higher education policies in European member states that, in turn, should include a strong emphasis on the freedom of research, teaching, and learning as well as the free movement of students and academic staff.

A network of European universities will also help to provide a basis for academic cooperation even in situations where political cooperation is difficult or—like in the case of Brexit—no longer possible on the terms that were agreed to previously. This is why some UK universities started to establish new links to Continental universities, like Oxford to Berlin, aiming at building bridges for academic cooperation even if Brexit will lead to cutting links that were of fundamental benefit for both parties.

Engaging with Civil Society and Rooting Universities in Their Local Context

It is evident that universities can no longer be considered neutral institutions at the margins of the political sphere—if they ever were. For quite some time we have focused on institutional autonomy and perhaps forgotten that universities are institutions that are deeply rooted in civil society and their local environment.

This topic of greater social engagement was discussed at a conference, the 15th Transatlantic Dialogue on Openness, Democracy and Engagement, organized by the American Council on Education, the European

University Association, and Universities Canada. It was held in July 2018 at the European University Institute in Fiesole, Italy. The participants agreed that European universities should shift from public or civic engagement as a third pillar to engagement as horizontally linking teaching and research.[31] Furthermore, the participants focused on the university as a socially responsible institution. This goes back to the notion of a civic university (among others) introduced by Goddard and colleagues, who identified the following dimensions of a civic university:

- Actively engaged with the wider world as well as the local community of the place in which it is located
- Holistic approach to engagement, seeing it as an institution-wide activity and not confined to specific individuals or teams
- Strong sense of place, recognizing the extent to which location helps to form its unique identity as an institution
- Sense of purpose, understanding not just what it is good *at*, but what it is good *for*
- Willing to invest time, people, and resources to have an impact beyond academia
- Transparent and accountable to its stakeholders and the wider public
- Innovative methodologies such as social media and team building in its engagement activities with the world at large[32]

The basic idea is to bring together the Anywheres and the Somewheres, the academic global elite with the people living in the region of the university who rightly expect that their local university is for their benefit, too. Examples for such universities are the Aalto University in Finland, the Karlstad University in Sweden, and the Leuphana University at Lüneburg, Germany, as well as the great public universities in the United States.

Moreover, some German *Länder* experimented with transforming state-financed universities into universities governed by independent foundations. This transformation was also combined with the idea of rooting these universities in civil society by integrating community representatives on university boards or activating local communities for further support of their universities, thus bringing them into a closer and mutual relationship with research, teaching, and learning.[33]

At the end of the conference minutes, the participants also identified five shared challenges to be solved in the future:

- Reaching out and communicating with all segments of the public
- Establishing a truly global curriculum combining engagement with internationalization of research and teaching, and integrating research cultures, techniques, and perspectives from non-Western research communities
- Providing lifelong learning opportunities enabling the local community to keep up with changing labor markets—meaning increased use of artificial intelligence, robotics, and digitized work processes
- Developing and providing information and communication technology and fostering digital literacy
- Measuring higher education's added value in a diverse way and not only focusing on standard research performance indicators[34]

Because all these challenges provide a suitable basis for further detailed consideration, the authors of this chapter want to focus only on the first aspect, which aims at a reliable and honest science communication involving trust, participation, and transparency.

New Modes of Science Communication: Trust, Participation, and Transparency

To a great extent, universities are still committed to a linear sender-receiver model of communication. Press releases, glossy university magazines, and annual reports—science communication often consists of researchers proudly informing the public about their capabilities and achievements. But raising expectations for scientific breakthroughs, and maybe even overselling the importance of one's research, can easily undermine trust. Academics should be careful not to mistake science communication for public relations; it should be conceived as an interactive mode of communication that starts with listening carefully to local voices.

The crisis of trust, a theme in the case studies provided in this book, is just as much a crisis of *the public*: its devolution into interest groups. Instead of speaking to the public, it will be essential for scholars and scientists to first of all listen to the people, to take their concerns seriously, to pay attention to the social pressures they are exposed to.

Given that neo-nationalists are skeptical of and even hostile to science and are at least partially successful in fueling general skepticism of scientific findings and facts, it is important embark upon new modes of interactions with the public. Interactive communication can play a key role in restoring trust in public institutions, and the science community, and in generating political and funding support for universities. The results of an Allensbach survey highlight the need for improved communication: 90 percent of surveyed scientists are convinced that they can communicate important scientific research findings in a way that is understandable to laypeople. Yet the survey response of journalists begs to differ: just 12 percent trust in scientists' ability to communicate in a way that is easy to understand.[35]

German psychologist Rainer Bromme formulated three criteria that scientists must fulfill if they want to be perceived as credible:

- Attribution of skills and expertise: a scientist possesses the necessary skills to produce knowledge and solve problems
- Attribution of integrity: a scientist follows justifiable rules and methods
- Attribution of good intentions (goodwill): a scientist focuses on the common good and benefits for others[36]

"Scientists are trusted less if they are associated with the intention of wanting to convince people," says Bromme. Certainly, the majority of researchers try to meet these criteria. But apparently, self- and external perception differ greatly. A nonscientific expert illustrated this in a lecture to the Volkswagen Foundation in October 2017. Stefan Wegner, one of the CEOs of the major advertising agency Scholz & Friends, spoke of a problem posed by four public perceptions of science and the science community:

- Science is incapable of self-criticism
- Science always claims to know what is good and what is right
- Science is merely simulating its openness to dialogue
- Science is too closely interlinked with politics[37]

What can scholars and scientists do to present themselves to the public in a more effective way? For far too long it was believed that facts simply had to be presented to the public, and billions in funding would flow from government agencies and the private sector. An open dialogue striving for more symmetric exchanges of views and opinions needs to replace the traditional monologue. Promoting scientific and technological innovation provides an example. Innovation is also a social process that cannot be solely developed through scientific progress; it has technological, economic, social, and ecological implications. As part of the German government's High-Tech Forum, the working group Participatory Agenda Setting in Research and Innovation Policy and a subsequent report noted that public participation could "build mutual understanding and trust and bring science and society closer together."[38]

The participation model certainly has its limits. Considering the scientific freedom guaranteed by the German constitution, citizens' participation is primarily consultative. Scientific freedom should continue to decide which subjects to focus on and which specific methods to use. After all, the knowledge asymmetry, especially in this highly specialized discourse, makes a dialogue on equal footing impossible. The experts' knowledge edge over laypeople generally cannot be overcome—although scientists should always attempt to bridge the gap and describe scientific matters in a way that is understandable for them and to take the questions posed by a nonexperts seriously.

For academics across Europe, it is increasingly urgent they see themselves as globally concerned citizens. In the light of increasing skepticism toward elites, the interaction between academia, politicians, and the public at large must be reviewed critically and realigned. Researchers need to enter into an open, transparent, participative, mutual, and critical dialogue with society. The fact that Germany came through the COVID-19 pandemic comparatively well is also due to a significant improvement in science communication. A Science Barometer survey showed that confidence in science rose in Germany. We hope that this will not remain a one-off effect of the crisis and that this success can be continued in the future.

6

Neo-nationalism in the European Union and Universities

MARIJK VAN DER WENDE

Our individual liberties are not givens. Democracy is not something we can take for granted. Neither is peace, and neither is prosperity. But if we break down the walls that hem us in, if we step out into the open and have the courage to embrace new beginnings, everything is possible.

Angela Merkel, Harvard Commencement 2019

NATIONALISM IS NOT new to Europe; it has characterized some of its darkest periods in the twentieth century. But since the end of World War II, European countries have lived in peace and moved steadily toward cooperation and interconnectedness. Their shared economic and political interests converged in the European Union, eventually as a joint response to globalization. Higher education is part of the process and became part of that response, supported by the creation of the European Research Area (ERA) and the European Higher Education Area (EHEA).[1] But the political winds seem to be shifting, and there are signs of a new age of populism and nationalism emerging in Europe—a development that challenges universities to rethink their social contract and missions in local, national, European, and global contexts, and that has real consequences.

This chapter discusses the character of current neo-nationalist movements in Europe and differing regional and age-related perceptions of the values of the European Union. Among many EU member states, there remains significant support for the European Union and for ensuring mobility, particularly among younger people. But at the periphery of the Union, the dynamics are different, and that translates into significant challenges for universities. This raises a number of related questions. First, as students search for opportunities outside of neo-nationalist-leaning countries on the EU periphery, how are nations with open higher education systems, specifically the Netherlands and Denmark, coping with increased enrollment demand and the budget and policy challenges that feed nativist politics? Second, how are universities, and the European higher education community, responding to neo-nationalist attacks on academic freedom and university autonomy? And third, how are universities in Europe reacting to this changing political landscape of populism, and how might their leaders mitigate its impact?

Neo-nationalism in Europe

The term *neo-nationalism* refers to the nationalism that emerged in the mid-2010s in Europe's political landscape and relates to anti-immigration and anti-globalization right-wing populism, protectionism, and euroskepticism. The fear of downward social mobility and the disproportional impact of globalization have fueled a political movement found throughout Europe.

In the Netherlands, right-wing anti-immigration parties such as the Centrum Party and later the Centrum Democraten emerged in the early 1980s. They dissolved after leaders were excluded from parliament and other "cordon sanitaire" strategies (similar to those in Belgium) were applied. In France, neo-nationalism gained strength when Jean-Marie Le Pen won a seat in the European Parliament in 1984. Since then, the Front National (called Rassemblement National since 2018) under the leadership of Le Pen's daughter has positioned itself as the anti-globalization party and champion of those who see themselves as its losers, manifested since 2018 as "les gilets jaunes." Anti-globalization evolved into an anti–European Union movement. France and the Netherlands surprised the rest of Europe in 2005 with an overwhelmingly negative vote (55 percent and 61 percent, respectively) in the referendum over the new EU Constitution.

Since 2005, populist parties have experienced significant political gains in more European countries,[2] including in Germany, Italy, Austria, Hungary, Poland, Sweden, and Denmark.[3] However, it is important to note that even though nationalist parties are on the rise, there is no universal trend toward nationalism within the European Union. Research finds that the increased visibility of nationalism in European politics is less attributable to a shift in global attitudes than to heightened political and social articulation of these attitudes via social media and political actors. The causes of this shift are country specific, but overall they are grounded in the resonance of anti-elite discourse and a crisis of liberal democracy.[4]

Contrary to what is often stated in the media, and as noted previously, among Europeans there is no significant negative trend in identifying with the European Union. Data from the autumn 2018 Eurobarometer reveal on average an upward trend in identifying with EU institutions (see table 6.1).[5] Overall the survey confirms that trust in the EU has risen considerably since 2015. On average Europeans trust the EU even more (42 percent) than their national government or parliament (both 35 percent). The overall image of the European Union has also increased significantly, which is likely related to its improved economic situation (49 percent consider it good) and related decrease in concerns about unemployment, which receives the lowest score (13 percent) in years (from 51 percent in 2009 and 2013).

Relevant to our discussion on the rise of nationalism, the data on identity, immigration, and freedom of movement displayed in table 6.1 are particularly striking. First, the highest proportion of people identify themselves as citizens of the European Union (71 percent); most express a dual European and national identity. Younger people express a stronger attachment to the EU than do the older generations. Second, concerns over immigration decreased strongly, although it still is the biggest concern, followed by terrorism and economic issues. Third, the free movement of EU citizens, who can live, work, study, and do business anywhere in the European Union, receives the highest level of support as a policy priority (83 percent) and is seen much more as a positive result of the EU (59 percent) than it was in 2015 (only 25 percent).

These trends indicate that the European Union recovered from the downturns caused by a series of crises—the global financial crisis, euro crisis, and refugee crisis—since 2007, although the full impact of the COVID-19 pandemic remains to be seen. More trust also indicates more confidence and expectation of the European Union providing solutions; for example, 69 percent favored a common European policy on migration, and 65 percent a common EU foreign policy.

These trends are based on averages for the European Union as a whole. It is important to look at the countries at the extremes of the spectrum. Smaller Nordic and Baltic states tend to be more on the positive end, while the United Kingdom, Greece, and some other countries in the southern and eastern parts of Europe appear rather frequently at the lower end. Even with the political tumult of Brexit, it is surpris-

Table 6.1. Selected scores on topics relevant to neo-nationalism discussion (in percentages)

Indicator	EU 2018	EU 2015	3 countries with highest scores	3 countries with lowest scores
Trust in the EU	42	32	Lithuania 65 Denmark 60 Sweden 59	Greece 26 United Kingdom 31 Czech Republic 32
Overall positive image of EU	43	34	Ireland 64 Luxembourg 56 Bulgaria 56	Greece 25 Czech Republic 28 Slovakia 33
I feel like a EU citizen	71	50	Luxembourg 89 Germany 86 Ireland 85	United Kingdom 58 Czech Republic 56 Greece 52
Main concern facing the EU: immigration	40	58	Estonia 65 Malta 61 Slovenia & Czech Republic 58	Romania 25 Portugal 30 United Kingdom 31
Political priority with most support: free movement of EU citizens who can live, work, study, and do business anywhere in the EU	83	n/a	Latvia 96 Estonia and Lithuania 94	Romania 69 Italy 72 United Kingdom 74
Most positive result of the EU: free mobility of persons to live, work, or study anywhere in the EU	59	25	n/a	n/a

Source: Eurobarometer 2018

ing to see that only 31 percent of UK citizens see immigration as the main concern facing the European Union, which is well below the EU average of 40 percent, and that the free movement of EU citizens still has the support of 74 percent. The anti-immigration argument was used extensively in the Brexit campaign, but the concerns of UK citizens shifted to state financial and economic issues, which may actually be a result of the uncertainty in the lead up to a hard or soft Brexit. Brexit is also mentioned sometimes as a cause for more support for the EU in other member states.

A survey by the University of Amsterdam carried out in 10 EU members states prior to the 2019 elections for the European Parliament confirmed that only some 10–25 percent of the population want to leave the European Union, despite their criticism of the current functioning of EU institutions. Interestingly, Poland and Hungary were at the lower end, with only 10 percent who would like to leave the European Union.[6]

Even though nationalist parties are on the rise in Europe, there seems to be no major shift of attitudes toward nationalism, a negative trend in identifying with the European Union, or a decline in European supranational identity.[7] Florian Bieber notes that this appears at first contradictory. But it might be explained by the political, and social, articulation of nationalist attitudes that has changed, and the polarization that has shifted in support of nationalist candidates.[8] In addition, I would argue that in Europe, nationalist parties articulate and fuel such attitudes, but more generally national politics may do so, as many national political leaders tend to blame the European Union, or "Brussels," for all sorts of problems. Attempting to keep nationalist parties at the margins, various centrist political parties adopted some of the nationalistic policy agenda, for example, on protectionism or even patriotism,[9] and seem at times also to borrow from the anti-elite discourse.

Many feared the election of a wave of nationalist party candidates with their anti-EU agendas to the European Parliament in May 2019. The dominant centrist parties, the Christian Democrats and Social Democrats, saw their 53 percent majority diminished to 44 percent. However, together with the Conservatives, the Liberal Democrats supported by President Emmanuel Macron's new party, and the Green

Party, the center, although more fragmented, still received the support of 76 percent of the voters. Euro-critical parties won less than feared and were scattered on both ends of the political spectrum. With a voter turnout much higher (51 percent) than in previous rounds (42 percent in 2014), the European Parliament strengthened its reputation as a public agora and representative body where all views are heard.

However, the arrival of the COVID-19 pandemic put the European Union's internal cohesion under great pressure and amplified existing internal tensions. With the virus outbreak in early 2020, all EU member states chose nationalist-protectionist solutions and closed their borders. The European Commission initially was unable to coordinate relief or provide much-needed medical supplies. Meanwhile, negotiations over the European Union's multiannual 2021–27 budget, complicated by Brexit, were overshadowed by much bigger tensions concerning solidarity between the North and the South, where countries were hit hardest by the pandemic. Their economic recovery became dependent on a substantial redistribution of the EU budget (€1,100 billion), as well as an additional package of loans and subsidies (€750 billion)—a deal negotiated during an exhaustive summit in late July 2020, under the remarkable leadership of German chancellor Angela Merkel.[10] The final agreement[11] was based on an initial and historic proposal by Germany and France, reached despite substantial concessions made to a group of smaller, high-GDP countries (Austria, Sweden, Denmark, Finland), also known as the "frugal" countries, led by the Netherlands.[12]

At the same time, events leading up to and during the pandemic did not affect support for the European Union negatively. Eurobarometer data from 2018 cited above emphasized EU citizens' high levels of trust in the European Union. This positive attitude was confirmed in 2019 Eurobarometer data, at the highest rates since 2014, and with higher trust in the EU than in national governments or parliaments.[13]

Further evidence is found in a dedicated survey, conducted in late April 2020, which focused on citizens' attitudes toward EU measures to fight the COVID-19 pandemic.[14] It showed that almost 6 out of 10 respondents were dissatisfied with the level of solidarity shown among EU member states during the pandemic. Nearly 7 out of 10 respondents wanted a stronger role for the European Union in fighting the crisis. Around two-thirds of respondents agreed that "the EU should have more competences to deal with crises such as the Coronavirus pandemic." In responding to the pandemic, European citizens wanted the European Union to focus primarily on ensuring sufficient medical supplies for all EU member states, on allocating research funds to develop a vaccine, on direct financial support to member states, and on improving scientific cooperation among member states.

A survey taken in the same period by the European Council on Foreign Relations also found that although people in nine member states believed the European Union responded poorly to the crisis, large majorities in these countries also said that they were now more firmly convinced of the need for further EU cooperation than before the crisis.[15]

How Are Universities Affected?

The plea for stronger cooperation within the European Union is, of course, a positive sign for the higher education sector, as well as for positive attitudes toward the EU, particularly among the younger population. The free movement of EU citizens to live, work, and study anywhere in the EU is viewed as the most positive result of the European Union and receives the highest level of support as a policy priority. The Erasmus Programme was rated the fourth-best outcome of the European Union, after peace and the euro. These opinions are crucial to sustain the beneficial conditions created in the European Research Area and the European Higher Education Area and for continued financial support for cross-border collaboration, exchange, and mobility.

However, and as noted before, these trends reflect averages for the European Union as a whole. Perspectives may be quite different in the countries toward the extremes of the spectrum or otherwise more on the periphery of the EU. Universities located there have more at risk. As shown in table 6.1, the United Kingdom is a clear and rather dramatic example. The Brexit process substantially affected the higher education sector, including a 26 percent drop in European students coming to the United Kingdom in 2019.[16] A further drop of 25 percent is expected for

2020 as a result of the UK government's decision to end home fee status for the European Union, other European Economic Area (EEA) citizens, and Swiss nationals following Brexit.[17] European research staff began an exodus back to the Continent.

Hungary is another sobering example. Although scores on European identity (80 percent) and in favor of free mobility (81 percent) are relatively high in Hungary, immigration is seen as an important threat to the European Union (54 percent), combined with concerns regarding the national health and social security system (40 percent). Citizens may thus be easily mobilized against immigration. However, the political conspiracy built against George Soros as the founder of the Central European University, which eventually forced the CEU to leave the country, cannot be attributed only to a shift in civic attitudes. It is also an anti-liberal ideological campaign of the government's increasingly autocratic leadership, posing a threat to liberal democracy itself.

At the same time, other institutions, such as the Academy of Sciences, the Constitutional Court, the free press, and certain nongovernmental organizations were attacked by the Hungarian government led by President Viktor Orbán (see chapter 5). This caused the European Union to trigger Article 7 in 2018, a disciplinary procedure against Hungary for undermining democratic rules and being "a clear risk of a serious breach of the values referred to in Article 2 of the Treaty on the European Union."[18] The Union is founded on the values of respect for human dignity, freedom, democracy, equality, the rule of law, and respect for human rights, including the rights of minorities. These values are common to the member states in a society in which pluralism, nondiscrimination, tolerance, justice, solidarity, and equality between women and men prevail.[19]

Shocking experiences also emerged on the EU periphery. After a failed coup in 2016 in Turkey, officially a candidate for membership in the European Union,[20] thousands of university deans and faculty members were fired or arrested (see chapter 7). Even in more moderate countries with nonauthoritarian leaders, higher education has been caught up in political polarization. The Netherlands and Denmark are, for instance, countries with overall moderate scores on the Euro-barometer indicators and with relatively high levels of trust in the European Union: 60 percent and 57 percent, respectively (although the Netherlands shows a striking rise since Brexit). Yet governments in both countries looked for measures to control or even reduce the number of international students at national public universities, and campaigns against teaching in English were launched.[21]

Another example is Switzerland, not in the European Union but a member of the European Free Trade Agreement (EFTA) and participant in ERA and EHEA. As a result of a 2014 referendum on immigration, Switzerland lost access to EU research funding (Horizon 2020) and mobility (Erasmus) grants.[22] The same may happen to the United Kingdom if it does break with the EU free movement principle, which is conditional on the EU side for such cooperation.[23]

Higher education in Europe is significantly affected by the COVID-19 pandemic. Academic mobility and cooperation activities under the Erasmus+ and Horizon 2020 programs were frozen or delayed since the outbreak. As of August 2020, various borders between member states were closed. And EU budgets for higher education and research for 2021–2027 were substantially reduced.

Consequences for Open Higher Education Systems

Neo-nationalist and populist movements, combined with the EU principles of the free movement of persons, created new challenges for national systems with open enrollment policies. The Netherlands, Denmark, Switzerland, and the United Kingdom have two particular features in common: first, they are highly internationalized and are among the strongest-performing research systems globally in terms of the quality and impact of their scientific output; second, they have the highest percentages of international students among Organisation for Economic Co-operation and Development (OECD) countries at the doctoral level (>40 percent).[24] These students are mostly in the STEM fields. In the Netherlands, for instance, the percentage of international doctoral students in STEM may be as high as 75 percent. Fifty percent of all scientific staff in technological universities are international, 40 percent on average across all fields in the research university sector.[25] In the United Kingdom, 40 percent of staff at the top universities were from the European Union prior to Brexit.

Clearly such "open systems" greatly benefit from open borders. Participation in EU programs adds to their academic quality and performance. These four nations, for instance, have achieved the highest return on investment from funding by the European Research Council by attracting many ERC grantees from other countries.[26] Yet, if they go without the European Union's free mobility rules, universities may face serious uncertainties regarding their ability to engage with the international community. More generally, closing borders would be detrimental to their corporate and cultural sectors, as much as to their universities.

At the same time, such protectionist trends are not shaped only by nationalist parties or by national governments. In some cases, the university sector itself may actually seek policies to influence the outflow and particularly the inflow of academic and student talent. In the Netherlands, for instance, universities may on the one hand plead for continued tax exemptions (30 percent reduction for ex-pats for the first years after arrival) for international staff, while on the other hand asking the government for more legally sound options to control and direct the inflow of international students.

The need for more effective steering of student flows is understandable, given the conditions in which universities and governments operate in Europe. The European Union provides them with major opportunities for internationalization (i.e., open borders) but may at the same time constrain their options to regulate consequences at the level of the system or the institution. This is because the right of free movement of persons in the European Union[27] implies that students from other EU member states basically have access to higher education on the same conditions as member states' domestic students have. Initially, this right provided a legal basis for student mobility and the start of the successful Erasmus program in 1987, which is based on short-term reciprocal student exchange. In the first decade of its operation, it was further facilitated by the introduction of mobility instruments enabling the transfer of credits and the recognition of degrees.

With the signing of the Bologna Declaration in 1998, a major step was taken to harmonize the degree systems of the member states, and since then through the so-called Bologna Process applied to a much larger range of 48 countries, together shaping the European Higher Education Area.[28] A decade of system reform introducing a bachelor's-master's degree structure,[29] led to greater degree mobility, or "free mobility" (i.e., without regulation through Erasmus learning contracts or grant support). But unlike Erasmus, there emerged no mechanisms for reciprocity and to balance the migration of students and faculty between countries. As a result, these migration flows are uneven.

The Example of the Netherlands and Denmark

Dutch research universities saw their percentage of international students more than quadruple after the introduction of the Bologna reforms (from 5 percent of all enrollment in 2000 to more than 20 percent in 2019).[30] With their generally high position on global rankings (virtually all are in the top 200)[31] and broad provision of programs taught in English (23 percent at bachelor's level and 74 percent at master's level),[32] it is expected that these numbers will continue to rise, even though Dutch universities charge higher tuition (around €2,000–€4,000 per year for EU-EEA students) than most other European countries, where enrolment is sometimes free.[33]

External events, such as Brexit, may further contribute to this growth of students in the Dutch system. The Netherlands is seen as one of the best and more affordable alternatives for English-taught higher education in Europe. Projections by the Ministry of Education, Culture & Science in 2018 anticipate a 25 percent increase in international students over five years. This would bring the enrollment of students from the EU-EEA up to some 50,000 in 2023—in other words, the equivalent of two midsize universities in a system of just 14 public research universities that currently command some 15 percent of the nation's public budget. In 2019, the number enrolled was already 43,706.[34] As the state contribution to universities is an institutional lump sum within a fixed macro-budget, the above forecast growth resulted in a significant decrease in per capita funding over the past years, and therefore the Dutch research universities feared that this trend would continue, diminishing the quality of teaching and learning.

This is one of the main reasons universities asked the government to enlarge the range of legal instruments available to them to better control the admission of international students. Additional arguments are related to the balance of nationalities within international groups, which may become too strongly biased toward, for instance, German students in certain social science fields, or Asian students, especially at technological universities and in STEM fields.

Universities in the Netherlands generally do not have the ability to set quantitative caps for access to study programs. All students who fulfill the formal entry requirements, be they Dutch or other EU-EEA nationalities, are thus admitted. Only in some specific (professional, performing, or liberal arts) fields are universities allowed to use a "numerus fixus," or cap, and select their applicants before admission. The number of graduate programs, especially those taught in English, use some form of selective admission, often using a combination of merit-based criteria (prior academic achievement) and background variables related to students' home country or region. However, Dutch students rallied against the evolving criteria for graduate enrollment, as these criteria would also apply to them, whereas they hitherto were admitted into master's programs simply on the basis of their bachelor's degree, without extra criteria for GPA or level of English. The national student union argued against that "as a Dutchman, it is difficult to compete with a multitude of foreign students, whose majority have better grades, *but who have developed less in other areas.*"[35] But admissions rules must be the same for all students under Dutch and EU legislation.

Denmark is facing comparable challenges. Unlike in the Netherlands, tuition is free for EU-EER students, and loans and scholarships are available. Over the past years, students from the rest of the European Union collected the same generous support packages and fee waivers as Danish undergraduates. But Danish ministers questioned the value of this spending. Danish officials asked the European Commission to help solve the problem of students who were unwilling to pay back study loans after leaving the country. But they found no support in Brussels. The Danish government then tried to restrict the inflow of EU students based national labor market needs, as allowed under EU rules. But this policy solution became too complex—once students graduate, some may choose to leave the country. Consequently, the government reduced the number of programs taught in English at Danish universities. University rectors criticized this policy choice, claiming that efforts to reduce numbers of international students by closing English-taught degree programs would limit the education of Danish students (i.e., programs may not be sustainable in Danish because of lack of interest among only domestic students) and widen skills gaps.[36]

The experience of the Netherlands and Denmark demonstrates the budget and political complexity of internationally attractive open higher education systems. It also shows how vulnerable universities are in the face of nationalist or populist parties that freely criticize their international aspirations as part of their anti-globalization and anti-elite discourse. A glaring example is the Dutch Forum for Democracy (FvD), a right-wing, national-conservative, euro-skeptic political party established in 2015. During its election campaign in 2019, the FvD launched a "left-wing indoctrination hotline" for students who suspect left-wing political bias on their campus.[37] They won the Dutch provincial elections. The FvD leader, who holds a PhD from Leiden University, attacked universities in his victory speech as "one of the institutions that undermine our society."[38] The FvD is popular among right-wing student groups.

It was difficult to explain to Dutch taxpayers why more than 22,000 German degree students need to be educated "on their purse" when only some 1,200 Dutch students study in Germany,[39] a country with a much larger economy, with only slightly lower GDP (6 percent less than the Dutch GDP per capita in 2019), and with virtually free higher education. The Dutch government actually prompted its universities to recruit German students in the 1990s, as part of its "cross-border higher education policy." Universities in border regions, for example, Maastricht and Twente Universities, were especially successful, introducing many English-taught programs; Maastricht began to change its entire operational language into English. However, Dutch students were less motivated to study in Germany, and efforts to balance these flows failed. A former ministerial official commented with hindsight in 2011, "Recruiting German students is absurd and socially irresponsible. Only some universities benefit, while the government has to pick up the bill and less budget is left for domestic students."[40]

Student mobility between the Netherlands and Belgium (3,600 to and 3,272 from Belgium) or with the United Kingdom (3,360 to and 3,100 from the UK) is better balanced, despite the unequal population size and bigger differences in GDP and tuition fees in the case of the United Kingdom. Countries smaller in population and with large neighbors, like Austria, may face similar challenges.

As much support as there is for subsidized short-term student exchange under the Erasmus program, it is clear that the free mobility of degree students within Europe is more difficult to sustain. A money-follows-student system at the European Union level could be a solution, but it does not seem feasible in the short term given the important differences between member states in terms of tuition fee levels and student financial support systems.

Universities in countries with open systems may greatly benefit from the inflow of international students. In the Dutch case, the continued existence of its research universities in border regions may even depend on these flows. International talent is also crucial for national research and development productivity, and Dutch universities receive strong support from the corporate sector for their 2018 internationalization agenda.

However, such countries also saw the support for nationalist and populist parties rise over the past decade. Ministers are then caught between issues of national interest, such as R&D performance and labor market demands for highly skilled immigrants required for economic growth on the one hand, and nationalist pressures from up-and-coming political parties on the other. In the view of neo-nationalist parties, solutions to national problems include closing borders rather than keeping them open: internationalization of higher education is a problem rather than an opportunity. But as noted previously, these pressures do not come only from external political parties or populist groups.

Universities may actually contribute to these trends. For instance, in 2018 the University of Amsterdam transitioned to English in courses taught in popular study programs such as business studies and psychology. This caused an overwhelming number of international applications and enrollments, which the university lacked the infrastructure to adequately handle. Amsterdam's municipal government was not able to provide proper housing for these students. This triggered criticism by student organizations and populist voices on the city council. Both groups argued for "domestic students first." In other student cities, including Groningen and Utrecht, student organizations spoke out against "international students as a business model" and occupied university squares to protest the lack of student housing. Conservative student fraternities tend to select their housemates from within their own circles, and "no foreigners" was frequently found to be a top criterion.[41]

These examples serve to further illustrate that, as stated before, universities cannot assume that nationalistic anti-internationalization or anti-globalization trends are exclusively manifest outside their walls. In balancing access, cost, and quality of a higher education system, governments face a trilemma, as they can generally only achieve two out of three politically desirable goals: low public and private tuition fee costs; mass access to higher education; and stable or improved quality in teaching, research, and public engagement activities.[42] The extent to which universities can effectively navigate this complex space depends on their degree of institutional autonomy and government financial support.

Institutional Autonomy and Academic Freedom under Siege in Europe?

The arrival of illiberal democracies in Hungary and Poland, and neo-nationalist movements more generally, raises new questions regarding the health of academic freedom and institutional autonomy in Europe. Although with limited powers related to national higher education policies, the European integration process has had a major impact on universities. European universities anticipated these changes in the late 1980s when they formulated their main principles and values under the concept of a common European inheritance. These were laid down in a charter in 1988, at the 900th anniversary of Europe's oldest university, the University of Bologna (founded 1088). This charter, called the Magna Charta Universitatum[43] includes institutional autonomy and academic freedom among its fundamental principles:

> The university is an autonomous institution at the heart of societies . . . to meet the needs of the world around it, its research and teaching most be morally and intellectually independent of all political authority and economic power. (fundamental principle 1)

> Freedom in research and training is the fundamental principle of university life, and governments and universities, each as far as in them lies, must ensure respect for this fundamental requirement. Rejecting intolerance and always open to dialogue, a university is an ideal meeting ground for teachers capable of imparting their knowledge and well equipped to develop it by research and innovation and for students entitled, able and willing to enrich their minds with knowledge. (fundamental principle 3)

The charter was originally signed by some 500 European rectors and later by many more university from around the world. To date, a total of 889 universities from 88 countries on all continents have signed, with more than a dozen others waiting to join at the next signing ceremony. In 1998, at its 10th anniversary, European university leaders decided to launch the Observatory Magna Charta on the universities' fundamental values and rights to more closely monitor the implementation of the principles outlined in the charter. On that occasion they noted:

> Indeed, Europe had changed since the fall of the Berlin Wall in 1989 and the new political situation of an open territory (in which national borders were less and less important) called for constant analysis of the changes

affecting academia, from within or from without, as the relevance of old references was being questioned by the sheer speed and extent of social transformations in the region—from Lisbon to Vladivostok.[44]

The Observatory continuously monitors the key values and fundamental principles of institutional autonomy and academic freedom. As result, formal statements of concern for Turkish scholars and universities were published in 2016 and for preserving institutional autonomy among universities in Hungary, with specific reference to the CEU, in 2017.[45] At the Magna Charta's 30th anniversary in 2018, the president of the Observatory remarked, "In times of political turbulence, competing claims and internal fragmentation, values matter more than ever for universities as they are they are foundational principles of institutional self-understanding and positioning in society."[46]

The European University Association (EUA), which represents more than 800 universities and national rectors' conferences in 48 European countries, is also concerned with monitoring and promoting institutional autonomy as a core principle of university governance and advocating academic freedom as the single most important basis for meaningful academic research and teaching.[47] It does so in close cooperation with other organizations such as the Magna Charta Observatory, the International Association of Universities (IAU), and Scholars at Risk. The EUA also monitors institutional autonomy through its Autonomy Scorecard.[48] Until 2017, the Scorecard analyses showed that the level of autonomy that universities in Europe have varied greatly, but it showed improvements.[49] However, in 2017 the EUA became concerned and noted:

> While earlier assessments showed promising developments towards more autonomy in Europe, there is currently no distinguishable uniform trend. . . . The Old Continent faces . . . rising populism, weakening solidarity and pressure on some of its most important values—all of which affect the ability of the higher education and research sectors in fulfilling their missions. In this scenario, university autonomy and academic freedom are of particular concern, as there is a growing tendency for governments to interfere. We have recently seen concrete

cases in countries in Europe. . . . This is worrisome as autonomy and academic freedom are crucial to the well-functioning of universities.[50]

The problems in Hungary represent extreme cases; they do not represent a general trend in all European countries. Nevertheless, the European university sector has found common ground to stand with colleagues under siege. A hashtag campaign, #IstandwithCEU, prompted many onto the streets of Budapest in 2017 and at the end of 2018 to protest the Hungarian government's attacks on the CEU. And the rectors' associations of 10 countries signed the Vienna Declaration[51] warning of neo-nationalist efforts to restrict academic freedom and threats to democracy. But what can be done beyond public statements, debate, and advocacy?

The Charter of Fundamental Rights of the European Union established in 2000 provides in Article 13 that "the arts and scientific research shall be free of constraint" and that "academic freedom shall be respected."[52] Institutional autonomy is generally promoted by the European Commission throughout its series of policy papers and agendas on the modernization of higher education in Europe. However, the European Union does not have sufficient legal competencies to directly interfere with what are national systems of higher education. Member nations are reluctant to directly intervene.

However, the events in Hungary, where the CEU was eventually forced to move from Budapest to Vienna, triggered the European Union to interfere in a broader and more drastic sense. It did so through Article 7 of the Treaty on the European Union with the European Parliament, adopting a Recommendation on Defense of Academic Freedom. Referencing Article 13 of the Charter on Fundamental Rights of the European Union, its Human Rights Guidelines, and UNESCO's definition of academic freedom, it stated, "The right, without constriction by prescribed doctrine, to freedom of teaching and discussion, freedom in carrying out research and disseminating and publishing the results thereof, freedom to express freely their opinion about the institution or system in which they work, freedom from institutional censorship and freedom to participate in professional or representative academic bodies."[53]

The European Parliament then recommended that the council, the commission, and other EU institutions express the importance of academic freedom in all aspects of the European Union's external policies and activities. The objective: to demonstrate active support for students and academics who are at risk. It also proposed that a similar commitment to academic freedom be part of the Copenhagen criteria for future accession to the European Union, and it specifically mentioned the attack on academic freedom in Hungary and supported initiatives to enhance academic freedom in existing programs like Horizon 2020 and Erasmus+.[54] However, despite a last-minute effort by the leader of the European Parliament's conservatives to broker a deal between the CEU and the Technical University Munich[55] to allow the CEU to stay in Budapest, the decision was made to move to Vienna. The CEU's president bitterly condemned Western powers for not having done enough.[56] "Academic freedom or even the university cannot be taken for granted," he warned.[57]

Universities as Followers or Leaders?

Many universities in Europe focused their attention on being globally competitive while at the same time often neglecting the consequences of globalization, including growing inequality and diversity in their local communities. One cause is the drive to become world-class universities, in particular the pursuit of positioning on global rankings, often at the cost of their "national mission and relevancy in the societies that give them life and purpose."[58]

The rise of neo-nationalist movements is a wake-up call. "What seems to have died is the European international education community's faith in the inevitability of the cosmopolitan project," noted one observer, "in which national boundaries and ethnic loyalties would dissolve over time to allow greater openness, diversity and a sense of global citizenship."[59] The signs of trouble came in the first few years of the twenty-first century, when students took to the streets in the south of Europe to protest European higher education policies, particularly the Bologna Process and the Lisbon aims to make "Europe the world's most competitive knowledge economy." This European response to globalization was perceived by some as a neoliberal, Anglo-Saxon effort that conflicted with European social values.[60] EU ambitions were seriously set back by the vote against the new EU Treaty in 2005 and then the 2008 global financial crisis.[61] Students protested in 2006 when ministers discussed future scenarios of higher education at an OECD meeting in Athens,[62] with the concern that globalization was creating economic imbalances with detrimental effects on social cohesion.[63]

I argued in 2007 that European universities need to broaden their missions to not only respond to the profitable side of globalization, but also to address problems such as migration and social exclusion, to be more open and inclusive, to balance economic and social responsiveness, and to redefine their "social contract" in a globalized context. In the local context, this means enhancing access for migrant and minority students; supporting the integration of student groups with different cultural, ethnic, and religious backgrounds; and thus embracing diversity in all its dimensions and make internationalization inclusive.[64]

UNESCO stated in 2015 that "the social contract that binds higher education institutions to society at large needs to be redefined in a context of increased global competition." The European Commission, alerted by the protests to the crisis around the euro mostly in the south, notably in Greece, revised its hitherto rather utilitarian education agenda by stating, "With regard to the recent tragic events related to radicalization in parts of Europe, a particular focus on civic democratic, intercultural competencies and critical thinking is even more urgent."[65]

Are universities sufficiently aware of the looming tensions that led to the rise of right-wing populism? The vice chancellors of Oxford and Cambridge both assured me during a conference dinner only 10 days prior to the Brexit referendum that they were not worried about it passing because "we wrote a letter to the Prime Minister!" Some 90 percent of people working in UK higher education voted Remain, but the majority of voters did otherwise.[66] Leading universities may be especially criticized for neglecting local needs, while pushing so hard for their global missions. But even at the system level it should have been obvious that higher education has largely ignored the growing inequalities resulting from globalization.[67]

European universities cannot assume that nationalistic anti-internationalization or anti-globalization trends are exclusively manifested outside their walls. Skepticism of internationalization also exists inside academia. There is concern over the use of English as a second or foreign language for teaching and learning, the increased focus on global rankings and the reputation race with its annual tables of losers and winners, and worries over the recruitment of international students for institutional income and more generally "academic capitalism." These internal voices do not represent the dominant academic perspective or the formal institutional view. But they raise the question of whether academia's internal debate has conservative traits that include academic nationalism, protectionism, or indeed isolationism.

Most universities have been followers rather than leaders (see chapter 2). The rise of populism is not only a wake-up call. It is also an opportunity to speak up more loudly for open societies and to recover their sense of social purpose. Various constructive responses are emerging in this respect. Notable is the increased attention to the issues of diversity, equity, and inclusion. For instance, the bottom-up initiatives launched by the EUA emphasize that increased migration has contributed to a more culturally diverse Europe.[68] This included a project for refugees with a refugee welcome map showing an overview of initiatives of higher education institutions and related networks and organizations supporting refugee students, researchers, and academic staff.[69] A major and early example is Germany's program for refugee students,[70] aligned with Chancellor Merkel's welcoming policy for refugees, for which German higher education was praised in a recent Eurydice report.[71] Another example is Ireland's universities of sanctuary.[72] There is also the program sponsored by Erasmus+ and the Council of Europe's European Qualifications Passport for Refugees to recognize refugees' qualifications.[73]

In the United Kingdom, where the top universities, specifically Oxbridge, were accused of "social apartheid,"[74] in 2018 the government boosted the universities' civic role with a £500 million fund and the launch of "civic university agreements,"[75] aiming to promote regional collaborations and more local student engagement.

For the first time in its 900-year history, the University of Oxford is offering places to students from disadvantaged backgrounds with lower grades.[76] The ultimate response to inequality and anti-elite discourse came from French president Macron, who proposed to abolish his alma mater, the elite École nationale d'administration.[77] Across Europe, the concept of inclusive internationalization is slowly beginning to resonate and becoming more widespread, although universities still seem to find an integration of diversity and internationalization agendas (and staff units) challenging.

Despite these recent initiatives, big questions remain. Phrases like "We have created Europe and now we have to create Europeans," which were first heard after the rejection of the EU Constitution in 2005, are being repeated, and role of universities in this is being questioned. Did we fail to develop European identity and citizenship—a goal of the Erasmus program—in our students? Should we expect to hear more from the over 3 million former Erasmus students, in defense of Europe, or have they all become the now-criticized cosmopolitan elite? Did we fail to educate them as critical thinkers about social responsibility, democratic citizenship, and civic engagement in support of an open society?

Despite all the European studies courses and mobility programs, young Europeans seem to take democracy, open borders, freedom, liberal values, and the institutions that protect them too much for granted. They understand the European Union just as an open market or trading zone, not as a peace project anymore. Yet some students are standing up as leaders of bottom-up initiatives in support of European values and open borders. Many others may be held back by ambivalence about complex and sometimes aggressive debates on identity, diversity, inclusion, and exclusion, or they may be reluctant to be seen in leadership roles as part of the "elite" themselves. It is very much in question whether the values of liberalism or liberal democracy can actually be defended on the basis of individualism, and how strategies intended to address multiculturalism, inclusion, and socioeconomic inequality can be effectively pursued by universities.

As the data from the Eurobarometer demonstrated, a large majority of Europeans are in favor of open borders and free mobility. Data from a recent survey done in France, Germany, Greece, Hungary, Italy, and Poland confirm that an overwhelming majority of Europeans support open society values, including freedom of expression, the rule of law, and pluralism.[78] But general support for immigration from outside the European Union has waned with the arrival of the 2015 refugee crisis. Is it naive to believe in a borderless world? Conservative historian Niall Ferguson pointed to many so-called failed states unleashing a wave of refugees. Consequently, more than 700 million adults are looking to emigrate, with Europe as their most favored destination (23 percent, compared to 21 percent for the United States).[79]

At the same time resistance to mass immigration is rising in many of the most popular immigration countries. This is certainly one of the main challenges for the European Union, which is still lacking an integrated immigration and foreign policy. Meanwhile, right-wing populist parties are targeting young voters with growing success. They are even establishing new academies. For instance, the Institut de sciences sociales, économiques et politiques in France, launched by the Rassemblement National, is aimed at training "a new elite to change the dominant beliefs in society." Donald Trump's former spin doctor Steve Bannon established an alt-right university to train nationalists, although it was shut down by the Italian government.[80] The Hungarian government continues to restrict the academic independence of the Academy of Sciences. To battle these neo-nationalist predilections, a network of such academies of Europe, the European Federation of Academies of Sciences and Humanities (ALLEA), joined forces to address the increasingly hostile political climate toward science in a growing portion of Western societies.[81]

We owe it to young Europeans to be optimistic. This is "a moral duty," as we learned from Karl Popper, the great defender of an open society. In this spirit Leiden University's rector wrote, "If history has taught us anything, it is that out of conflict comes collaboration. Brexit won't hold back science because the challenges the world faces are bigger than the fights between nations and it is in everyone's best interest to work together."[82]

The COVID-19 pandemic has shown that global scientific cooperation is essential; it has resulted in an unprecedented push for global collaboration and open science. At this time it is too early to fully assess the implications of the pandemic on higher education in Europe. Will it lead to a further de-globalization or re-globalization and does this imply a rebalancing of the global higher education landscape? Will it bring the European Union closer together or drive toward it toward further fragmentation, re-regionalization, or even re-nationalization?

Institutional autonomy and academic freedom are stated as values in the European Treaty and the European Charter on Human Rights, but they are under pressure in some parts of Europe. The European Union is after all a collection of sovereign member states, lacking a consolidated foreign affairs policy and with only limited competencies to act internally in research policy, and even less so in education. Only with stronger internal cohesion will the European Union be able to play a significant role. Let's hope that this pandemic, despite its many victims, will eventually contribute to that.

7

Turkish Academics in the Era of Erdoğan

BRENDAN O'MALLEY

UNDER AN INCREASINGLY repressive neo-nationalist regime, large numbers of Turkish academics have been targeted for arrest and detention, universities closed, and thousands of academics fired. Officially these actions were carried out in response to several key events challenging the authority of the Turkey's president Recep Tayyip Erdoğan. The intensity of the purge increased dramatically following the July 2016 coup attempt. Erdoğan blamed his former ally turned rival, the moderate Islamist leader Fethullah Gülen, for the failed coup.

Events prior to the coup provide evidence of a deeper, systematic attack on academic freedom and civil liberties in an effort to restrict political opposition and criticism of Erdoğan's ruling party, the Justice and Development Party, or AKP. Some six months before the coup attempt, many Turkish academics signed an Academics for Peace petition demanding an end to military operations against Kurdish militants in civilian areas and asking for the opening of a peace dialogue. This led to the first significant wave of faculty persecutions. Prior to that, Istanbul's Gezi Park civil society demonstrations in 2013 spiraled into repeated protests nationwide that included faculty and students and led to restrictions on free speech.[1] Since the Gezi Park demonstrations,

141

Erdoğan and his party successfully sought administrative pathways for gaining greater control over the leadership and management of universities.

Erdoğan used these and other events as opportunities to silence voices critical of the AKP, including those in academia, as part of a slide into authoritarianism. Universities in Turkey, both public and private, had been home to a significant number of academics who opposed the AKP's drift away from the secular principles that defined the nation under its founding president, Mustafa Kemal, later dubbed Atatürk (father of the nation), and enshrined in Turkey's constitution. In doing so, Erdoğan was, in fact, following a familiar path. Atatürk had used constitutional restrictions on criticism of him, his government, and the principles of the secular constitutional republic he founded.

In his early years in power, Erdoğan was embraced as a source of hope for an improvement in human rights and freedom of expression in Turkey—a country with a record of extrajudicial killings and disappearances in the 1980s and 1990s. He initially sought EU membership, which requires an adherence to human rights. Over time, however, Erdoğan showed that his real interest was in achieving greater religious rather than political freedom. His political power, and his popularity, was rooted in his Muslim identity and his appeal to the mass of conservative rural voters and conservatives who had moved in large numbers to the cities and urban centers. In his drift to an authoritarian government, he rode a wave of religious revivalism previously suppressed by government leaders. He also leveraged a rising sense that the Turkish state was under threat from enemies within and outside its national borders—specifically Kurdish nationalism—and fears that supporters of Western-style secularism, including in Turkey's "deep state," were trying to take him down.

Erdoğan consolidated his political power by garnering support across the country in successive elections while presiding over an unprecedented period of political stability and economic growth. But after years of taking on more and more debt, fueled by a construction boom that enriched AKP partisans, Turkey's economy entered a period of instability. Beginning in 2018, Turkey experienced hyperinflation and a declining currency. This, plus the conflict in Syria and renewed military attacks on Kurdish nationalists, increased the regime's desire to restrict civil liberties and suppress Erdoğan's political opposition.

This chapter considers the origins of Erdoğan's shift toward authoritarian rule. Erdoğan and his party offered a vision of a nation whose society is more sectarian and oppressive. Particularly after the attempted coup in 2016, but before that as well, universities, faculty, and students represented a real and potential source of opposition that Erdoğan wanted to manage. The following also explores the question of whether Erdoğan offers a new form of Turkish nationalism or a merely a redeployment of the tools of nationalism to consolidate a different elite.

The Gezi Park Protests

Three years before the coup attempt, Erdoğan faced the first major challenge to his authority as prime minister with the Gezi Park protests in Istanbul. Erdoğan was a former mayor of Istanbul, and the city had previously proved important to his political popularity. But the planned development of Gezi Park, one of the last remaining green spaces in central Istanbul, into a shopping center sparked a major protest that lasted from May into June 2013. The plan, pushed personally by Erdoğan, followed his imposition of constraints on civil liberties; the protests reflected discontent with his rising authoritarianism. But they did not dent his ambition to elevate the position and power of Turkey's presidency and win the office for himself, which he duly did in 2014. Until then, power had been shared between the offices of prime minister, which he had held for three terms, and president.

In the months leading up to the Gezi Park demonstrations, a march in Ankara to celebrate the official anniversary of Turkey's establishment as a secular republic was blocked and the ensuing protest was attacked by riot police; and a series of new policies that restricted the sale of alcohol and that reduced the rights of women generated increased public concern, particularly in the more liberal cities and among academics. Inspired partly by the events in Ankara, the Gezi

Park protests began as a small sit-in by environmental and political activists. Over a matter of days, and after police used tear gas and burned down protesters' tents, the event evolved into a nationwide protest against the government's conservative agenda. Within a fortnight, it was reported that 3.5 million people had taken part in thousands of related protests across the country that left 5 dead and 8,000 injured.[2]

These protests united disparate political groups who opposed the increasingly authoritarian Erdoğan government and saw the demonstrations as an opportunity to defend civil rights and freedoms in Turkey. Erdoğan described the protesters, many of whom where university students, as "atheists, leftists, and terrorists." Turkeys' news media, largely controlled by AKP associates, harshly condemned the demonstrations. Individuals who tweeted support for the protestors were fired from their jobs or faced criminal charges in an effort to crush dissent.

Turkey's Tradition of Autocratic Rule

Erdoğan and his supporters saw enemies throughout Turkish society, with some good reason and with an eye to history. Atatürk's nationalism had reformed Turkey and imposed a form of cultural homogeneity that officially denied or restricted the expression of Muslim identity for a large portion of the country. This was the path that Atatürk chose in his efforts to turn Turkey from a socioeconomically backward country into a modern state, to create a national identity, and to build the institutions that would sustain it.

Atatürk's leadership relied on his close relationship with the military. The Turkish armed forces helped enforce Kemalism and played a central role in the political and economic life of the country. During and after Atatürk's rule, the military leadership saw themselves as guardians of the state—a view widely shared in the country—with a duty to put the nation back on track whenever politicians strayed from Republican-Kemalist ideals. The threats they perceived included Kurdish nationalism, Islamism, and any attempt to reduce the power of the military-bureaucratic elite established under Atatürk. Competing for political power was an emerging counter-elite with conservative, traditional values, Islamic in viewpoint, and based largely in rural Turkey.

When Turkey's government had seemed to stray from the secular vision of Atatürk, the military generals intervened by either staging a coup, forcing a change of government, or forcing a change in government policies. This occurred in 1960, 1971, 1980, and 1997. One result was that between 1960 and 1973 university staff were subjected to constraints on academic freedom, arbitrary punishments, and sanctions. The 1981 Turkish constitution instituted by the military made it very clear that academics were not allowed to challenge the political status quo. Article 130, which remains in the Turkish constitution, states that "universities, members of the teaching staff and their assistants may freely engage in all kinds of scientific research and publication. However, this shall not include the liberty to engage in activities against the existence and independence of the State, and against the integrity and indivisibility of the nation and the country."[3]

Erdoğan and his supporters had learned a lesson from the 1997 military "postmodern coup" that forced then prime minister and Islamist leader Necmettin Erbakan to step down, in large part because of his sectarian leanings. Erbakan led a coalition government, and some of the leaders of Erbakan's Islamist Welfare Party had called for an Islamic Common Market to rival the European Union, with some members backing the imposition of Sharia law. The generals and the political establishment initially perceived the Kurdish nationalist movement as the greatest threat to Turkey's security. But political Islam was increasingly viewed as even more dangerous.

In 1998, the Welfare Party was declared unconstitutional. A follower of Erbakan and a popular mayor of Istanbul, Erdoğan was jailed for 10 months, convicted of inciting hatred by reciting a line from the Turkish poet Ziya Gökalp: "The mosques are our barracks, the domes our helmets, the minarets our bayonets and the believers our soldiers." The conviction forced him to step down as mayor of Istanbul, but his incarceration turned him into an anti-establishment hero. By 2001, Erdoğan sought a new path to power. He created the Justice and Development

Party, which he described specifically as not Islamist but as promoting "conservative democracy." The party was backed by Fethullah Gülen. It was swept into power in the 2002 elections with Erdoğan as prime minister, and the AKP has remained in power ever since, surviving four general elections.

Initially, and as noted previously, Erdoğan was embraced as a source of hope for an improvement in human rights in Turkey because of his push for EU membership. Countries wishing to join must have "stable institutions guaranteeing democracy, the rule of law, human rights and respect for and protection of minorities."[4] Like populist leaders in other countries, Erdoğan was viewed as someone who cares for the lower and middle classes, whom previous leaders had ignored. As Asli Aydıntaşbaş, Turkey analyst at the European Council on Foreign Relations, noted, many Turks saw the AKP's rise to power as a means to wrest control of the institutions of democracy from political and business elites. Erdoğan also received the support of religiously minded people who considered themselves sidelined by the Atatürk's secularism. He invested in infrastructure that boosted economic development. When the AKP first emerged, the party appealed to other excluded groups, including liberals and center-right conservatives seeking more freedom and pluralism.[5]

Buoyed by their second general election victory in 2006 by promising to bring constitutional change, the AKP government set about reversing the headscarf ban in universities, which allegedly excluded tens of thousands of women from higher education in Istanbul alone. This was a widely popular action among Erdoğan's supporters. But many academics and students viewed the ban as a symbol of Turkey's modernization and feared a slide toward Islamism.[6] In the process of consolidating his power, Erdoğan and the AKP sought pathways to reduce the influence of the military generals, delegitimizing their extralegal interventions in politics as "guardians of the secular republic," lowering their membership in the National Security Council, and downgrading the council to an advisory body making recommendations rather than decisions.

Exerting Control

Erdoğan's initial political success stemmed from his appeal as a religious moderate. But his vision of nationalism is deeply rooted in his Muslim faith and Turkey's history as the heart of the Ottoman Caliphate. In the aftermath of the 2013 protests, then prime minister Erdoğan ruthlessly began a more overt effort to consolidate his power. General İlker Başbuğ, the former head of Turkish military forces, and five other generals were charged with being part of the Ergenekon coup some fifteen years earlier and for being part of an alleged contemporary conspiracy by secular ultranationalists within the "deep state" to topple Erdoğan's government. They were jailed and sentenced to life imprisonment. The venue of their trial and conviction was a specially constructed courtroom west of Istanbul to help avoid protests by supporters of secular republicanism. Still, as Jiyar Gol of the BBC reported, protesters did find the location, and "around 1,000 people tried to reach the court. But security forces successfully blocked the area."[7]

Erdoğan also shut down a major corruption inquiry that brought charges against the sons of two ministers by transferring judges and prosecutors, including the chief prosecutor, to remote jurisdictions and sacking or moving police officers who had launched the investigation. The scandal exposed a growing rift with Gülen, whose supporters included members of the police and the judiciary.

The Gezi Park protests led Erdoğan to place greater limits on civil liberties, including the right of assembly and selective detention of opponents. He viewed university students, faculty, and staff as largely opponents of the AKP and his efforts to reintroduce conservative Muslim practices into society. Prior to 2013, many of Erdoğan's attempted reforms in higher education were viewed as marginal or symbolic changes, although one, the 2010 rescinding of the ban on women wearing the Muslim headscarf at university, was hugely controversial. The ban emanated from the Atatürk era but was implemented in modern times on the insistence of the generals in the 1997 postmodern coup. It had the effect of excluding large numbers of religiously minded women from higher education—including many who were partway through their degrees when it went into force. But lifting the ban was strongly opposed by pro-secular students who believed it would lead to pressure on all women students to wear a headscarf.

After the Gezi Park demonstrations, marshal law–style constraints on dissent and arbitrary arrests of real or perceived dissidents had a chilling impact on universities. At the same time, Erdoğan was pursuing changes in the governance and management of universities while also significantly expanding the number and geographic location of Turkish higher education institutions, with the idea that they would boost socioeconomic mobility, as well as support for the AKP. Erdoğan found some supporters in the university community, many of whom were attracted to a greater emphasis on Turkey's Muslim cultural heritage, others who saw that their professional survival required aligning with the priorities and demands of the AKP. He also had an administrative structure to help manage the university community. The Council of Higher Education (YÖK) was established by the 1982 constitution after Turkey's 1980 coup d'état. YÖK had broad authority, like that of a ministry of education, with appointments to the council made by the Turkish president.

Erdoğan sought to solidify his influence over the growing university sector through YÖK. Legislation passed in 2014 took tenure and promotion decisions away from the Interuniversity Council, an independent body that included academics, and handed them to YÖK. New regulations also allowed campus administrators to punish academics and students who participated in discussions, debates, declarations, and statements that were not "scientific" in nature.[8] YÖK was given the power to appoint board members of private universities—it already had this authority for public institutions. YÖK also acquired the authority to review and grant approval for degrees obtained abroad for appointment of faculty in Turkish universities. This meant that the council, with its politically appointed members, could deny those with master's and doctoral degrees from foreign countries if they lacked the "right" frame of mind.[9]

The Academics for Peace Petition

Concerned with the conflict between Turkish troops and Kurds in southeast Turkey, the organization Academics for Peace was formed by Turkish academics with supporters internationally. In January 2016, the group published a petition entitled "We Won't Be a Party to This Crime" criticizing the military crackdown on Kurdish rebels by Turkish troops, calling for military operations in civilian areas to be halted and for the opening of peace talks. The petition also urged the government to proceed with negotiations and prepare a "road map that would lead to a lasting peace." Some 1,128 academic from 89 universities signed, among them distinguished international scholars, such as US linguist and philosopher Noam Chomsky, French philosopher Étienne Balibar, British anthropologist David Harvey, American philosopher and gender theorist Judith Butler, and the Slovenian philosopher and cultural critic Slavoj Žižek.

Erdoğan accused those who signed the petition of engaging in "terrorist propaganda" on behalf of the Kurdistan Workers' Party (PKK), membership in which is illegal, and failing to condemn violence by Kurdish militants. He also said they were "the darkest of people" and that "everyone who benefits from this state but is now an enemy of the state must be punished without further delay."[10] Istanbul's Chief Public Prosecutor's Office launched an investigation of the signatories with the expectation that anyone found guilty would be charged with violating Article 301 of the Turkish Penal Code, under which it is illegal to insult the institutions of the Turkish nation.

A number of universities that employed the academic signatories launched administrative inquiries, including Kocaeli University, Selçuk University, Mersin University, Trakya University, Istanbul Arel University, Giresun University, and the Gaziantep University. Within four days of the publication of the petition, at least 41 academics faced punishment, including suspension and dismissal. Some signatories received death threats from ultranationalist groups.

A warning for academics supporting Kurdish rights had been issued two months before the petition. YÖK was given the authority to close private universities "that have become a focal point for activities against the state's indivisible integrity," which is code for separatism. Commenting on the investigations of the signatories, John Bass, the US ambassador to Turkey, stated, "We are seeing reports of academics being investigated and subjected to penalties for expressing their opinions about the conflict in the South-East. While we may not agree with the opinions expressed, we are nevertheless concerned about this pressure having a chilling effect on legitimate political discourse across Turkish society regarding the sources of and solutions to the ongoing violence."[11]

The International Human Rights Network of Academies and Scholarly Societies, with 80 member organizations around the world, issued a statement voicing alarm at the "increasingly repressive and inflammatory reaction by Turkish government leaders, many university officials," urging them to desist from "threatening academics who are performing their civic duties" by expressing humanitarian concerns about the crisis in southeast Turkey. A coalition of 20 higher education networks from around the world, coordinated by Scholars at Risk, issued a joint public letter expressing concern over reports of widespread pressure on members of Turkey's higher education research community: "Actions reportedly taken against these scholars raise serious concerns not only for [the scholars'] professional and personal well-being, but for the overall well-being of the Turkish higher education and research community, and for the ability of intellectuals and institutions in Turkey to undertake world-class scholarship."[12]

In July 2019, the Constitutional Court struck a blow against the prosecution of the Academics for Peace petition signatories, finding 10 convictions in violation of the right to freedom of expression. As a result, by November 2019, 491 signatories were acquitted of charges of "terrorist propaganda" for signing the petition. Some were acquitted after a retrial, but others had their retrial request turned down by the court in Istanbul.[13] It is a measure of how polarized academia had become that three Turkish universities—İbrahim Çeçen University in Ağrı and the Aydın and Medeniyet Universities in Istanbul—actually launched a petition against the Constitutional Court's decision, titled, "The Constitutional Court Cannot Legitimize Terrorism."[14]

The 2016 Coup

The Academics for Peace petition along with growing criticism of Erdoğan significantly raised political tensions in Turkey. But few anticipated the events that would follow. On July 15, 2016, a faction of the military attempted to overthrow Erdoğan, reportedly seeking to capture or kill him. The unsuccessful coup included military jets bombing Parliament and the Presidential Complex.

As those in the military loyal to the AKP fought the rebels, Erdoğan used social media to appeal to his supporters, asking them to take to the streets of major cities to block the tanks and soldiers deployed by coup leaders. Some 240 people were killed and more than 1,500 were wounded in the fighting. The faction attempting the coup called themselves the Peace at Home Council, citing concerns over the erosion of secularism, pervasive corruption, the erosion of democratic rule, and the disregard for human rights—despite their own act being a clear example of the latter two.[15]

When the streets of Ankara were cleared of rebel tanks and troops, Erdoğan declared a state of emergency. He apportioned the blame for the putsch attempt on some, but not all, of the country's generals, but more specifically on his political enemy Fethullah Gülen. Gülen denied any involvement. A centrist Muslim religious leader exiled in the United States, Gülen remained the leader of a faith-based social movement spanning 140 countries. He was very influential in Turkey. His movement funded community work and schools with the stated aim of promoting intercultural and interfaith dialogue, a pacifist and modern-oriented version of Islam. Gülen had extended his influence through large investments in Turkish media, finance, and for-profit health clinics, and via his followers rising to key positions in the military, judiciary, and municipal police departments. Erdoğan's supporters viewed Gülen as a threat to the AKP's control of Turkey. In May 2016, the government designated the movement a terrorist organization (FETÖ) and a "parallel state structure."[16]

Erdoğan survived the poorly conceived coup attempt. With the brief and dramatic period of street fighting over, on July 21 he returned to the Presidential Complex, declaring a three-month state of emergency. The president could now bypass parliament in establishing laws and could restrict or suspend rights and freedoms. He vowed that "all the viruses within the armed forces will be cleansed." Over the next two years Erdoğan extended the state of emergency seven times and issued 32 emergency decrees, under which more than 80,000 people were detained and 160,000 dismissed from their jobs. Amnesty International reported that up to a third of Turkey's judges and prosecutors were detained or dismissed in 2017–2018.[17] Some 131 media outlets were closed or taken under state control, including 16 TV channels.[18]

Incidents of torture or ill treatment by the police were widely reported in the international press in the weeks after the coup attempt. Erdoğan's purge, the biggest in Turkey's modern history, targeted not only alleged followers of Gülen but also Kurdish activists and leftists. Although there was some anecdotal but questionable evidence that some individuals who were followers of Gülen were involved in the coup, according to a UK Foreign Affairs Select Committee report, there was scant evidence that the Gülen movement as a whole was behind it.[19] The coup was used as an excuse by Erdoğan to consolidate power. The scope and arbitrary nature of his acts of retribution were startling. As the UK MPs concluded, the scale of purges, and the fact that most of those affected were in the education sector or civil service rather than the military or security forces, meant that they could not be considered a necessary and proportionate response.

Persecution of Academics

Perhaps there were some faculty and administrators, and students, associated with the coup. But the scope of the purge is reminiscent of the most egregious purges by autocrats. More than 23,420 academics were dismissed from jobs or lost tenure for allegedly supporting Gülen. Some universities were simply closed. Many university rectors, beholden to the Erdoğan regime, worked with members of the intelligence services to fire faculty and staff. Most dismissals followed the government publication of the *Official Gazette*, listing people who are "terrorists" or affiliated with terrorist organizations, with no right to recourse.[20]

Many who had signed the Academics for Peace petition six months earlier were among those listed for immediate dismissal.[21] Between December 2017 and October 2018, court proceedings began against more than 390 academics who signed the petition, nearly all of them charged under Turkey's anti-terror act for "making propaganda for a terrorist organisation." Some were charged with "insulting the Turkish nation." Under the terms of act, anyone who publicly insults the Turkish nation, the state of the Republic of Turkey, the Grand National Assembly of Turkey, the government of the Republic of Turkey, or the judicial bodies of the state is subject to imprisonment for a term of six months to two years. A person who publicly insults the military or security organizations can be sentenced to a similar prison term.[22]

Erdoğan's government took measures to ensure that those who were dismissed from their jobs were banned for life from working in public service. At the same time, the stigma attached to being found guilty of terrorism offenses effectively blacklisted the victims from securing comparable jobs in the private sector. In many cases the authorities indefinitely blocked or canceled the passports of the accused and reportedly prevented severance or employment insurance and terminated pensions. In some cases, government officials froze bank accounts; if the accused lived in public housing or housing owned by a foundation, they were evicted within 15 days.

The collective result is what some academics described as a "civil death," where they are condemned to a socioeconomic no-man's-land, unable to claim benefits or pensions, unable to work, and unable to travel to take up opportunities abroad. Even relatives of the accused academics were blocked from traveling abroad. This forced some to try illegal methods of fleeing the country; there are also reports of suicide. The evidentiary bases behind the dismissal orders remained undisclosed or vague. However, one announced reason for prosecution was the use of an encrypted smartphone messaging app, Bylock, that was associated with the Gülen movement. In December 2017, for instance, Turkish authorities issued warrants for 171 former personnel of Fatih University, ultimately detaining at least 54, based on alleged use of the app. The next day, detention warrants were issued for 23 personnel from Hacettepe University, also based on alleged use of Bylock, and at least 7 were detained.

Yet forensic studies cast doubt on the ability of investigators to identify individual users or decrypt messages exchanged with Bylock. Authorities also accused academics and students of connections to the coup attempt based on their liaisons with private institutions, including universities, schools, and banks.

The fate of a number of leading academics provides case examples of the scope of Erdoğan's purge. Sedat Laçiner, then a professor of international relations; a former rector at one of Turkey's largest state higher education institutions, Çanakkale Onsekiz Mart University; and a former adviser to the minister of the interior and to YÖK, was highly critical of government policy and the use of authoritarian methods to restrict freedom of expression. Laçiner was arrested in the days after the coup attempt and held at Çannakle's high-security prison. He shared a cell designed for 4 people with 20 other inmates. "I am under arrest for more than three months," he wrote in October 2016, "and I don't know how long I will be kept imprisoned. I even haven't been told what the reason for my imprisonment is." He was held until his conviction in September 2018 of being a member of the Gülenist movement and given a nine-year sentence.[23] A well-known liberal secular author, Laçiner strongly denied being a Gülenist.

Scholars at Risk (SAR), an organization devoted to monitoring academic freedom globally, described Laçiner's case as "the arbitrary prosecution and imprisonment of a scholar as a part of sweeping actions taken by the state against members of the higher education community." Turkey is a signatory to the Universal Declaration of Human Rights and the International Covenant on Civil and Political Rights, SAR stated, and is obligated to adhere to due process. Noting Laçiner's and other cases, SAR observed that "such incidents have a chilling effect on academic freedom and undermine democratic society generally."[24]

Some two months after Laçiner's arrest, Candan Badem, an associate professor of history at Munzur University, Tunceli, was dismissed, also for being an alleged Gülenist. "As an openly secular, atheist person and a vocal critic of Fethullah Gülen and political Islam in general, my dismissal as a Gülenist was like a bad joke," he stated. "Three days after the dismissal, my office and home were searched by the police and I was detained." The police found a book by Gülen that Badem used in a course on political Islam. He had also used passages from the book against Gülen in statements on social media. "Although the court released me the next day," he noted, "it cancelled my passport . . . and placed a block on my credit cards, bank accounts and on my car." He accused the ruling party of condemning its opponents to a "civil death" because, due to prisons overflowing, they could not imprison them all.[25]

A year and more after the coup, the intensity of purge and restrictions on civil liberties continued. Mehmet Ünlü, a former professor of medicine at Afyon Kocatepe University, was sentenced in October 2017 to 12 years in prison, based on his alleged attendance at Gülen-related religious gatherings and possession of an account at Bank Asya, a national banking institution founded by Gülen's followers—a bank closed by state authorities shortly after the coup attempt. In June 2018, police raided student dormitories in the city of Adana and detained 25 students, based on allegations that the residences were supported by members Gülen's network. Even possession of US dollar bills was cited as evidence of membership of the movement.[26]

Government security officials also identified academics who allegedly had links to a prominent funder of civil society activities, philanthropist and businessman Osman Kavala. Kavala is likened by Turkish newspapers to Hungarian-born billionaire and American philanthropist George Soros. Kavala chaired the Anatolian Culture Foundation, which sought to bring people from different ethnicities and nationalities together through culture and the arts. He was arrested on October 18, 2017, accused of "attempting to overthrow the government wholly or partially preventing its functioning," and put on trial in June 2019. This followed an indictment accepted by an Istanbul court that reimagined the Gezi Park protests as a conspiracy to overthrow the government. According to Human Rights Watch, there was "absolutely no evidence that Kavala or the others were involved in planning the protests, let alone conspired to foment an illegal uprising."[27]

A number of academics associated with Kavala were the victims of a coordinated raid on November 19, 2019. Istanbul academic Yiğit Aksakoğlu, a former education researcher at the private Bilgi University and Turkey representative of the Netherlands-based Bernard van Leer Foundation, was jailed. So was prominent mathematician Betül Tanbay of Boğaziçi University and Turgut Tarhanlı, dean of Bilgi University Law School and professor of law and human rights. All the suspects were accused of "creating chaos and mayhem" and "seeking to overthrow the government" and faced a sentence of life in prison without parole.[28] Other victims included Ali Hakan Altınay, director of the Boğaziçi European School of Politics in Istanbul and founding president of the Global Civics Academy, and Gökçe (Yılmaz) Tüylüoğlu, executive director of the Soros-funded Open Society Foundation in Turkey.[29]

YÖK and Universities

Besides the purge of individual faculty and students, Erdoğan's government sought greater control over the management of Turkey's university sector. In the weeks after the coup attempt, the Council of Higher Education, YÖK, ordered university rectors to investigate all academics and employees, from the vice rector down, for ties to the Gülen movement and report back just three weeks after the coup attempt. By July, the council required such reports on a continuous basis.[30]

But Erdoğan and his political appointees on the council did not intend to rely only on rector loyalty to consolidate the government's power over universities. In October 2016, under Presidential Decree 676, Erdoğan abolished rector elections at public universities. Henceforth, rectors at state universities were to be appointed by Erdoğan from among three candidates recommended by YÖK. If one of the recommended candidates was not appointed within one month and YÖK did not present new candidates within two weeks, the president would directly appoint the rector.[31]

In 2017, Erdoğan issued a new decree ending the right of academic staff at a university to even nominate candidates for the post of rector. Now only YÖK provides the three nominations from which the president chooses. Then in July 2018, a newly reelected President Erdoğan issued Decree 703, which among other things ended the council's role in vetting rectors completely. Erdoğan would make all decisions, and he lowered the requirement that nominated rectors hold a professorship from five to three years. The proportion of staff that could be foreign personnel was restricted to 2 percent, with the apparent hope of limiting international influence at Turkish universities.[32]

The Impact of Erdoğan's Nationalism

The introductory chapters in this book describe how neo-nationalism comes in many different forms, with different meanings and consequences for universities (see chapter 2). A spectrum of neo-nationalisms and their impact on universities is identified, with four overlapping types: nascent populism, nationalist-leaning governments, illiberal democracies, and authoritarian regimes. President Erdoğan's assault on academia straddles three of them, but it encompasses five out of six of the sub-criteria of an illiberal democracy (restrictions on free speech, firing of academics, controls on management, restrictions on travel for academics, targeting nationals in foreign universities for sedition), and three out of five sub-criteria of an authoritarian regime (limits on or censorship of social criticism, ministerial controls on leadership and faculty hires and advancement, arrest of academics for sedition). But interestingly, it meets fewer of the criteria of nationalist-leaning governments and none of nascent populism.

Erdoğan's agenda is not anti-immigrant—quite the opposite. He welcomed 3.5 million Syrian refugees into the country. Nor is he opposed to international students, with the number of Syrian students at Turkish universities increasing to 15,000 in 2017. Nor does he seem particularly nationalist leaning in terms of restricting visas for incoming students and faculty. Erdoğan is a nationalist in the sense of employing a post-Atatürk version of Turkish nationalism as a means, in part, to consolidate power and to attack his enemies. The methods he employed are not entirely new to Turkey—suppression of dissent, arrests, and organizational control over public and private institutions. Having built a cult of personality much like Atatürk's, Erdoğan is engaged in an existential battle to shift power from the Western-oriented secular republican elite, the heartlands of whose support are the big cities, to the mass of current and formerly rural religiously minded conservatives, most of whom support the AKP. They include millions who moved from rural areas into towns and cities in the past generation.

Erdoğan's plan is to reshape the Turkish state and society into a more overtly Muslim country, and his enemies are those who do not share his or the AKP's vision. Well before the 2016 coup attempt, Erdoğan openly accused the Gülen movement of operating a "parallel state" and conspiring to bring down the government. The Gülenists accused the government of trying to hide corruption by spreading conspiracy theories.[33] The Arab Spring and Gezi Park protests influenced the AKP to become more conservative, more nationalist, and less tolerant.[34] Berk Esen and Sebnem Gumuscu observed that Turkey no longer satisfies even the minimum requirements of democracy and that it is part of a "broader trend of global authoritarian retreat observed in the weakening of political institutions and the erosion of the rule of law by leaders who had initially come to power through the ballot box."[35]

Universities and the ideals of academic freedom have become a central focus of attack by Erdoğan, in part because, if left unmanaged, they pose a threat to the state. Universities were a symbol and vehicle for a modern Turkey; now universities are a place of suppression and party control. The report *Free to Think 2018* stated that for three consecutive years, Turkey's higher education community suffered from a "state campaign of debilitating attacks on the freedom to think, question, and share ideas."[36]

With tens of thousands of academics and students forced out of Turkish universities or put in jail, the productivity of Turkey's universities has markedly declined. According to Freedom for Academia, an analysis carried out by the Turkish government of the first 5,295 academics dismissed by decrees, more than 40 percent were professors or assistant professors. Their dismissal correlates with a reduction of 11.5 percent in peer-reviewed journal articles between 2016 and 2017. It was also reported that many of the posts of these sacked academics were then filled by AKP partisans. And many of the academics who retain their faculty positions fear for their jobs.

The attack on higher education in Turkey also had a wide societal impact. Academic freedom depends on pluralist democracy, but the opposite is also true: effective pluralist democracy requires academic freedom, along with press freedom and freedom of expression for the population in general and politicians in particular. Under Erdoğan, Turkey has veered in the opposite direction on a scale that deserves far greater international attention. The result for universities, particularly in the social sciences, is a relentless pressure on academics to self-censor in front of students and in seminars.[37]

Thus universities, reflecting the constraints of a relatively new Turkish state still fixated on threats to its existence, are no longer places of critical analysis and reflection. Erdoğan's government effectively isolated many academics, placing some in jail and many in limbo with no recourse to find employment, even abroad. In turn, the world is in a meaningful way isolated from Turkey. Meanwhile, Turkey's government appears immune to international condemnation regarding its mass violation of human rights.

Erdoğan was reelected for a second presidential term in 2018. In early 2020, the fragile economy was expected to experience sluggish growth and a continuing decline in the Turkish lira. This is a formula for Erdoğan to continue his sectarian agenda and continue to clamp down on political opposition. The COVID-19 pandemic will not likely change this political trajectory.

As Erdoğan tightens his grip on universities, and as long as he is in power, it is difficult to see Turkey's higher education institutions achieving the type of autonomy and academic freedom required for them to be productive national universities—leaders rather than followers. Universities will not be able provide the critical thought and innovations that Turkey needs. And perhaps that is exactly what Erdoğan wants.

8

Nationalism Revived

China's Universities under President Xi

KARIN FISCHER

ON MAY 4, 1919, thousands of Chinese students streamed into the streets of Beijing in protest. The precipitating event was the decision by the victorious Allied powers meeting for postwar peace talks in Paris to allow Japan to keep colonial territory seized from Germany in eastern China. But the protests, which soon spread, were about more than land. The students marched under the banner of "Mr. Science" and "Mr. Democracy," advocating that a new China should be built on the ideals of a free society and modern science. Many scholars, too, embraced the idea that open expression, intellectual exploration, and scientific inquiry would lead China into the future. "We believe only these two gentlemen can bring salvation from all the darkness in China," wrote Chen Duxiu, a Peking University dean who was a leading figure in the May 4 Movement, "be it political, moral, intellectual, or spiritual."[1]

One hundred years later, China's president Xi Jinping heralded the May 4 demonstrations, which are seen as having paved the way to the founding of the Chinese Communist Party (CCP). But Xi's May 2019 speech, in the Great Hall of the People, adjacent Tiananmen Square, notably lacked any mention of the intellectual ferment or rejection of tradition that had spurred the protests. Rather, Xi cast the events a century earlier in decidedly nationalistic and patriotic terms. And his remarks included a clear admonishment to the current generation of students to fall in line and not to buck the system—unlike their predecessors. "Those who are unpatriotic, who would even go so far as to cheat and betray the motherland, are a disgrace in the eyes of their own country and the whole world," Xi said. "Chinese youth in the new era," he warned, "must obey the party and follow the party."[2]

Taken together, the two events—the anniversary and the episode it celebrates—embody the paradoxical relationship between the Chinese government's nationalistic impulses and Chinese higher education. Universities, both as institutions and through their students and scholars, played a significant role in building modern China. Chen Duxiu, the Peking University dean, would go on to become one of the founders of the Chinese Communist Party. Research helped fuel China's remarkable rise to become the world's second-largest economy and a global superpower.

Yet the partnership has always been an uneasy one. Universities, with their principles of unfettered inquiry and open discussion, always existed uncomfortably within a political system that demands ideological adherence. Their international ties were periodically viewed with suspicion, as conduits for outside ideas that could potentially undercut the Communist orthodoxy. As Sinologists Merle Goldman and Rudolf Wagner wrote in the *New York Review of Books*, "Since the Party came to power in 1949, it has sought the cooperation of intellectuals in developing the economy, but it has also insisted that they conform to every shift in the Party's political and ideological line."[3]

Under Xi, those tensions are at their highest point in decades. He sought to project a new era of confident Chinese power, one that plays on a longstanding, and particularly Chinese, narrative, that the world is a dangerous place and China needs a strong government to protect it, says Jeffrey Wasserstrom, professor of history at the University of California, Irvine. The most authoritarian leader since Mao Zedong, Xi consolidated power. In 2018 the National People's Congress rubber-stamped a constitutional amendment abolishing presidential term limits, allowing him to remain in office beyond the end of his second term in 2023. His tenure stretches ahead indefinitely.

Underpinning Xi's resurgent nationalism is the idea that innovation and knowledge are central to global power in the twenty-first century and thus should be harnessed to serve national aims. This makes universities pivotal in the new vision for China, in this new scientific or technological nationalism. But even as Xi elevated one of higher education's roles, he sought to rein in universities in other ways, through centralizing government control, imposing a more ideological curriculum, and cracking down on dissident scholars.

The following narrative explores Xi's evolving nationalist policies that seem to contradict broader announced goals for higher education—policies that constrain both teaching and research even as China's best institutions strive for international excellence. They also threaten partnerships with foreign universities and the exchange of students and scholars at a time when higher education worldwide is more intertwined than ever. There is a pronounced trend toward greater Communist Party control of universities, including the repression of critical dissent. The current moment could be a pivotal one: Is this the beginning of a long-term trend, an anti-Western form of intellectual isolationism? Or is it simply a short-term adjustment to solidify party control and reset China's version of civil liberties before some form of relaxation—two steps forward, one step back?

Before we consider the implications for China's future, it's worth examining nationalism and its historic impact—some good, some bad, some devastating—on universities in modern China. In many ways, today's developments mimic and hark back to the trials and tribulations of universities, and of academics, during the Mao era.

Nationalism's Anti-intellectual Moments

Although the May 4 Movement helps illustrate some of the underlying tensions, a clearer starting point is 1949 and founding of the People's Republic of China. The Chinese Communist Party swiftly sought to assume control over universities, nationalizing the entire system of education and reorienting it toward a more Soviet style of specialized institutions serving discrete sectors as part of a planned and centralized economy.[4] Though there was an effort to integrate Marxist teaching into the curriculum, an emphasis was placed on the value of universities for national defense and economic advancement. While Mao Zedong and other Communist leaders were skeptical of longstanding Western influences on the universities, they also believed that "only the institutions of higher education could be counted on to produce cadres capable of building a powerful state and an industrialized nation. Without cadres, the CCP government would be weak and the nation poor."[5]

But the embrace, even a hesitant one, wouldn't last long. The first significant break, as would be the pattern in decades to come, followed a period of relative openness. The Hundred Flowers Campaign was, in part, a response to the Hungarian Uprising of 1956, which raised concerns about the Soviet Union's influence throughout the Communist world. In China, Mao decided to loosen the taboo against speaking out about the Communist Party and its ideology and invited intellectuals to share criticisms and critiques, both about the university and about wider society. The slogan: "Let a hundred flowers bloom and a hundred thoughts contend."[6]

Scholars and students were initially hesitant to speak out. (Indeed, some believe that the Hundred Flowers Campaign was a cynical ploy by Mao to smoke out dissent—something he later admitted.)[7] But once they gained the courage, intellectuals expressed strong views. On the educational system, they complained about copying the narrow Soviet approach, about the neglect of the social sciences, and about the lack of critical academic discourse about Marxist-Leninist doctrine. Broader social criticism centered on the authoritarian and far-reaching role of the party in everyday life and on the rise of a privileged new political elite.[8]

The brief period of liberalism did not last. The backlash was harsh and swift, coming just a few weeks after the first critiques. Students and scholars who had spoken up were forced to repudiate their views; at Peking University, more than 12,000 students, faculty, and staff gathered for a two-day condemnation meeting in which student activists had to make self-criticisms.[9] The university's president was himself later pressured to resign and went into exile after he refused to disavow statements he had made about economic and population theory. Labeled "rightists" or "counterrevolutionaries," some critics lost their teaching positions or were forced to abandon their studies. Many were sent to labor camps for "reeducation," thrown into prison, or sent into exile. But it was just a precursor to what would befall students and academics, and universities themselves, a decade later with the Cultural Revolution.

While the Cultural Revolution was sparked by successive struggles for control of the party and the country, it deeply scarred higher education. A wave of purges and counter-purges turned students against teachers, professors against colleagues, classmates against one another. Indeed, such factionalism was repeated throughout all corners of Chinese society. Still, higher education became a particular target. Academics were viewed with immediate suspicion because they were seen as representative of an old, more conservative social order and because campuses had the potential to give rise to competing, and therefore dangerous, ideas. Hundreds of thousands of students and scholars were "sent down" to the countryside to engage in mandatory manual labor. Some professors were beaten to death by their own students, while others killed themselves in response to unrelenting persecution.[10] Libraries and laboratories were damaged or destroyed.

As Ruth Hayhoe of the University of Toronto writes, "The general climate was one of fear and a sense of the worthlessness of academic knowledge." All universities were closed for four years, and some, such as People's University and the regional institutes of finance, economics, political science, and law, for even longer. Graduate programs were halted for more than a decade. College enrollments fell from a high of 961,000 in 1960 to just 47,800 when classes resumed in 1970.[11] With the national college entrance exam halted, many of those who were admitted gained access based on political connections, ironically making China's universities even more elite than before. The Cultural Revolution robbed a generation of students of a college education; estimates are that just half of those who would have normally gone on to postsecondary education earned a degree.[12]

Of all the repressive movements against Chinese students and academics, however, the 1989 Tiananmen Square protests and the subsequent crackdown may be the one most indelibly burned into the global consciousness—even as it is not openly discussed at home. While the iconic images of students and their fellow protestors are instantly recognizable abroad, three decades later, Tiananmen—or Liu Si, June 4, as it is referred to in Chinese—remains such a taboo subject that even the actual number of deaths from the military crackdown remains unknown.

The wave of mass protests was sparked by the death of the reformist former general secretary of the Communist Party Hu Yaobang. While Tiananmen is popularly characterized as a prodemocracy movement, as Rowena He, a historian of modern China noted, the protesters' grievances were broader: They were concerned about corruption, frustrated by the limitations of economic reform, and dissatisfied with conditions on campus. They also were not opposed to the government or the Chinese Communist Party but rather interested in reform from within. As He wrote, "They wanted a genuine dialogue (*duihua*) with the government regarding their calls for a free press, free speech, and an end to corruption and inflation, a dialogue in which they would be treated as equal and legitimate partners."[13] A peaceful march from Beijing-area universities led to occupation of the square, which, when the government refused to engage in a dialogue with the demonstrators, led to a hunger strike. Citizens joined the students in protest. But China's leaders declared martial law, and troops moved into Tiananmen Square, breaking up the demonstration and killing an unknown number of protesters.

In Tiananmen's aftermath, nationalism was again a tool of repressing dissent. The Patriotic Education Campaign was launched in college classrooms, and textbooks were revised with a nationalistic bent. Students were forced to attend weekly political study sessions, confess the number of times they had joined in the protests, inform on classmates, and read the speeches of leader Deng Xiaoping. Enrollments in higher education, particularly in the social sciences, which were viewed as more politically threatening, were limited. Student leaders and intellectuals were imprisoned or forced into exile overseas. In the United States alone, some 80,000 Chinese were granted "June 4 green cards."[14]

But as Hayhoe writes, "what was perhaps the most surprising about the aftermath of the Tiananmen events was the relative brevity of the period of increased political conservativism and control" over universities.[15] That again speaks to the inherent contradiction in the relationship between China's Communist government and its universities— campuses are at once "dangerous places," in the words of Andrew J. Nathan, an expert on Chinese politics at Columbia University, and one of the most potent tools to achieve national greatness. Just as Tiananmen and the Cultural Revolution left an imprint on Chinese universities, so, too, have they been shaped by leaders who saw them as integral to China's rise.

Nationalism and Educational Investment

Deng Xiaoping showed up to shovel dirt at the groundbreaking ceremony for China's first particle accelerator.[16] It was 1982, and China had only begun to emerge from the shadow of the Cultural Revolution, its economy still in tatters. Many people questioned why such a poor country was investing in high-energy physics, said Yangyang Cheng, a postdoctoral researcher at Cornell University and a frequent writer on science and her native China. Deng replied that a country this poor can't afford not to do it. "Investing in science," according to Cheng, "was a matter of national pride."

Deng's embrace of education was also pragmatic—it was an instrument to achieve social and economic change. Enrollments in the recently reopened universities were rapidly expanded, doubling between 1977 and 1985, and the *gao kao*, the national college-entrance exam, was reinstated.[17] Government slogans—"emancipate the mind" and "seek truth from facts"—elevated education as a patriotic duty. Under Deng, universities were given more autonomy, in areas including admissions, job assignment on graduation, investment of capital, personnel administration, job evaluation, teaching administration, scientific research, and international academic exchange. In 1998, a higher education act was passed, stipulating university autonomy under law.[18] With that newfound freedom, university leaders modernized the curriculum, broadened majors, and increased support for research.

Higher education also played a critical role in reconnecting China to the world after a decade of isolation. Denis Simon, executive vice chancellor of Duke Kunshan University and a longtime China expert, points out that the 1979 agreement signed by Deng and President Jimmy Carter normalizing relations between the two countries included an appendix that laid out provisions for sending students and midcareer academics to the United States for education and training. The inclusion of provisions for sending students abroad highlights the priority Deng put on replenishing a generation of scientists, researchers, teachers, and administrators lost to the Cultural Revolution. At a time when just 3 percent of high school graduates went on to college, jumpstarting the pipeline of trained professionals was crucial to economic revitalization, according to Simon. With the Tiananmen movement, the pendulum then swung back, as the government reasserted control of universities, political surveillance on campus was stepped up, and international projects were suspended.

But as Hayhoe noted, the years immediately following the Tiananmen protests proved to be an aberration. By the early 1990s, Deng had recommitted to a path of economic opening and privatization, highlighted by his famous trip to Shenzhen, which was experimenting with free market economic reforms. Higher education was seen as necessary to achieving those national aims. The urgency only increased as China sought to join the World Trade Organization and move firmly into the ranks of middle-income countries. That is not to say the Chinese government did not place limits on academic freedom—there continued to be red lines that students and scholars could not, or did not, cross. However, in general, for the better part of two decades, China's nationalistic ambitions and its goals for its universities were largely in concert. That included a push toward massification—between 1999 and 2010, higher education enrollment soared, from 4 million undergraduates to 22 million.[19]

But Chinese leaders did not merely want more; they wanted better. A series of multiyear reform programs earmarked special funding in an effort to elevate a top echelon of universities to world-class status. Indeed, the Academic Ranking of World Universities, now one of the primary global educational rankings, was started by researchers at Shanghai Jiao Tong University who were trying to benchmark Chinese universities against their competitors in other countries. "From a national perspective," Simon said, "having great universities is a point of national pride."

Research funding is a major component of global rankings, and so the Chinese government invested heavily in it and incentivized scientists to publish in well-regarded international journals. In 2017, for the first time, China overtook the United States as the largest producer of scientific publications, according to the US National Science Foundation, although American researchers still produce a greater share of the most highly cited papers.[20] Through the Thousand Talents Plan, the Chinese government sought to attract top faculty to China to lead generously funded research institutes. And it opened the doors to partnerships with elite foreign universities, including Duke, New York University, and the University of Nottingham. These joint institutions and programs were part of an embrace of Western academic traditions, most notably the liberal arts, that were meant to improve the quality of the Chinese higher education system. Those who advocated for a Chinese-style liberal arts education had as a central argument the idea that producing creative, nimble thinkers would help power China's already humming economy in the twenty-first century.[21]

Four decades after Deng broke ground for the particle accelerator, China's leaders again are dreaming about greatness through science, specifically physics. As the Large Hadron Collider, built by the European Organization for Nuclear Research, or CERN, comes up against limitations, there is a need for an even more massive, more powerful supercollider. China is moving forward with plans for a behemoth facility, some 34 miles in circumference, at a cost of billions of dollars.[22] The first supercollider to be constructed outside of the liberal democracies of the United States and Europe, it would help researchers from around the globe answer fundamental questions about the makeup of the universe—and it would cement China's position at the center of the world in a key area of scientific discovery.

Xi Jinping and the China Dream

There is broad agreement among scholars of China that the 1990s and early 2000s were a high-water mark for Chinese universities' autonomy and engagement. It can be tempting then to see the November 2012 accession of Xi Jinping as president of China and general secretary of the Chinese Communist Party as a definitive slamming of the door on that openness. In fact, there had been earlier signs of tightening.

One of the most notable instances surrounds Charter 08, a petition signed in late 2008 by hundreds of intellectuals and activists calling for democratic reform. In the crackdown against signatories, many were interrogated and arrested. He Weifang, a lead signatory and a prominent law professor, was effectively exiled, transferred from Beijing to a remote university. Liu Xiaobo, a professor and poet, was sentenced to 11 years in prison for writing the manifesto. He was awarded the Nobel Prize in absentia and later died of cancer that went untreated in prison.[23] Others who signed, like law professor Teng Biao and economist Xia Ye-liang, lost their teaching posts; both eventually moved to America.[24]

Foreign academics also ran afoul of Chinese political sensitivities during this period. Scholars who contributed to a 2004 book about Xinjiang, a region in western China that agitates for autonomy, found themselves blacklisted, unable to get visas to China for a number of years. (Some have since been able to visit China.) Nor has Xi revived a wholly dormant sense of patriotism. During the leadup to the 2008 Beijing Olympics, the government exploited nationalistic pride to counter protests against China's political and human rights record, a strategy that included mobilizing college students to participate in seemingly spontaneous pro-China demonstrations.[25]

But from the outset, Xi—the son of one of the first generation of Chinese leaders, or a princeling—elevated nationalism as a guiding star of his government. In his first speech to the nation, he called on the Chinese people to "strive to achieve the Chinese dream of great rejuvenation of the Chinese nation. To realize the Chinese road, we must spread the Chinese spirit, which combines the spirit of the nation with patriotism as the core and the spirit of the time with reform and innovation as the core."[26]

There are multiple reasons for the rise of nationalism under Xi, and they are both distinctive to China and a product of the broader moment. Foregrounding nationalism is a way to assert control, paper over divisions, and coalesce popular opinion in pursuit of a singular goal. It is a tool to strengthen the Chinese Communist Party and Xi's leadership of it. "To stay in power, the CCP needs an ideology," said Teng Biao, the human rights lawyer, "and nationalism is that ideology." Like President Donald J. Trump, Xi is tapping into a sentiment genuinely held by at least a segment of the population; after all, several generations of Chinese children grew up with patriotic education in the schools.

Nationalism is also a response to threats both real and perceived, internal and external. The Chinese government's moves against its Uighur Muslim minority, more than 1 million forced into reeducation camps, was framed as a way to suppress "extremist" ideas viewed as a danger to the country. Likewise, the recent trade war with the United States took on a nationalist tone. And nationalism is a way to distract from the increasing inequality of Chinese society, where just 1 percent of the richest households now control a third of the country's wealth. Those economic tensions could deepen as China's economic growth falters, and the post-Tiananmen bargain of fewer political freedoms but greater personal prosperity appears at risk.[27]

Like his predecessors, Xi Jinping both eyed higher education warily and recognized it as a way to achieve his Chinese Dream. If students and academics, with their history of fomenting change, were a potential threat to his legitimacy, they also offer one of the surest paths to global prestige. Scholars of Chinese education often talk about it as a pendulum oscillating between greater engagement and exploration on one side and repression and government control on the other. Now, there is an attempt to, somehow, do both extremes at once. Under Xi, higher education is subject to the harshest crackdown since the Tiananmen protests—and, some say, since the Cultural Revolution. It also is a centerpiece of the country's aspirations.

Western Thought versus Xi Jinping Thought

The opening salvo didn't take long. In the spring of 2013, a communiqué began to be circulated within the Communist Party and then on university campuses. Known as Document 9—it was the ninth policy paper of the year—it laid out a list of topics that could no longer be discussed publicly, including in the classroom. Among the newly off-limits subjects: civil society, constitutionalism, economic neoliberalism, press freedom, universal values, the historical mistakes of the Chinese Communist Party, and anything questioning the validity of Chinese economic reforms and socialism. The communiqué called on party members to resist "infiltration" by outside ideas, to prioritize their work in the "ideological sphere," and to be vigilant against ideas, institutions, or people who could threaten party rule.[28]

Document 9 greatly enlarged the list of taboo topics; professors previously knew steer clear of the "3 Ts"—Taiwan, Tiananmen, and Tibet—but otherwise were able to conduct relatively open class discussions. Initially, it was unclear how seriously faculty members would take the directive. "I don't think it will be possible for the government to push forward the seven taboos on a large scale," a historian told the *Chronicle of Higher Education*. "If it is carried out, the rights of speech of public intellectuals will be deprived."[29]

Instead, Document 9 proved to be the first volley in a broader ideological campaign. In the words of one scholar, it "expanded the scope of unacceptable ideas," signaling that potentially any subject could be subject to censorship.[30] The government began to push to restrict the use of foreign textbooks, with the education minister warning university presidents that they needed to limit the spread Western values. Professors must "stand firm and hold the political, moral, and legal bottom line,"

Yuan Guiren said during the 2015 meeting. In one high-profile case, a constitutional law textbook written by Zhang Qianfan, a Peking University law professor and prominent advocate for judicial reform, was apparently pulled from bookstores after education authorities ordered a nationwide review of all law textbooks; Zhang was said to have excessively promoted Western ideas in his writing.[31]

There were also multiple instances of the Chinese government seeking to censor or restrict Chinese users' access to articles in international academic journals. Cambridge University Press came under heavy criticism in 2017 for agreeing to block 300 articles in the Chinese studies journal *China Quarterly*. CUP, the world's oldest publisher, said it had complied with Chinese censorship of the articles, on sensitive topics such as the Cultural Revolution and the prodemocracy movement, in order to ensure access in China to the rest of its publications. But after an international outcry, including threats of an authors' boycott, it reversed course.[32] More recently, the academic publisher Brill terminated its relationship with Beijing-based Higher Education Press to produce four China-focused journals after an entire essay in *Frontiers of Literary Studies in China*, on a Chinese political satirist, was removed without alerting editors. Scholars said they were led to believe that the journals would be published according to international standards of academic freedom when really they were subject to Chinese state censors. Other journals, including the *American Political Science Review* and the *Journal of Asian Studies*, have also been subject to censorship demands.[33]

Some publishers, however, acquiesced. Springer Nature agreed to remove 1,000 articles from the websites of two journals, *International Politics* and the *Journal of Chinese Political Science*. Like CUP, Springer Nature said it weighed the benefits of limiting access to "less than 1 percent" of its content in China to having all of its materials become out of reach to Chinese readers. LexisNexis withdrew an academic research database from the Chinese market after being asked to take down some content.[34]

Scholars were taken aback by Chinese efforts to suppress or redact content in academic publications, given their small audiences and being written in English. International specialized publications were previously largely left alone by Chinese censors, and the new attention further signals the intent of the Communist Party to curb public discourse and critical writing, according to James Millward, a Georgetown University professor who penned an open letter condemning concession to Chinese censors as "craven, shameful, and destructive." But in an unsigned editorial, the progovernment newspaper *Global Times* argued that China had a right to block ideas that are "harmful" to Chinese society: "This is for the sake of China's security and is within the scope of China's sovereignty. . . . If they don't like the Chinese way, they can stop engaging with us."[35]

It's not only the works of Western liberal thinkers that become impermissible—Karl Marx, whose thinking is the official ideology of the Communist Party, is seemingly off the table, too. Though the government feted the 200th anniversary of Marx's birth in May 2018, it also began cracking down on Marxist student groups. Clubs organized to study Marx's works—students read excerpts from Marx during political thought courses but rarely entire essays or books—were threatened with closure at several institutions. Peking University effectively dissolved its student Marxist society for its support of workers' rights, removing the club's leader and several of its members and installing new leaders chosen by university officials in their place.[36]

The concern seems to center on students putting Marx's ideas into action in a way that could threaten government or social stability. Such apprehension is grounded in precedent—joining a Marxist study group, after all, inspired the thinking of a young university librarian named Mao Zedong. In this new generation, Marxism is invoked by #MeToo activists, and Marxist student groups campaigned for better employment conditions for laborers. Over the past year, students were detained for organizing workers (labor unions are illegal in China) and said they were monitored on campus. Ahead of the celebration of the centennial of the May 4 protests, a half-dozen student leaders went missing.[37]

If at first Document 9 was met with a shrug, the sustained campaign had a chilling effect in the classroom and may narrow the research interests of scholars, particularly in disciplines like history, law, and political science. This will be discussed in greater detail later in the chapter. If many topics now are verboten, what is meant to take their place? The answer: Xi Jinping Thought.

The political doctrine associated with the president, more formally called Xi Jinping Thought on Socialism with Chinese Characteristics for a New Era, is enshrined in the constitutions of both the country and the Chinese Communist Party. A blueprint for consolidating and strengthening power around the nation, the party, and Xi himself, the doctrine has become part of the curriculum of ideology courses all university students must take. (For those who have already graduated, Xi Jinping Thought is also the subject of an edX course and China's most popular smartphone app.)[38]

Days after the party constitution was amended, in October 2017, Renmin University established the first official center for Xi Jinping Thought. Since then, at least 30 such centers have been established in universities, local governments, and government ministries, each with a different area of specialization. The center at Peking University, for example, focuses on connecting Marxist doctrine with Xi Thought, while the one at Renmin is dedicated to crafting curriculum. Another center, in Shanghai, has a mission of developing more sophisticated technologies to distribute Xi's doctrine. And even though it's just being developed as a discipline, students in at least one institution, Yunnan Minzu University, can already earn a master's degree in Xi Jinping Thought.[39]

There is real money behind such efforts. Beijing's Xi Thought institute had a 2018 budget of 16 million yuan, or US$2.5 million, according to the Beijing Federation of Social Sciences. Researchers who apply for awards through the center can receive 80,000 to 300,000 yuan per project. One of the most prestigious annual grants in China, the National Social Science Fund, awarded funding in 2018 to 90 research projects with Xi's name in the title; to 240 projects on the "new era," which is a signature Xi slogan; and to dozens more on other Xi Thought–related policy initiatives.[40]

Wasserstrom said when he asked colleagues in China about building a curriculum and academic research centers around a collection of Xi's public statements, they made the comparison to religious-affiliated colleges in Europe and North America. "After all," he is asked, "don't Catholic colleges have divinity schools?"

The Party Line

As in past pendulum swings toward authoritarianism, Xi sought to reassert governmental control over higher education, a message he delivered bluntly during a December 2016 meeting with university leaders and top Communist officials. Higher education, he said during the two-day session on ideological and political work in Chinese universities, must be the "stronghold of the Party's leadership."[41]

If it was not clear enough that Xi expected universities to pledge allegiance to authorities in Beijing, the point was underscored in late 2018 when China's State Council abruptly removed the president of Peking University, one of the country's most elite institutions, and replaced him with a Communist Party loyalist. Like most Chinese college presidents, Lin Jianhua was an academic, while Hao Ping, his replacement, was the university's Communist Party chief. While Lin was officially dismissed for being past retirement age, the message was unmistakable—universities should not expect autonomy, even if they are among China's best. Peking is historically the center of student activism—both the May 4 and Tiananmen movements began on campus—so the move, months before important anniversaries of both protests, carried political symbolism as well. If Xi and his government were concerned about campus unrest tied to the two anniversaries, the new university leadership was an insurance policy.[42]

For Robert Daly, director of the Kissinger Institute on China and the United States at the Woodrow Wilson Center, the installation of political allies at the helm of academic institutions was a sign that Xi was "going back to the Maoist playbook" in a way that the earlier government edicts about Western ideas had not as forcefully signaled. It suggests a tightening of the government's control of higher education, he said.

Hao's replacement as Peking's party boss raised additional alarms. Qiu Shuiping was previously the head of Beijing's State Security Bureau, the local branch of the ministry responsible for espionage and counterespionage, leading to fears that he could introduce more sophisticated surveillance methods to check academic speech. But such practices may already be routine. A party official at South China Normal University, for instance, said the Guangdong-based institution built a database to track and analyze the political opinions of more than 2 million college students in the province.[43] Students throughout China reported that college authorities required them to register personal data, including social media accounts, suggesting that such monitoring may be widespread.

Some institutions, including Beijing's China University of Political Science and Law and Sun Yat-sen University, a top institution in Guangzhou, installed closed-circuit cameras in classrooms and lecture halls. Although students and law faculty challenged the installation of the cameras, authorities claimed they are there to improve teaching quality and to cut down on cheating on examinations. However, it is broadly believed that the devices are there to ensure that class discussions do not cross into off-limits subjects. And institutions relied on low-tech means, too, of keeping both faculty members and students in line, by recruiting a growing network of student informants. While the practice of using students to spy on their teachers and fellow students is long-standing—as discussed previously, it was a means of control during the Cultural Revolution—under Xi, the practice expanded and become more systematized, with some universities having regular evaluation forms for students to fill out.[44]

The result, say Chinese professors, is to feel that you are constantly being watched. "We are more on guard," said one professor, who asked not to be named. "You do not know who will report you." The government indicated that ideological adherence will assume greater primacy in evaluation of both institutions and individual instructors. In a 2018 interview, China's minister of education Chen Baosheng said the government planned to overhaul the university curriculum, add new assessment criteria, and seek better qualified teachers who will be specially trained in ideological education.[45] Whereas before ideological instruction was mainly confined to mandatory sessions on political thought, now it will be throughout the curriculum. "Courses of all kinds should be in the same direction as political courses," Xia said in the December 2016 meeting.

According to a new Ministry of Education guide for universities, issued in December 2017, "ideological and political performance" will be the single most heavily weighted criterion in assessing professors' job performance. The notion that political correctness, more than research publications or teaching quality, could determine career prospects alarmed academics and would seem counter to the government's ambitions for global technological and research primacy, especially in the sciences, a tension that will be addressed more fully later in the chapter. In the past, issues of ideology mattered more in certain social sciences and humanities disciplines, where there are more delicate political lines to trip. Yet the Ministry of Education guide seems to indicate that ideology will matter in the appraisal of all university faculty, including in the sciences. Government officials will regularly visit universities, the guide states, to check on professors' ideological performance and to make sure that universities are complying in their evaluations.[46]

Some universities adopted, at least on a trial basis, evaluation systems that credit faculty members for the online publication of ideologically correct articles in much the same way that publication in reputable academic journals counts toward promotion. At Zhejiang University in Hanzhou, professors and graduate students can earn credit for publishing articles that reflect "core socialist values" and influence public opinion with "correct thinking" in outlets such as the *Global Times, China Youth Daily*, or *Beijing News*. Credit will also be given for articles, of not less than 1,000 words, that are carried by 10 or more mainstream media outlets, that are published in provincial-level papers with a readership of 400,000, or that attract at least 100,000 readers on the Chinese social media app WeChat. At Jilin University, in northeastern China, placement of articles that laud China's achievements in the foreign press also can win a professor points.[47]

In interviews with Chinese academics and with foreign researchers who study the Chinese educational system, it is not clear how fully or methodically the directives to reward ideological performance were taken up in the promotion system. As a means of advancing an academic career, they may, so far, be more aspiration than acted upon. Whether ideological performance is a plus factor, what is certain is that failure to toe the line has costs.

A New Era for Faculty

If publishing progovernment propaganda online can help faculty members get ahead, public criticism, the questioning of Xi or of the Chinese state, can get them fired. Beijing Normal University lecturer Shi Jiepeng, for example, had his contract terminated in 2017 after he was accused of writing "inappropriate comments" on social media, according to a copy of his termination letter posted to Twitter. Li Mohai, a deputy professor at Shandong Institute of Industry and Commerce, was fired the same year after criticizing the government on his microblog.[48]

These two academics are not alone in being penalized for running afoul of Communist Party orthodoxy, whether online, in lectures, or in their research. In just a 12-month window, between May 2018 and May 2019, more than a dozen academics lost their positions or faced some other sort of censure. Zhai Juhong, an associate professor at Zhongnan University of Economics and Law in Wuhan, was fired for raising questions about presidential term limits in class.[49] You Shengdong, a professor of international trade and world economics at Xiamen University, was dismissed after a student reportedly informed authorities about comments he made during a lecture.[50]

Another Xiamen professor, historian Zhou Yun-Zhong, was dismissed for a pseudonymous post on Weibo calling China an "inferior nation."[51] Tang Yun wrote Chongqing Normal University's school anthem, but the university nonetheless demoted him and revoked his teaching credentials for discussing a revolutionary author.[52] Yang Shaozheng was first suspended and then expelled by Guizhou University for "long-running publication and spreading online of politically mistaken speech, writing a large number of politically harmful articles, and creating a deleterious influence on campus and in society." Among his essays was one that questioned the economic cost of sustaining the Chinese Communist Party infrastructure.[53] And Zhao Siyun, the deputy head of the School of Literature at Zhejiang University of Media and Communications, was disciplined for remarks he made at a freshmen welcoming ceremony, in which he criticized the Chinese school system for failing to nurture students' creativity and innovation. Zhao was issued a "severe internal Party warning" by the university's Communist Party Committee for his speech, which also called for more public intellectuals with "the spirit to criticize and the willingness to uphold morality."[54]

The accusations against the faculty members may differ, says Teng Biao, the law professor who signed Charter 08, but at root the issue is that "China does not tolerate any critical ideas, especially public criticism of the government and its monopoly on power." Nor is the academic crackdown limited to Chinese nationals. Peking University did not renew the contract of Christopher Balding, an American and a nine-year member of the business school faculty, over public criticism of the Chinese government. Balding, who later returned to the United States because he said he did not feel safe in China, had launched a successful online petition about the *China Quarterly* incident calling on Cambridge University Press not to assent to censorship by Communist authorities.[55]

For some, the penalties for speaking out extend beyond those meted out in the workplace. In June 2018 Chinese authorities raided the home of Wenguang Sun, a well-known scholar and retired professor of economics at Shandong University, and detained him during a live telephone interview with Voice of America.[56] As of this writing, he remains under house arrest. Guo Quan, a former associate professor at Nanjing Normal University imprisoned for a decade for his prodemocracy activism, was rearrested because of his social media posts questioning, among other things, Chinese government transparency in a deadly chemical explosion.[57]

As a group, however, Uighur academics and intellectuals were singled out, part of the Chinese government's persecution of its separatist Muslim minority. Authorities imposed an extensive surveillance apparatus throughout the western region of Xinjiang and, since 2017, interned an estimated 1 million Uighurs in forced reeducation camps. Members of the Uighur cultural, academic, and business elite, including the editors of local newspapers and top administrators of universities, were targeted for detention, noted Millward in the *New York Review of Books*.[58] The Uighur Human Rights Project estimated that nearly 400 students, scholars, and other intellectuals were taken into custody.[59]

While most of those who are sent to the camps disappear without warning—when writing on the closely surveilled messaging app WeChat, friends and family say a missing person has "gone to study"—the detentions of several higher-profile professors and administrators drew notice. Rahile Dawut, a celebrated ethnographer and professor at Xinjiang University, went missing in December 2017 after abruptly telling relatives she was taking a trip to Beijing.[60] The same year, Tashpolat Tiyip was removed as president of Xinjiang University and arrested, accused of being a "two-faced official," a term used to describe Communist Party members who are suspected of supporting separatist efforts. Tiyip was reportedly sentenced to death with a two-year reprieve, meaning that at the end of two years, officials can decide whether to carry out or reduce his sentence. A similar sentence was given to Halmurat Ghopur, a professor of medicine and a former president of Xinjiang Medical University Hospital.[61] And Ilham Tohti, a writer and economist at Minzu University, is serving a life sentence after advocating for Uighurs' peaceful resistance to Chinese policies.[62]

While China's anti-Uighur campaign drew headlines, perhaps the individual case that attracted the most international attention is that of Xu Zhangrun, a law professor at Tsinghua University. Xu rose to prominence in 2018 when he published a series of essays rebuking Xi Jinping and warning of deepening repression under his government. "People nationwide, including the entire bureaucratic elite," Xu wrote, "feel once more lost in uncertainty about the direction of the country and about their own personal security, and the rising anxiety has spread into a degree of panic throughout society."[63]

Despite warnings from authorities after his first essay, which called on lawmakers to reestablish presidential term limits, Xu continued to write; despite Chinese censorship and strict control of the internet, his pieces continued to be read. In March 2019, he was ordered by Tsinghua officials to stop teaching and conducting research, told his pay would be drastically cut, and was questioned for an hour and a half. "I don't know what they'll do next," he told the *New York Times* in a mobile phone message. "I've been mentally preparing for this for a long time. At worst, I could end up in prison."[64]

Xu's suspension led to an outcry outside China, where hundreds of scholars signed an open letter to Tsinghua's president and party secretary calling for Xu to be reinstated and warning of the damage being done to the university's reputation.[65] But it may be even more closely watched inside China as a measure of how far Xi's government is likely to go to bring the country's universities ideologically in line.

When Xia Yeliang was fired in 2013, Peking University initially said it was for poor teaching, claiming that he was the institution's worst-ranked instructor and the source of 340 student complaints since 2006. But Xia maintained that he was let go for his political views, including signing Charter 08, and an email to the professor from the Communist Party chief of the School of Economics shows just that, chiding him for his activism and making no mention of teaching or scholarship. When Xia was fired, university officials invented an excuse, "but now they don't even care to do that," he says. "They just come out and say that you're teaching bad ideas."[66]

That may be exactly the point that the government is trying to send—that bad ideas, or ones that cross political lines or question the authority of the Chinese state, can bring scholars big headaches. "People now feel that they need to do a calculation, a risk analysis, when they decide what to say," said an American academic now teaching in China. "Before they would not have done that."[67]

Another scholar of China who asked not to be identified because of the sensitivity of the issue for his Chinese collaborators noted that most of the Chinese academics who publicly spoke out for Xu were more senior faculty members; in fact, he said that some senior faculty members at Tsinghua advised younger professors not to sign a letter supporting Xu because of its potential long-term effect on their careers. He said he had noticed that younger Chinese academics in his field, Chinese law, were steering clear of hot-button issues, like constitutionalism or judicial reform, in favor of technical or theoretical areas of scholarship. The push for professors to conform to Communist Party ideology had a chilling effect on scholarship, rendering more and more topics off limits, he said. But he also perceived that younger legal scholars—unlike the two previous generations, who were students or young professors in the aftermath of the Cultural Revolution and during the Tiananmen protests— had already seemed predisposed not to gravitate toward sensitive topics, perhaps because they had grown up in a period of relative affluence and one in which there was a greater feeling of national pride. "They just seem more likely to play it safe," he said.

That said, there also may be a general sense, and a long-standing one, among Chinese academics that they have little to gain by wading into contentious areas. A 2000 survey of Chinese academics found that 67 percent thought their research results could have no effect on policy making at a national or even university level.[68] Still, many worried that the current crackdown could cast a long shadow, one that will shape Chinese higher education for future generations. "What dissertations won't be written because of problems and pressures?" said Sophie Richardson, the China director for Human Rights Watch. "There's a real cost to knowledge."

International Relations in a Time of Nationalism

In the spring of 2019, alarmed about the impact of China's rising nationalism on academic freedom at home and abroad, Human Rights Watch released a set of guidelines for universities working with China.[69] The fact that the organization developed an entire code of conduct specifically for China highlights the country's importance in today's global higher education landscape, its preeminence made even more notable by the fact that it has been only four decades since President Carter and

Deng Xiaoping signed a historic agreement reopening China, and its universities, to the world.

For Western scholars who work in and on China, the Xi era at first had relatively minimal impact on their research, but now there is significant heightened concerns that it could. Two China specialists, Sheena Chestnut Greitens now at the University of Texas at Austin and Rory Truex of Princeton University, decided to survey more than 500 of their colleagues about their experiences working in China. By and large, they found what they called "repressive research experiences" fairly rare—in the past 10 years, the majority, 57 percent, said they had no such experiences. Just 5 percent reported having any difficulty in obtaining a visa, while 2 percent had been blacklisted from the country for an extended period of time. Nine percent had been temporarily detained or questioned by authorities, a process known colloquially as "being taken for tea."[70]

Even though a not-insignificant number of scholars were "taken for tea," Truex said in an interview that it was unlikely that the questioning was related to Xi's push for tighter control over higher education. Most such interviews are conducted by local officials and are not spurred by concerns over a particular scholar's work but rather occur because the researcher is a stranger in the community. "It's not like they've been reading our papers in an academic journal," Truex said. "Usually the question is, 'Are you a journalist?'"

Overall, Truex and Greitens concluded that repressive experiences are a "rare but real phenomenon," with one exception—one in four of those who conduct archival research report being denied access. Because the survey asked whether the respondents had a repressive experience at some point in the past decade and not for the particular year, it's not possible to compare incidents pre- and post-Xi. However, Truex, whose research focuses on Chinese politics and theories of authoritarian control, said he was told anecdotally that denials occurred with more frequency in recent years, not surprising under a leader who is seeking to control both the present and the past narratives about China. Projects that were feasible 10 years ago just aren't today, he said.

The study's other finding that received attention is the response to a question about self-censorship: Nearly 70 percent of respondents agreed with the statement, "Self-censorship is a problem in the China field." Truex said the self-censorship concerns were reported, simplistically, as "China scholars cave to the Chinese Communist Party." However, he and more than a dozen other scholars interviewed for this chapter said they found themselves in a research environment that became increasingly complicated and ethically fraught to navigate, for themselves, their Chinese collaborators, and for their research subjects. Truex said he had recently called off a project in China because it could put participants at risk. "That's not self-censorship," he said. "That's research ethics." He still planned to take an upcoming research trip to China, albeit with a little uneasiness, especially since the December 2018 arrest of Michael Kovrig, a former Canadian diplomat who now works at a major international think tank. "The tension has slowly crept into academia," he said, "and I have a one-year-old kid."

If individual scholars are proceeding with caution, what about universities? In a 2017 American Council on Education survey, Mapping Internationalization on U.S. Campuses, China was named the country with which American colleges had the most existing academic partnerships. It also was their top target for expanded activity.[71]

There is little past evidence that issues of academic freedom or political repression will curtail Western colleges' relationships in China. In 2013, a group of faculty members at Wellesley College pressed administrators to reconsider student and scholar exchanges with Peking University after it fired Xia Yeliang, the economics professor and activist. Although the liberal arts college did not cut ties with Peking, it did overhaul its process for striking international partnerships to, among other things, place a great emphasis on academic freedom.[72]

Cornell University did actually end a six-year-old research and exchange relationship between its School of Industrial and Labor Relations and Renmin University after Renmin punished a dozen Marxist students who had campaigned for workers' rights. Eli Friedman, an associate professor at Cornell who oversaw the program, said the Chinese university's actions, which included compiling a blacklist of student activists to be monitored by national security officials, represented a "major violation of academic freedom" that Cornell could not tolerate. "Their complicity in detaining students against their will is a serious red line for us," he told the *New York Times*.[73]

But Cornell and Wellesley may be the exception that proves the rule. Many colleges see China as simply too big and too important—geopolitically, culturally, scientifically—to disconnect. More cynical observers like Teng Biao, the former law professor, also noted that American universities have a financial incentive to continue to work with China, which sends more foreign students to US campuses than any other country, a critical source of revenue for colleges, particularly as state funding for higher education has eroded. If anything, from a late-summer 2020 perspective, it is a global pandemic, which grounded flights and closed national borders, that has the greatest potential as a disruptor, not concerns around ideology or expression.

For many academics, the fact that academic freedom is being restricted in China is reason to engage more, not less. At Wellesley, one professor who had signed a petition protesting Xia's dismissal and questioning the Peking partnership said he came to believe that Americans would have a better chance of influencing the academic environment in China by continuing to work together. "I think positive results are better achieved by being engaged than by condemning from afar," said Philip L. Kohl, an anthropology professor.[74]

When Harvard president Lawrence Bacow visited China in March 2019, he used a speech at Peking University to talk about the value of academic freedom and free speech. He mentioned the May 4 Movement, calling it "a proud moment in your history that demonstrated to the world a deep commitment on the part of young Chinese to the pursuit of truth—and a deep understanding of the power of truth to shape the future." He ended his remarks by quoting a few lines of verse by a celebrated Uighur poet, a provocative move in the midst of China's crackdown on the minority group.[75] Chinese news reports edited out the references to both May 4 and the Uighurs, but they were just as surely heard by the (likely intended) audience in China's government as by the students in the Peking lecture hall.

Perhaps the question is, will China continue to view such partnerships as worthwhile, or will it move to cut its international ties? Dating back to Deng's time and earlier—before Communist rule, top Chinese students were routinely sent abroad for graduate training—China saw working with foreign universities as a shortcut to building up its scientific and research capacity. But does it need the assistance any longer? A May 2019 report showed China on track to surpass the United States in total research and development expenditures. It already awards more degrees in science and engineering and leads the United States in its production of scientific papers.[76] As noted previously, American researchers produce more highly cited papers.

It's also a matter of optics. Even as the government issues edicts warning Chinese universities against teaching Western ideas and values, it hosts more international branch campuses than any other country in the world. Beyond those institutional-level partnerships, its universities have many more joint schools, institutes, and degree programs with foreign universities.

There are signs of waning enthusiasm. In 2018, the Chinese government announced the closure of 234 joint programs, a fifth of its partnerships between local and foreign universities. Six were with China's most prestigious universities, Peking and Tsinghua. Foreign partners in the shut-down programs included the University of Florida, the University of Melbourne, and Bournemouth University in the United Kingdom. In its announcement, the Ministry of Education cited a variety of reasons, including poor quality, lack of enrollment, and financial mismanagement.[77] Even so, there had not been similar mass closures of foreign programs in past years, leading many to wonder whether this was a further sign of the government's tightening grip on its universities. "There's a growing hostility to foreign expertise," said Jiang Xueqin, an educational consultant based in Chengdu. "Right now, China is looking inward."

The government also exerted more control over the remaining partnerships, ordering all foreign-funded universities to start Communist Party units and to grant decision-making power to a party official.[78] International programs previously were exempt from such requirements, raising fears that Xi's government could limit academic freedom on foreign campuses as well. Thus far, administrators at two of the best-known joint-venture campuses, New York University–Shanghai and Duke Kunshan University, say they experienced no curbs on their autonomy. "We have never had to compromise on academic integrity in what we do," said Denis Simon of Duke Kunshan, whose agreement with China's education ministry includes a legally binding guarantee of academic freedom. The universities' very prominence draws extra attention to the question of whether China will continue to interfere with foreign universities, Simon noted. "Eyes are on us."

Students as Vessels for Global Learning or Nationalistic Impulses?

If such joint programs like those at Duke and NYU draw scrutiny because of the institutions' selectivity, Chinese students abroad attract attention simply because of their numbers. More than 600,000 Chinese students study overseas in 2019, some 370,000 in the United States alone.[79]

China's neo-nationalism affected students within its own higher education system, as detailed previously. They were subjected to patriotic education, surveillance, and, in the case, of the Marxist students, government suppression. As movements from May 4 to Tiananmen demonstrate, students can be potent advocates for openness, free thinking, and similar values, leaving leaders vested in autocratic control in a perpetual state of wariness. As the Cultural Revolution shows, they, too, can be weaponized as a tool of nationalism, a corrosive force that can be turned against professors, fellow students, and even education itself.

As a case study for nationalism, however, China is complicated because of the sheer volume of students it sends overseas. For some perspective, there are more students from China in the United States than from the rest of the top five sending countries combined. Over the past decade, hundreds of thousands of Chinese parents invested their savings in sending their children abroad, motivated by a belief in a better education, a hope for a more secure future, or some mix of the above. Xi Jinping is one of them—his daughter graduated from Harvard University in 2014.[80]

But as with joint campuses, Chinese student mobility has the potential to run counter to the country's nationalistic goals. Xi's government attempted to dictate the curriculum in its own universities and sought greater control over branch campuses and foreign degree programs on its own soil. Influencing what students study overseas is more difficult, although the Chinese government has tried to do so, as will be addressed below. When you send your children to Western or Western-influenced universities—every one of the top study destinations for Chinese students is a liberal democracy, with the exception of Hong Kong—it is inevitable that they will get a Western education, be exposed to Western values, and meet Western people. If one of the hallmarks of Chinese-style nationalism is to posit love of country as a bulwark against hostile foreign powers, it's hard to portray a country like the United States as big and bad when more than a half million students study there. "Every Chinese student in university today has a classmate in America," said Jiang.

The Chinese government did not move in any meaningful way to restrict the flow of students to the United States or elsewhere, although it took steps on the edges. Some of China's larger cities moved to more strictly regulate international programs within elementary and secondary schools that prepare students to go abroad for higher education.[81] Such programs had expanded rapidly in recent years as parents sought to give their children an advantage in applying for college abroad through early exposure to Western-style teaching, additional English instruction, and a curriculum oriented to the SAT rather than the *gao kao*. There were rumors that Chinese authorities issued a secret order forbidding children of high-ranking Communist Party officials from sending their children to study in the United States, in response to Trump administration criticism of Chinese students.[82] Whether or not that's true, some parents with party connections had already opted to keep their children in the Chinese educational system because they didn't want to be perceived as embracing Western values—a shift from a few years earlier when even Xi's daughter went abroad.

That doesn't mean Xi couldn't decide to prohibit Chinese students from studying abroad in general or in the United States in particular, a threat that suddenly became more real as Beijing and Washington engaged in a tit-for-tat trade battle in 2019 and 2020. Education is the United States' fifth-largest service export, according to the US Department of Commerce, and China its largest consumer. An abrupt halt to Chinese enrollments would mean big trouble financially for many American colleges. But a trade war could have given Xi a ready-made excuse to cut short a phenomenon that seems in many ways incompatible with his nationalist aims.

There is already some precedent for such a move: After the University of California, San Diego, invited the Dalai Lama to speak at commencement in 2017, China retaliated by banning students and scholars with funding from the Chinese government's China Scholarship Council from attending the university.[83] In 2018, Saudi Arabia ordered 7,000 of its citizens at Canadian universities to immediately leave after the Canadian foreign minister criticized the Saudi human rights record.[84] (Some who were close to earning their degrees were eventually allowed to stay.)

The most significant threat to Chinese student flows may be the pandemic, not politics. But while new enrollments slowed to a trickle at the beginning of the 2020 academic year, it's far from clear whether such a downward trend will be sustained long term. And a more robust neo-nationalistic pursuit of academic self-sufficiency on the part of the Chinese government could, paradoxically, help mitigate such sentiments elsewhere around the world. As will be discussed in greater detail later in the chapter, China's rise as an intellectual and research force contributed to neo-nationalism in higher education systems in the United States and Europe, leading to protectionist actions around intellectual property, the questioning of research collaborations, and the singling out of Chinese students as suspicious. If Xi's government were to pull back on any of these academic relationships, it could lower the temperature on nationalistic impulses.

However, the real restrictions came mainly from the American side. In 2018, the Trump administration changed visa rules for Chinese students in certain science and technology fields, forcing them to renew their visas annually. It also considered, but did not act on, a proposal to bar all Chinese nationals from studying in the United States. In fact, President Trump made Chinese students and scholars the target of his own nationalistic rhetoric, accusing them of being spies in American higher education, poised to steal intellectual secrets. "We're on the verge of a U.S.-government-driven demonization of Chinese students and scholars," Millward says. "That's really dangerous."[85]

The fact that Chinese students abroad are caught in the nationalist crossfire between the United States and China gets at a tension: Are students a vessel for Western ideas or a vehicle for exporting Chinese nationalism? Young Chinese are frequently said to be more nationalistic than older generations, although a 2017 paper by Harvard researcher Alastair Iain Johnston, based on longitudinal surveys of Beijing residents suggests that nationalist sentiment over time has actually diminished among young residents. In 2015, barely a quarter of young respondents voiced strong support for nationalist statements such as "Even if I could choose any other country in the world, I would prefer to be a citizen of China than any other country"; "In general, China is a better country than most others"; and "Everyone should support their government even when it is wrong."[86]

Despite Johnston's findings, instances of Chinese students at American universities protesting events or speakers that diverge from nationalist ideology or the Communist Party line are routine. At UCSD, for instance, the Chinese Student and Scholar Association, or CSSA, demanded that the university rescind its invitation to the Dalai Lama, writing on WeChat, "If the school insists on its actions by inviting the Dalai Lama as a commencement speaker, our association will take further tough measures and resist the school's unreasonable contact." When UCSD refused, they protested at the ceremony. When Yang Shuping, a graduating senior from China, praised the fresh air and freedom she found studying in the United States in a 2017 commencement address at the University of Maryland, she faced a backlash and even death threats.[87] And at Canada's McMaster University, students tried to shout down a Uighur activist then filmed her and took down the names of people in attendance, apparently at the behest of the Chinese consulate.[88]

In some cases, these students employed the language of American campus free speech political discourse in their protests. For example, a group of Chinese students at Smith College insisted that faculty member Jay Garfield remove a Tibetan flag hanging in his office, saying that it "hurt their feelings"—despite the fact that they had never taken any of his classes or visited his office before.[89] Although it is possible these students are expressing authentic views, they often argue that they are silenced in order to silence others.

The students involved in these cases are certainly a tiny fraction of the many Chinese students abroad, and there's no reason to think that they are representative of Chinese students as a whole. But one thing that troubled observers in many of these episodes is the involvement of Chinese embassies or consulates. An investigation by *Foreign Policy* found that CSSAs regularly accept funds from their local consulates; at Georgetown, it amounts to about half the group's budget. The Chinese consulates are in regular contact with CSSA leaders, sending them safety information and occasionally political directives. When Xi Jinping came to the United States in 2015, for instance, Washington-area colleges organized 700 students at the embassy's request to line city streets holding banners and flags to welcome him. (The students were later paid $20 apiece.)[90]

The links between consulates and CSSAs raise the specter that the Chinese Communist Party was able to extend its long ideological arm all the way onto American campuses. In many cases, the CSSAs are primarily social clubs, but a few of the student groups vet their members along party lines. Some club leaders told *Foreign Policy* they felt growing pressure to promote "patriotic" ideas, along much the same timeline as the push for ideological education ramped up back home. "It's hard to know if students from the mainland are participating in nationalistic activities because of their views," says Human Rights Watch's Richardson, "or because someone has told them they must."[91]

Although Human Rights Watch has urged colleges to monitor CSSAs and other organizations linked to the Chinese government as part of efforts to ensure academic freedom, higher education officials did relatively little to challenge the groups or curtail their activities. At McMaster, for example, it was the student union that revoked the CSSA's privileges as a student club, not administrators. This raises questions about the extent to which Western universities will forcefully push back against Chinese neo-nationalism.

Could the presence of Chinese students compromise what is taught or create a chilling effect in American classrooms? There are no cameras in US lecture halls, but that does not mean students here are not being monitored as well. A University of Minnesota professor said when he tried to get Chinese students in one of his courses to discuss a film that was an allegory about corruption in China, he was met with silence. After the professor chided the students, a student who typically participated in class finally spoke up. "We're uncomfortable talking about that because we don't know who might be listening to us," he said.[92] Indeed, in some cases, Chinese government authorities visited students' families in China to warn them about their children's allegedly subversive statements abroad.[93]

Soft Power: Projecting an Image Abroad

The Chinese government doesn't simply keep its own students in check overseas. It also seeks to project its national image on a global stage. Using education as a form of soft-power diplomacy is neither a new idea nor unique to China, of course.

Germany's Goethe-Institut promotes the country's language and culture abroad. The American Fulbright Program was born in the wake of World War II with the belief that building educational and cultural ties could help avert future carnage. Through the US Agency for International Development and the Department of Agriculture, American grants helped build critical research capacity, and sometimes entire university faculties, throughout Asia and Africa. But China's educational diplomacy stands out for its current scope and scale—and because of the not always diplomatic way in which it is carried out.

In the West, China's signature program is the Confucius Institute, the government-funded Chinese language and cultural centers located primarily on college campuses. First opened in 2004, there are now nearly 500 Confucius Institutes worldwide and about 100 in the United States, although the latter number is shrinking as the centers come under political attack.

In practice, the CIs typically had a fairly narrow mandate, offering cultural programming and language courses, often not for credit. Although the centers are based on college campuses, many of the instructors actually teach Chinese in the local public school system. Nonetheless, CIs, as the Chinese-branded entity on campus, came to crystallize American concerns about Chinese Communist Party influence in higher education. Indeed, they've managed to accomplish the rare feat of uniting conservative Republican lawmakers and the American Association of University Professors in opposition.[94]

In 2018, Congress approved a rider to a defense spending bill prohibiting colleges with institutes from using federal funds for Chinese-language training. Although colleges could apply for a waiver, the Defense Department granted none of the dozen applications; as of this writing, six Confucius Institutes have shut their doors. A key Senate committee called on the Justice Department to investigate whether the remaining CIs should be required to register as foreign agents.[95] In August 2020, the State Department designated the Confucius Institute U.S. Center, the DC-based administrative and coordinating office, a "foreign mission," recognizing it as an entity under the control and direction of the Chinese government and requiring it to report detailed information about personnel, real estate holdings, and funding.

Confucius Institutes often get lumped in with problematic behavior such as intellectual property theft, espionage, and intimidation of Chinese students and scholars on American campuses, but, in the words of Mary E. Gallagher, a professor of political science at the University of Michigan, they've gotten "a bad rap for the wrong reasons." The right reason, Gallagher and others argue, is structural—the CIs, in both their establishment and their operation, run counter to American higher education's principles of academic freedom.[96] A Government Accountability Office review of 90 agreements setting up the centers found that half contained confidentiality clauses. The agreements also give the Hanban, the Chinese government agency that administers the worldwide network, disproportionate weight in decisions about both programming and personnel.[97]

There are actually few prominent examples of speakers or topics running afoul of Hanban, but that may be because academics simply aren't proposing them. Gallagher, who is director of Michigan's Center for China Studies, told this author that she regularly gets requests from faculty to support symposia or research projects that they never bother to submit to the campus's CI, assuming up front that the issue would be too sensitive. This behavior might not be consequential at an institution like Michigan where there are multiple opportunities for learning about China, but at colleges with tight budgets or without other China studies centers, it means that the Chinese government, through the Confucius Institutes, is able to set the agenda on how China is taught, Gallagher said. That amplifies the Chinese perspective.

Critics of the institutes worry that their presence may make administrators hesitant to host speakers—like a talk with the Dalai Lama or a forum on Uighurs—that Chinese authorities might object to for fear of jeopardizing the partnership, even if the event was wholly separate from the CI. There's evidence of the Chinese government using such programs as leverage to express dissatisfaction—it temporarily halted a long-standing exchange program with the University of Maryland after the university invited the Dalai Lama to speak.[98] At the same time, the Chinese government was not receptive to similar American attempts at soft diplomacy, shutting down 29 American Cultural Centers on Chinese campuses or blocking them from opening.[99]

Despite American disapproval, the Chinese government is moving forward with plans to expand its network of institutes. A February 2019 document on modernizing the Chinese education system affirmed that CIs would continue to be a key government policy and that their growth would be "optimized" around the globe.[100]

Confucius Institutes may get much of the ink because of their presence on American and other Western campuses, but a perhaps more ambitious educational diplomacy effort is aimed elsewhere. Named for the old Silk Road, the Belt and Road Initiative, started in 2013, attempts to link China to southeast and central Asia, the Middle East, Europe, and Africa through education, trade, infrastructure, and investment. As part of the effort, China established university campuses in four countries—Japan, Laos, Malaysia, and Thailand—and set up another 100 joint educational programs abroad. The new campuses and programs are meant to support China's economic ambitions by training a skilled local workforce for its companies.

In Malaysia, a satellite campus of China's Xiamen University expects to eventually enroll 10,000 students from that country as well as Indonesia and China in a dozen academic programs tied to local economic demands. In Laos, an outpost of Soochow University is just the country's fifth college campus.[101] The Belt and Road Initiative represents a recalibration of China's international collaborations away from Western universities, which often called the shots in such partnerships. Instead, the new effort allows China to project its brand of educational nationalism and Xi's vision of the nation as an intellectual superpower abroad.

The government also seeks to attract more students to China. Through the Belt and Road program, the Ministry of Education has pledged to support 10,000 students a year over a five-year period. Overall, more than 440,000 foreign students, most from elsewhere in Asia, now study in China, compared to just 55,000 a decade earlier. That puts it third, behind only the United States and Britain, as a higher education destination.[102]

Although some of the noneducational Belt and Road projects—such as a Chinese-financed industrial park in Sri Lanka condemned for its environmental impact—were controversial, its educational efforts avoid local opposition. Still, some worry that China's emergence as an educational hub could come at the expense of other destinations for international students. Australian universities in particular have become concerned that Chinese scholarships may be siphoning off students who might have otherwise gone to Australia for China or for Chinese-funded institutions in their home countries.[103]

Still, the Belt and Road has not, so far, received the same kind of pushback as Confucius Institutes. A journalism professor at the Malaysian campus said the leaders of the new initiative were conscious about repeating the same mistakes. "We don't want to become another Confucius Institute carrying a strong China label," Wang Changsong told the *South China Morning Post*. "We want to position ourselves to be truly international, meaning we wouldn't force anyone to accept our perspectives."

Nationalistic Goals Meet Nationalistic Fears

Though the original focus of the Belt and Road's educational efforts was on building student access and educational capacity, China sought to position itself in the center of a research Silk Road as well, using science to develop links between countries. The Chinese Academy of Sciences alone invested close to $270 million in science and technology projects as part of the Belt and Road Initiative and supports nine joint research and training centers around the globe. Each year, the academy funds the doctoral studies of 200 promising students from Belt and Road countries, talented young scientists who might have previously gone to American or other Western universities for their graduate work.[104]

The full scope of the Chinese effort is difficult to gauge because the Chinese government has not released a full list of projects or partners, but the push to establish collaborative agreements and offer scientific assistance is on par, observers say, with American and Soviet efforts to ramp up scientific output during the Cold War. In doing research on clean drinking water in Sri Lanka or rice cultivation in Pakistan, China is positioning itself as a new scientific-development superpower. "Science, technology, and innovation are the core driving force for the BRI development," said Chinese Academy of Science president Bai Chunli.[105]

China's Belt and Road research thrust was welcomed by emerging countries that may not be able to undertake ambitious scientific projects on their own, although Chinese universities are working in some countries and regions with a solid scientific track record. The University Alliance of the Silk Road has 150 members in nearly 40 countries, including Washington University in St. Louis, the University of Liverpool, and the National University of Singapore.

But China's effort is viewed with some skepticism as an authoritarian state looking for another tool, in this case, scientific outreach, to expand its sphere of influence. There were complaints that projects that match China's economic aims too often did not take environmental concerns to heart. Are science and innovation a way to put a gentler face on Beijing's ambitions to be an economic and geopolitical force? University involvement can help build "positive attitudes," says Mike Gow, a lecturer in international business at the University of Coventry and a longtime China watcher. "If [the Belt and Road initiative] is seen as a hegemonic move to spread Chinese influence around these countries, it is going to encounter a lot of resistance. If you get the academy onside, it becomes a different proposition altogether."[106]

Without question, the Belt and Road Initiative attests to China's ambitions to move the center of scientific research eastward. "The Chinese government values power," says researcher and writer Yangyang Cheng, "and it sees science and technology as contributing to the power of the state."[107] During the 2017 Party Congress, even as Xi Jinping was warning academics to toe the academic line, he reaffirmed that education must play a key role in spurring China's economic growth and boosting its international reputation. "We will strengthen basic research in applied sciences, launch major national science and technology projects, and prioritize innovation in key technologies," he said during the quinquennial meeting. China must be a "country of innovators," he said, pledging that the coming years "will be an era that sees China moving closer to center stage."[108]

China's plan to do that is called the Double World-Class Project. Its goal is to elevate 42 Chinese universities into the top 200 globally ranked universities by midcentury, as well as to build some 450 elite programs in individual disciplines, most in the sciences. Over the past two decades, China had several higher-education development plans, but the

Double World-Class Project is more ambitious than its predecessors: The 211 Project, begun in 1995, aimed to raise the educational quality of 100 Chinese universities, while 1999's 985 Project hoped to create 40 research-intensive universities with an international impact. China, the new plan says, should become a center of learning worldwide.[109]

There are signs that it is on its way. In 2019, Tsinghua became the first mainland Chinese institution to rank as the top university in the Asia-Pacific region. Globally, it is just outside the top 20, while Peking is on the cusp of the top 30.[110] No other country produces as many scientific papers or undergraduates with STEM degrees or as many of the world's fastest supercomputers. China is on its way to matching the United States in its number of STEM doctorates and to surpassing the United States in global R&D expenditures, according to the OECD.[111]

But China's march to educational and technological greatness had a perverse effect of politicizing the one area of academe that historically was a refuge from politics, the sciences. Although there may be nothing inherently political in the nature of hard science research, Cheng says, using science as a tool to advance the interests of a single authoritarian nation seems at odds with its foundational principles of openness and cosmopolitan collaboration. (Though there is, of course, plenty of precedent for countries using science for their national interests.) If China becomes home to and finances the bulk of the next supercollider, will a previously international effort become "owned by China" and answer to Communist Party interests? she asks. "If you take the government money and use government-funded equipment, are you inherently complicit in the aims of the government? Scientists are not supposed to pledge allegiance to the state." Cheng also worries that the Chinese government could use global science as geopolitical leverage. China was willing to punish foreign universities that host speakers unfriendly to government stances with the loss of funds or suspension of exchange programs, she points out. It could use access to the supercollider to keep colleges, and even governments, in line.

Even as China publicly declares its ambitions for scientific primacy, there are concerns that it is cutting corners, using intellectual property theft to augment its own investments in indigenous science and technology. Intelligence experts say Beijing offers rewards of cash, tax breaks, research grants, or even university tenure to those willing to acquire technology and exploit the openness of overseas universities and laboratories. "China takes advantage of the commitment to intellectual freedom on campus, which strongly resists government scrutiny of the activities of foreign students in hard science programs and international academic cooperation," concluded a 2018 Hoover Institution commission examining Chinese influence in the United States. "China's aggressive policy is threatening the advantages the United States has long enjoyed a scientifically creative nation."[112]

Such suspicions threaten to sour key international research collaborations. Both Europe and the United States began investigations into Chinese theft of technology, and universities were put on the defensive as intelligence agencies warned that campuses may be the soft spot in the national security armor. Fears that China may be poaching American know-how led the Trump administration to limit the duration of visas for Chinese students and researchers in sensitive STEM fields. Anecdotal reports suggest that students are experiencing delays as their applications are subject to greater scrutiny. Chinese enrollments at American colleges, which grew at a breakneck pace for more than a decade, had already begun to slow, and the additional hurdles could speed a decline, educators worry. This may have an especially deleterious effect on certain departments and disciplines—nearly a quarter of the physics doctorates awarded in recent years by American colleges, for instance, go to Chinese nationals.[113]

If visa restrictions could make it more difficult for Chinese students and scholars to come to the United States, Congress also considered measures to stymie connections in the other direction. An amendment to the 2018 defense spending bill that was considered but not adopted blocked any university researcher who had ever participated in a foreign-talents program from receiving Defense Department grants. The proposal seemed aimed at China's Thousand Talents Plan, which offers lucrative short-term joint appointments to experts and academics based abroad. At least one college, Texas Tech University, put the hiring of a star biologist who had worked with Nanjing Agricultural

University on hold while the measure was being considered and warned other employees about accepting foreign research positions.[114]

As the trade war between the two countries heated up, so did a visa war, with each country denying entry to academics. In one case, FBI agents blocked a Chinese scholar at his airplane gate, marking a big *X* to cancel the 10-year visa in his passport. "Go back to China," he was told.[115] American academics who know Zhu Feng, a professor of international relations, dismiss notions he was doing anything secretive in the United States, noting that it's commonplace for foreign-affairs experts at US colleges and think tanks to have connections in the government. "It doesn't make him a spy," said Robert Daly of the Woodrow Wilson Center.[116]

At the time of the 2020 US presidential campaign, the Trump campaign sometimes seemed to run against China as much as Democratic challenger Joseph R. Biden Jr. While many of the Trump administration's actions, such as the threat to shut down the popular Chinese social media app WeChat and the closure of the Chinese consulate in Houston, were aimed more broadly, other policy moves targeted academic ties more specifically. Among them are the "foreign mission" designation of the Confucius Institute U.S. Center, the ending of the flagship Fulbright Program in Hong Kong and mainland China, and a threat to expel graduate students and researchers suspected of ties to the Chinese military (see chapter 4).

The COVID-19 pandemic, which originated in the Chinese city of Wuhan, added fuel to the administration's sometimes fiery critique of China, with the president repeatedly dubbing the infectious disease "kung flu." Chinese students studying in the United States, many of whom were not able to go home during the height of the pandemic, reported experiencing an uptick in discrimination.[117] The sense that they are not welcome, combined with an ongoing travel ban that made it impossible for new Chinese students to come to American colleges for the fall 2020 semester, could depress Chinese enrollments. Even with a vaccine, pressure for decoupling the higher education partnership could persist. After all, there was bipartisan support in Washington for measures that would increase scrutiny of foreign research collaborations and restrict Confucius Institutes.

While China sought to develop new academic partners and expand its sphere of intellectual influence, a chilling of Sino-American exchange and research could damage both sides. Yet it's precisely because leaders in both countries take a similar view that innovation and knowledge are key to twenty-first-century power that higher education is at the center of the current global standoff. "Universities," Daly said, "can't sit this one out."[118]

Like-minded American and Chinese visions of scientific and educational nationalism reinforced the two nations' mistrust. But China's greatest challenge may well be internal: the government's nationalistic impulse to restrict dissent and speech in academe could be the very thing that ends up undercutting its nationalistic ambition to become a world-class higher education system. If certain ideas are off limits, if some lines of research are too sensitive to pursue, it could affect who wants to teach at Chinese universities as well as who studies there. Without the ability to write, to research, to inquire, to speak critically, China risks sabotaging its own vision of building a great university system. This moment is a critical one and could cement China's future as an intellectual superpower. The coming years will answer the question, When one nationalistic impulse drives toward control and the other seeks innovation, which will win out?

9

Balancing Nationalism and Globalism

Higher Education in Singapore and Hong Kong

BRYAN E. PENPRASE AND JOHN AUBREY DOUGLASS

HONG KONG AND Singapore are island city-states that exude the complicated tensions of postcolonial nationalism. Both are influenced directly or indirectly by the long shadow of China's rising nationalism and geopolitical power and, in the case of Hong Kong, subject to Beijing's edicts under the terms of the 1984 Sino-British Joint Declaration. Both have productive economies dependent on global trade, and each has similar rates of population density—Hong Kong's population is 7.4 million and Singapore is home to 5.8 million people. Both also face the difficulties of a declining domestic population.[1] Both built and leveraged their growing network of universities to attract students and talent to fuel their knowledge-based economies. And both, for different reasons, are exposed to growing social tension caused by autocratic-leaning governments, with implications for academic freedom and the autonomy of universities.

At the same time, nationalism manifests itself in different forms on these two islands. The dramatic protests in Hong Kong in 2019 and 2020 reflect a peculiar and nascent sense of nationalism, shaped by the fear of mainland China's growing political suppression and nationalist agenda. In effect, neo-nationalism in China has shaped and conditioned Hong

Kong's tenuous sense of identity—what is termed "peripheral national-ism" experienced by other regions where "residents of an ethnically, linguistically, or culturally distinctive periphery resist incorporation by a centralizing state."[2] For example, Hong Kong, with its Cantonese-speaking population and different Chinese character set, has a linguistic identity distinct from that of mainland China. But it lacks the cultural traditions built over many centuries that other separatist regions share, like those in Catalonia, the Basque territories, Wales, and Brittany.

It remains to be seen whether Hong Kong's peripheral nationalist identity will be retained, or whether the increasingly assertive influence and control by mainland China will prevail and fully assimilate Hong Kong. But it is apparent that Hong Kong is at a turning point. Throughout 2019, protesters filled the streets of the city, worried about declining civil liberties, specifically Beijing's refusal to provide universal suffrage as promised previously in law and the disqualification of prodemocracy candidates, along with the growing control of Hong Kong's government and universities by Chinese central government designates and fears of an ever-expanding crackdown on dissent.

Where does that leave Hong Kong's universities? A question presented in the introductory chapters of this book is, When are universities leaders or followers of society (see chapter 2)? In the case of Hong Kong, students engaged in the larger protest movement blamed university leaders for failing to defend their civil liberties.[3] Universities on the island are dependent on government funding and rules, and on the income and networking advantages of enrolling a large number of mainland Chinese students. University leaders, it seems, share a fear of retribution by Chinese officials if they voice support for protesters. Most university presidents sought neutral ground as a path to navigate competing visions of Hong Kong's future (the protesters and Beijing), sending a message to students and faculty—beware of voicing dissent. One observer stated, the "failure to speak up on the extradition bill and during the early days of the protests does not bode well for academic freedom."[4]

The worst fears of the political activists, and many academics, came true with the passage of the National Security Law for Hong Kong by

Beijing. Effective on July 1, 2020, it prohibits "secession, subversion, terrorism and collusion with foreign or external forces." Xi's government then established a new security office in Hong Kong with its own law enforcement personnel. This office can extradite those who violate the new law for trial on the Mainland. As a result of this law, plus a mainland China–induced reorganization of the management of universities, the future of academic and personal freedom in Hong Kong and the vitality of its universities are very much in doubt. Where Hong Kong's universities were once a magnet for attracting talent globally, now there are the initial indicators of the flight of talent.[5]

Singapore has its own form of nationalism, conditioned by its status as an island and strategic location in Asia, its impressive economic growth, its own increasingly complex ethnic identity, and its colonial past. Since assuming power in 1959, the People's Action Party has ruled Singapore with restrictions on dissent. Is Singapore an illiberal democracy? Yes, but in its own unique form and with a slow movement toward greater civil liberties. Greater tolerance is, in part, a necessity. The Republic of Singapore has welcomed immigrants since its establishment as a nation in 1965 independent of Malaysia. Immigration has helped fuel its economy, which requires interaction with the larger world. To help attract talent and grow its economy, the ruling government built a higher education system and an international higher education hub dubbed the "Global Schoolhouse" that includes numerous high-profile university collaborations. And to attract students, largely throughout Asia, and international businesses and investment required some form of liberalization.

Singapore provides a less dramatic but relevant example of the tension caused by the influx of foreign national students and academics who often displace native citizens, combined with government-enforced efforts to control dissent in universities. And like Hong Kong, the long shadow of China influences the role universities are allowed to play in civil society.

The following further explores the implications of nationalist movements on universities in Hong Kong and Singapore. In both, university leaders, and their academic communities, value academic freedom and the idea of independent scholarship. Yet the political environment is severe enough, and the opportunity costs great enough, that they, thus far, remain generally neutral institutions in a debate over civil liberties and the future of their island states. The exception is the key role students have played in the protest movement in Hong Kong, but for how long?

Protests and Hong Kong Universities

In the early 1980s, China's president Deng Xiaoping outlined the principle of "One Country, Two Systems" for the reunification of Hong Kong with China as part of the negotiations with the United Kingdom. There would be "One China," with distinct Chinese regions such as Hong Kong and Macau, which would retain their own economic and administrative systems. Mainland China would continue to pursue "socialism with Chinese characteristics."

What the One China, Two Systems policy truly meant for Hong Kong remained a question—a vague promise or a true commitment by Beijing? In the negotiations with the United Kingdom, there was an assurance stated in Hong Kong's new constitution: "The socialist system and policies shall not be practiced in the Hong Kong Special Administrative Region, and the previous capitalist system and way of life shall remain unchanged for 50 years."[6] This became known as Hong Kong's "Basic Law," which also included a guarantee of academic freedom under Article 137.[7]

Yet with Xi's election in 2012 as China's president, the One China, Two Systems concept began to erode, at first slowly, and then rapidly. Beijing sought greater political control of Hong Kong, including expanded authority to extradite those who criticized the mainland Chinese government. In early 2019, capitulating to Beijing's desires, the Hong Kong government proposed a bill allowing extradition. This fueled a remarkable response. The protest movement began in March 2019 and escalated into the summer and fall. Police and plain-clothes gangs systematically assaulted protesters, prompting a general strike and citywide protests that included an estimated 1.7 million people. Pro-China protests also were organized by the government. As the conflict grew, radical wings of the protest movement became violent when protesters were confronted by riot police bent on dispersing large crowds; civil disobedience became rampant, including the closing of Hong Kong's international airport for a period.

Public support was largely behind the protestors. The violence caused initially by police and undercover agents seemingly organized by Beijing authorities was widely condemned. Over 20 percent of the population (2 million by some estimates) engaged in both peaceful and violent protest marches in the Hong Kong central region in June and July 2019, placing extreme pressure on Hong Kong's leaders to respond.[8] One group of protesters broke into the Legislative Council and defaced the city's emblem (now a crime punishable by up to three years in jail) and vandalized the chamber with spray-painted slogans.[9] Protesters stormed offices used by the Chinese government. Clashes between police and protesters came to include rubber bullets and tear gas.[10]

Students played a significant role in organizing the mass demonstrations and in developing what became known as the "five demands" of the protest movement: the withdrawal of the extradition bill, the introduction of universal suffrage and an end to Beijing government appointments, an investigation into alleged police brutality and misconduct and the release of all the arrested, a retraction of the official characterization of the protests as "riots," and the resignation of Hong Kong's chief executive Carrie Lam—an appointment made by Beijing. In early September, student protest groups successfully called for the boycott of classes in Hong Kong universities, which were generally supported by faculty and staff. The boycott began even after Hong Kong's chief executive Lam stated she was withdrawing the extradition bill.

Student unions at 11 universities organized the event and issued a joint declaration of "unforgivable atrocities" by Hong Kong police and "gangsters" and demanded an inquiry into police conduct as one of their five demands. "Hong Kong people have been very clear that there are five demands and we accept not one less. Students' unions of higher institutions will continue our strike," they said, adding, "We have reached the point of no return."[11] Thousands of students wore helmets, goggles, and masks at the Chinese University of Hong Kong, holding black banners saying, "Boycott for freedom" and periodically shouting, "Reclaim Hong Kong."[12]

For the large number of students who participated in the often-dangerous mass protest movement, the lack of vocal support by university leaders was a source of consternation. Most university leaders initially chose to largely ignore the pivotal issues of freedom of speech and opinions, and made no public statement for or against the five demands. The focus of university leaders was on condemning the violence.

In late October 2019, a group of University of Hong Kong (HKU) students delivered a petition calling on HKU president Xiang Zhang to issue a statement condemning police brutality and demanding a bar on police searches on campus of students and faculty, legal and financial support for arrested students, and a forum scheduled to listen to students' concerns.[13] Pressure grew for universities to be more active proponents, if not on the central issues of academic freedom, then on protecting students. Zhang proceeded to send a brief, four-paragraph email to HKU students, staff, and alumni stating, "I am against any form of violence by any party," noting the availability of legal advice, counseling, and other support for students in need. He also outlined the university's policies covering police entry onto campus. He closed by writing, "We have held discussions with students at various occasions in different manners and will continue to do so."[14]

Chinese University of Hong Kong president Rocky Sung-chi Tuan did offer a more significant statement of support for students. Prodemocracy students had met in his office, claiming that police brutality included the sexual assault of a student. In an open letter, Tuan stated, "I was able to see personally and up close the pain and suffering of the students, how they were driven to a state of hopelessness, and why they had turned to the university for help." He also noted that, "in teaching students to accept responsibility for their own action, the university shall also help them assert their rights." He would establish a team of alumni volunteer lawyers to support arrested students.[15] Yet Tuan was quickly criticized for his efforts. "It should come as no surprise," observed Phil C. W. Chan in the *South China Morning Post*, that the former head of Hong Kong's university system, Leung Chun-ying, criticized Tuan "for agreeing to condemn the police for 'any proven case' of brutality."[16]

In China's Shadow

One might have hoped for greater leadership in the great debate on Hong Kong's future by university leaders and faculty. But there were significant forces at play, including an increased financial dependency on Chinese student enrollment and the changing nature of university governance in Hong Kong that made vocal dissent increasingly difficult.

China's resurgent nationalism under Xi brought measures for greater control not only of Hong Kong's government but its public universities—changes in governance that mirrored similar reforms on the Mainland. All Hong Kong universities are formally under the direction of the chief executive of Hong Kong, who serves as the official chancellor of all the city's universities and 6 of the 23 members of the university councils. These councils hold the power to block faculty and staff appointments and to steer selection of academic leaders, including university presidents, toward individuals sympathetic to the People's Republic of China (PRC) government. The "councils" (read: governing boards) were increasingly populated by those who supported Xi's policy agenda.

As in China, a systematic effort emerged to constrain academic freedom, buttressed by not only threats of penalties and, in some instances, imprisonment but financial incentives to voice and publish pro-mainland policies. In turn, this created a relatively new environment of self-censorship among academics. Prior to Xi's ascendency, Hong Kong encouraged open debate and had policies that attempted to attract academic and professional talent to Hong Kong. Like Singapore, Hong Kong formulated a strategy to become a "higher education hub" for Asia as a means to bolster Hong Kong's rapid economic expansion and booming financial and business sectors.

Prior to the higher education hub strategy, Hong Kong's higher educational institutions included two major universities, the University of Hong Kong, established in 1911, and the Chinese University of Hong Kong, established in 1963. A new technical university, the Hong Kong University of Science and Technology, was added in 1991, and five additional universities were created from existing colleges or institutes in the 1990s. In 2007, Donald Tsang, then chief executive of Hong Kong, explicitly stated his intention to recruit nonlocal students to Hong Kong schools and universities. Hong Kong increased admission quotas for international students, relaxed employment restrictions, and provide scholarships for nonlocal students from mainland China.[17] Hong Kong's universities flourished.

But since Xi's election as president of China, infringements on academic freedom became more frequent and severe. Hong Kong's government wrestled with its difficult mandate to reconcile China's increasing authority and insistence on Communist Party–defined civil order with the expectations of academics and the public for continued freedom of speech and extensive legal rights under the One Country, Two Systems doctrine. For Beijing, universities appeared as one of the primary sources of fomenting unrest and political opposition. This, in turn, triggered the selective removal of controversial academic figures from their positions, government interference in promotions and appointments, selection of politically connected and Chinese-aligned figures as presidents of Hong Kong's universities, and increasing pressure to limit speech on campuses. The examples are numerous.

The 2014 Occupy protests that briefly paralyzed Hong Kong were originally advocated by two professors (one at the University of Hong Kong and one at Chinese University of Hong Kong), and the Occupy and Umbrella protests were led and implemented by students. The two professors, law professor Benny Tai at HKU, and professor of sociology Chan Kin-man at CUHK, were imprisoned by the Chinese authorities.[18] At Lingnan University, Professor Chin Wan-kan, author of the 2011 book *Hong Kong as a City State* and proponent of complete autonomy for Hong Kong, was informed that his political activism "severely hurt the reputation of Lingnan." His contract was not renewed in 2016.[19] Cheng

Chung-tai, a lecturer at Hong Kong Polytechnic University, was fired after he was accused of "desecrating the flag" by displaying upside-down versions of the PRC and HKSAR (Hong Kong's Special Administrative Region) flags on the legislator's desks in the Legislative Council.[20]

One well-publicized case involved HKU law professor Johannes Chan. In 2014, Chan was recommended by a faculty committee for a position as pro–vice chancellor, but his candidacy was attacked by Hong Kong state-sanctioned media because of his political views on human rights and Hong Kong's constitution. HKU's governing board then blocked his appointment, against the recommendation of HKU faculty and its administration.[21] Peter Mathieson, the president of HKU, stated that the board had acted against the "best interests of the university."[22]

Hong Kong's government ministry overseeing universities has numerous methods for influencing tenured faculty. For example, they can deny the extension of contracts beyond the mandatory retirement ages, set for between 60 and 65 at Hong Kong's universities. Several politically active faculty were denied extensions, including faculty supportive of the Occupy protests. Concerns about contract extensions raised questions about Hong Kong's competitiveness with universities in the United States and Australia in hiring and retaining faculty: prospective faculty became concerned that they might labeled as "troublesome faculty," fired, and possibly jailed.[23]

It is difficult to project what Hong Kong's higher education system will look like in the near future. How can it attract and retain academic and professional talent? Can Hong Kong's institutions remain competitive with other leading world universities?[24] The future of Hong Kong's universities is tied to the outcome of the larger question of the island's political future and the sustainability of Xi's form of neo-nationalism, which increasingly punishes dissent.

Singaporeans First

Singapore has its own particular form of nationalism. Singapore is ruled by a semi-autocratic government that systematically constrains dissent, although to a much lesser degree than in Hong Kong. The phrase "Singaporeans First" became a rallying cry for government officials and those citizens who have a sense of socioeconomic displacement caused by the influx of foreign nationals.

Like Hong Kong, as well as the other "Asian Tiger" nations, Singapore pursued a long-term policy of increasing educational attainment rates of its citizens, while welcoming foreign investment and talent viewed as a necessity to generate and sustain a globally competitive economy. Higher education is a key part of this successful policy. Beginning in 2002, Singapore's government launched its Global Schoolhouse—the first "higher education hub," which was later imitated in many other nations. The initial plan was to bring international students to Singapore to attend existing and dozens of new institutions, many of them established in partnership with foreign universities.

Teo Chee Hean, then minister of education, outlined this ambitious strategy in a 2000 address, emphasizing that "in a knowledge economy, intellectual capital is a prized resource. As traditional seats of scholarship and learning, universities are now seen as valuable sources of 'brainpower' needed to drive the new economy." As Minister Teo described it:

> Our vision, in shorthand notation, is to become the Boston of the East. Boston is not just MIT or Harvard. The greater Boston area boasts of over 200 universities, colleges, research institutes and thousands of companies. It is a focal point of creative energy; a hive of intellectual, research, commercial and social activity. We want to create an oasis of talent in Singapore: a knowledge hub, an "ideas-exchange," a confluence of people and idea streams, an incubator for inspiration.[25]

From this Global Schoolhouse vision came an initiative that some called Singapore's "open-door" policy. The objective was to attract 10 world brand name universities to establish branch campuses or partnerships with local institutions. This would form the means for Singapore to recruit up to 3,000 globally recognized scholars as well as 150,000 international students by 2015. International students would be eligible for grants, and the government would waive a portion of their tuition in exchange for three years of work in Singapore after graduation. International students could also work during their studies and for one year after graduation.[26] The Singapore government increased university funding to help attract foreign talent, often offering lavish research grants to international scientists. Singapore's government also made new governance arrangements that established universities as semiautonomous corporations—a trend found in other parts of Asia that reflected norms in the United States.

From 2002 until 2015, many of the goals of the program were realized. Prior to 2000, Singapore featured two major universities: the National University of Singapore (NUS), established in 1980 by merging Nanyang University and the University of Singapore; and Nanyang Technical University (NTU), established 1991. These two universities offered degrees at the bachelor's, master's, and doctoral level, with NTU specializing in technology. Singapore's higher education network of institutions grew to include the new Singapore Management University in 2000, the Duke-NUS Medical School campus in 2009, LaSalle College of the Arts in 2009, Singapore Institute of Technology in 2009, and Singapore Institute of Management University in 2005.[27] Other successful international partnerships included a branch campus of the international business school INSEAD, the new Singapore University of Technology and Design campus developed in collaboration with MIT in 2012, and the Yale-NUS College—a partnership between NUS and Yale University, which opened in 2014.

Some ventures failed. The University of New South Wales opened a campus in 2007 but soon withdrew, and the Tisch School of the Arts and the University of Nevada, Las Vegas, opened campuses, which closed in 2014 and 2015, respectively. The University of Chicago opened a campus of its Booth School of Business in 2000 and continued operations until 2014, when it moved to Hong Kong.

But overall, Singapore's Global Schoolhouse initiative was a tremendous success. Singapore attracted international students, increasing from 50,000 in 2002 to 90,000 in 2010, seemingly on the way to the 150,000 goal. The evolving links with China played a part in this increase: students from China represented over a third of all international students, and China became Singapore's largest trading partner. The recruitment of international scholars and increased funding also revitalized NUS and NTU, and both rose steadily in the international global rankings of universities that focus on research output, with NUS ranked 1 in Asia and 11 internationally, and NTU ranked 2 in Asia and 12 internationally, according to 2019 QS World University Rankings.[28]

However, another outcome was a growing sense of resentment among Singaporeans. Many objected to the subsidies given to international students and their increasing numbers in prestigious universities, seemingly at the expense of local Singaporean students. Political pressure grew on the ruling People's Action Party, or PAP, to reduce the number of international students. Singapore's press and politicians expressed concern about the increasing numbers of foreign workers and academics, triggering a backlash to Singapore's "open door" policies. Immigrants arrived in Singapore on two tracks: one as mostly unskilled workers and the other as highly compensated "foreign talent." Singapore's population of 5.5 million included 3.38 million Singaporean citizens, 0.53 million permanent residents, and 1.63 million nonresidents.[29] The large influx in the number of foreign residents strained funding for Singapore's public services, housing, and educational institutions, and generated increased resentment.

When a 2013 white paper outlined a government plan to grow Singapore's population to 6.9 million by 2030 through increased immigration, the result were large demonstrations (an unusual event in Singapore) and the first major political pressure to reduce immigration. In response, the government sharply curtailed work visas. Net migration to Singapore dropped from its peak of 228,000 in 2008 to less than 50,000 in 2014.[30] The government also provided 2,000 extra university places to Singaporeans at public universities over four years, starting in 2014, and capped foreign placement at 18 percent of the island-state's total enrollment.[31] By 2019, international student enrollment dropped to about 65,000 students, and scholarships for these students were reduced to $130 million (a decrease from $210 million in 2014).[32]

The Singaporean parliament and Ministry of Education began to express concerns about the small proportion of native Singaporeans in tenure-track faculty positions, which in 2014 stood at 25 percent at NUS and NTU—the result of the prior "pro-foreigner policy."[33] The government responded by urging universities to "do more" to hire a "local core" of Singaporeans as faculty.[34] The Singaporean government also shifted its emphasis in educational funding away from international students and toward continuing education for Singapore's citizens. The new policy took the form of the ambitious 2015 SkillsFuture initiative, which the Singaporean government described as "a national movement to provide Singaporeans with the opportunities to develop their fullest potential throughout life, regardless of their starting points."[35]

SkillsFuture represented a massive US$1 billion per year investment by the government. All Singaporean citizens were eligible for grants for early and midcareer training to update their skills, switch careers, obtain career guidance, and prepare for the new "automation economy."[36] This investment was paired with a program for Singaporean adult learners, including large reductions in fees to enroll in undergraduate courses.[37]

The rise in the international reputation of Singapore's universities was impressive. But there emerged concerns about an overreliance and focus on quantitative measures of excellence, known as key performance indicators, or KPIs. International rankings of universities rely heavily on the citation count of academic publications, for example. To move up the rankings, Singapore's universities adopted policies for hiring, promotion, and tenure that relied heavily on these metrics. Critics contended that such practices favored research by foreign academics while discouraging research on local political and social issues that were much less likely to be publishable in prestigious international journals.[38]

In January 2019, an online article titled "Opaque Policies, Fixation with KPIs, Rankings: Why Arts and Humanities Academics Quit NUS, NTU" criticized Singapore's "incessant pursuit of rankings" and the "relative lack of academic freedom when it comes to certain projects or research initiatives." The article appeared in the online newspaper *Today* but was taken down after just four days after the threat of a legal challenge by NUS administrators.[39] Rather than suppressing concerns, the legal challenge triggered an international response, and the article was quickly reposted by a number of online sites outside of Singapore.[40] Since then, NTU and other universities have broadened the criteria for faculty advancement. But the fact remains that global rankings drive much of the research behavior away from regional and local needs, and thus engagement with local communities.

Fake News and Academic Freedom Tested

Singapore has the semblance of a democratic republic yet, as noted previously, with one-party control since 1959. The government mandates constraints on social behaviors and on academic freedom that, while not as egregious as the situation in Hong Kong or in China, pose challenges for university leaders, faculty, and students.

One example is a 2019 controversy at the Yale-National University of Singapore's College—a liberal arts college that represents one of many joint academic teaching and research programs with foreign universities. The Yale-NUS College is governed by a board that includes Singaporean leaders from business and government, Yale administrators and corporation members, as well as the presidents of NUS and Yale. When the Ministry of Education noted concern regarding a scheduled weeklong program at the college titled "Dialogue and Dissent in Singapore" to be led by Alfian Sa'at, a Singaporean playwright, it was canceled. The short class was to feature screenings, panel discussions, and conversations with prominent dissidents. In canceling the event, Yale-NUS College professor Tan Tai Yong stated his concern over the possibility of international students enrolled in the class losing their visas for engaging in political activity. There was also concern within the college of the academic value of the class with its focus on political activism. "The fundamental reason why we took the decision," he said to the *Octant*, Yale-NUS's campus newspaper, "was risk mitigation."[41]

In response, Yale's president Peter Salovey stated that "Yale has insisted on the values of academic freedom and open inquiry, which have been central to the college and have inspired outstanding work by faculty, students and staff."[42] Salovey requested that Yale's vice provost for global strategy (and former Yale-NUS president) Pericles Lewis investigate. In a detailed report that included interviews with Yale-NUS administrators, faculty, and the instructor of the course, Lewis concluded "that the decision to cancel the module was made internally and without government interference in the academic independence of the College."[43] In founding the college, the agreement with NUS and ministerial officials stated guarantees on academic freedom and autonomy in setting the curriculum and hiring of academic staff.

The reality or appearance of capitulation by Yale-NUS president Tan Tai Yong raised long-simmering worries at Yale and elsewhere about academic freedom when operating programs under semi- or fully autocratic governments. Cancelling the Yale-NUS class generated international attention. An editorial in the *Washington Post* stated, "Although only 16 students were enrolled, the decision has revived a debate on whether American liberal arts colleges and other Western universities are compromising their values of academic freedom and the free exchange of ideas when they expand into places with restrictive political climates such as Singapore, the Persian Gulf states and China."[44] Such are the constraints on personal freedom that even if students at Yale-NUS wanted to protest the cancellation of the class, they were prevented from doing so: Singapore's government allows for protests and demonstrations only in a section of a specific park in the city and does not allow non-Singaporeans to participate.

Shortly before the events at Yale-NUS, Singapore's government aggressively sought new powers to constrain freedom of speech, with implications for universities. In May 2019, parliament passed the Protection from Online Falsehoods and Manipulation Act, also known as the "Fake News Law." It gave government ministers sweeping powers to remove online articles if they are deemed to be "false or misleading, wholly or in part," and if the minister concludes that the removal is "in the public interest."[45] Before drafting the bill, Singapore created a Parliamentary Select Committee on Deliberate Online Falsehoods. The committee heard testimony from faculty, including former Rhodes scholar P. J. Thum. He strongly objected to the bill and claimed that the ruling People's Action Party itself had used "fake news" repeatedly.

Thum's testimony was rebuked by government officials. More than 170 academics signed a letter stating their concerns about the bill and the suppression of academic freedom in Singapore.[46]

The Fake News Law gave Singaporean ministers the power to order "corrections" to "false and misleading" content anywhere in the world, not just in Singapore, and required internet service providers to block censored content. With the arrival of the COVID-19 pandemic, ministerial officials claimed the new law would help block false information about the pandemic, thereby better protecting public health. But more than 100 academics from throughout the world thought otherwise, signing a letter protesting the threat to academic freedom.[47] One of the first usages of the law was to block a Facebook page known as the "States Times Review" run by an Australian-based Singaporean political activist named Alex Tan.[48]

Singapore's partial shift away from international students and foreign ventures in higher education reflects its own nationalistic approach to education. Singapore's unique history, with its very recent national origin that fused diaspora populations from India, Malaysia, and China into a nation in 1965, defies traditional notions of nationalism that rely on common ethnic, linguistic, and cultural origins. As an island-state, Singapore is likened to a local dish known as *rojak*, a salad-like mixing together of peoples, which predates its formation as a nation. As a result, nationalism in Singapore is formed in a context of what P. Yang has called a "constitutive sociocultural hybridity" in which authenticity is derived differently than it is in other nations with more easily identified markers of cultural inclusion.[49]

Divergent Futures?

China's assertive global presence, rising economic strength, and dogmatic nationalism are major influences on both Hong Kong and Singapore, but with significant differences. Seemingly with little choice, Hong Kong's government responded to Xi's increased nationalism by cooperating with mainland Chinese authorities, including a pivot in policies to favor mainland Chinese students and increasingly for suppressing dissent. There is an emerging sense of the inevitable integration with China; the future of Hong Kong may be less as a "global city" and instead as one of many Chinese cities, with economic activity coming increasingly from trade with the Mainland.

Beijing's new National Security Law for Hong Kong bodes ill for the independence of Hong Kong's universities, severely eroding the One China, Two Systems promise. The vastly expanding power of Beijing to forcibly limit the civil liberties of Hong Kong's citizens promises a further crackdown on university faculty and students similar to that experienced in China's Mainland. As observed by Amnesty International, "Under this new law 'secession, subversion, terrorism and collusion' with foreign forces incur maximum penalties of life imprisonment. . . . [T]hese offences are so broadly defined they can easily become catch-all offences used in politically motivated prosecutions with potentially heavy penalties."[50] The law also resulted in changes in the governance of Hong Kong universities, further stacking their governing boards with mainland Chinese appointees.

Where once there was a hope of two separate university systems between Hong Kong and Beijing, that seems on the brink of dissolution. If this continues to be the case in a post-COVID-19 world, we should expect a flight of talent from the Chinese city-state and a real decline in the vitality of its universities. The erosion of academic freedom and enforcement of political orthodoxy will degrade the competitiveness of Hong Kong's universities as part of the cost of complying with mandates from China.

China's influence on Singapore includes a dependency on high number of fee-paying Chinese foreign students, but more specifically Singapore's dependency on China as a trading partner and, at the same time, economic competitor bent on dominating Asia and beyond. As an independent state with limited resources, Singapore knows that its economic competitiveness depends on high-quality academic institutions, an ability to attract global talent, and a well-educated population. This awareness resulted in high levels of funding and growing international reputations for its research universities, fed initially by increasing numbers of international students and faculty.

But over the past few years, Singapore has moderated its investment in higher education and curtailed the recruitment of foreign students and faculty, and the government has decreased civil liberties with a direct impact on its higher education sector. The Fake News Law and other efforts to control dissent have a chilling effect. But one might speculate that these increased controls on civil society will only partially erode Singapore's reputation as a global powerhouse for higher education. They are difficult but navigable.

Both Hong Kong and Singapore face their own economic slowdowns, exacerbated by the COVID-19 pandemic. When combined with their aging and declining domestic populations, this makes innovation and excellence in higher education even more important for sustaining prosperity. In both city-states, universities played a key role in boosting their economic competitiveness. Both need to manage the external reality of China *and* seek political support from their native populations. It is a balancing act. In theory, the solution for both requires increasing numbers of foreign or nonresident students and workers, and an energetic and global higher education system to maintain a competitive workforce. Yet it appears that the trajectories of their two higher education systems are going in different directions under the long shadow of a powerful China. The political environment for universities in Singapore is much more positive and sustainable than it is in Hong Kong.

10

The Role of Universities in Putin's Russia

Reinforcing the State

IGOR CHIRIKOV AND IGOR FEDYUKIN

RUSSIA IS ONE OF the international leaders of the neo-nationalist movement. Russia's president Vladimir Putin cultivates close ties with avowed neo-nationalists abroad, including Turkey's president Recep Tayyip Erdoğan and Hungary's president Victor Orbán. He gives encouragement and support to aspiring neo-nationalist politicians in France, Germany, and elsewhere. The actual extent and effectiveness of this support is a matter of debate. But more importantly, Russia's leader does not hide his connections with neo-nationalists around the globe. On the contrary, he flaunts them as a personal projection of Russia's power and influence.

Russia's neo-nationalist credentials found publicity on the *Economist*'s November 2016 iconic cover portraying President Vladimir Putin among the front men of a rising neo-nationalist movement, alongside Donald J. Trump and Nigel Farage. In June 2019, in an interview with the *Financial Times*, Putin reaffirmed his role as a champion of neo-nationalism, proclaiming the end of liberalism and lambasting migrants, minority rights, and gender equality as threats to nations and traditional values.[1] In Russia, government-run media sharply and noisily blamed (neo)liberalism, "Brussels bureaucrats," "globalist elites," immigration, and the "Gayrope" ("Gay Europe") for the world's ills. Putin also plans to make Russia great again—in its Russian version, the motto calls for the country to "Rise Up from Her Knees." Putin's "Fortress Russia" posturing and hostility to all things "Western" dates to the 2014 absorption of Crimea and the conflict in eastern Ukraine, but it has deep roots Russia's Soviet past.[2]

How has Russia's version of neo-nationalism influenced the behavior and status of Russia's universities? Answering this question entails a conceptual challenge: What is the difference between the resurrection of Soviet legacies of control over higher education, "generic" authoritarian practices, and those associated specifically with neo-nationalism? In a number of countries, especially in the West, it is easier to ascribe certain developments—such as cracking down on the inflow of international students or attacks on the "liberal bias" at universities—to neo-nationalism. However, autocratic regimes throughout the world have sought to limit academic freedoms, to police international contacts and mobility, and to impose a nativist agenda long before the contemporary global wave of neo-nationalism.

After the collapse of the Soviet Union, Russian universities did gain a semblance of greater institutional autonomy and academic freedom, although often mired in the difficulties of a higher education system characterized by patronage and corruption. Paradoxically, the first steps toward reasserting greater control over universities by the government initially came in the late 1990s to early 2000s as part of a larger agenda to modernize and "Westernize" higher education. Since Vladimir Putin's emergence as Russia's undisputed leader, some of the very same policies intended to modernize universities were employed to impose limits on political activism and dissent.

In this chapter, we explore the tensions between different policy objectives related to higher education in Russia, such as a modernization agenda versus tighter ideological and political control by the state. We also explore the scope and the meaning of increasing "re-Sovietization" of higher education,[3] as elements of Soviet higher education system are being brought back to life. The COVID-19 pandemic, and the financial difficulties it will impose, may simply reinforce the power of the state in controlling the university sector for the Russian state's political needs.

Institutional Autonomy and University Governance

The collapse of the Soviet regime in 1991 heralded a new era of institutional autonomy for Russia's universities. This included the 1992 Law on Education No. 3226 that explicitly banned the old Soviet practice of appointing university rectors in civilian state-run institutions of higher education (Article 35, Paragraph 3). It mandated that rectors be elected by the faculty members themselves, while university councils were to exercise "overall governance."

The weakness of the central government in the early 1990s meant that many of these elections were truly competitive, sometimes fiercely so; the elections of faculty deans and department chairs were also competitive. While these latter positions were elective even in the Soviet era, at least in theory, these "sleeping institutions" now became the sites of genuine and open political competition between rival faculty groups. Legislation also allowed for the first time the establishment of private universities where governance was left to the founders' discretion (with the downside that many of these universities were simply money-making diploma mills). At the same time, state funding of higher education dwindled dramatically; public universities then became increasingly reliant on their own ability to attract fee-paying students and on other sources of income, such as renting out their facilities to commercial enterprises. This meant that Moscow's financial leverage over universities declined.

By the late 1990s, however, reformers in the federal government were increasingly convinced that Russia's higher education system was in a deep crisis and its problems required a reassertion of federal government control over rectors, many of whom were viewed as corrupt, incompetent, too conservative, beholden to equally corrupt interest groups in their universities, and generally unwilling to implement any changes that might be painful for their constituents—that is, their faculty.

This Moscow-led program of higher education modernization called for making university management more transparent and faculty more research oriented and more international. This included introducing measurable indicators of faculty research performance, including the number of peer-review publications indexed in international databases, such as Web of Science and Scopus. The government also began a shift toward competitively awarded research funding, much stricter enforcement of quality controls and regulations, and changes in university governance. Just as with other elements of modernizing agenda, this latter objective was to be supposedly based on "best international practices": for example, the rectors were to be made accountable to independent boards of external trustees, rather than to their own faculty.

One outcome of these efforts, however, was the erosion of university autonomy. "Neoliberal" reforms were consistently, though selectively, implemented as a way to assert greater central government control. This included incremental changes in the wording of the 1992 Law on Education No. 3226 and the 1996 Law on Higher and Postgraduate Professional Education No. 125-FZ. Amendments included a provision for the establishment of special vetting commissions that certified candidates for the position of rector before they would be allowed to run in the election. These commissions were composed of outsiders: half of their members were to be appointed by executive agencies that supervised a given institution, and the other half were to represent various other external interests.

The cumulative result of this legislative fine-tuning dramatically increased the powers of the so-called founders (*uchrediteli*)—the executive agencies empowered to supervise these institutions on behalf of the state (in most cases, the Ministry of Science and Higher Education; but also some other ministries, such as Health or Transportation; or regional governments). This turned rectors into de facto appointees. While elections were still held, the government now had ample opportunities to block undesirable candidates from running. The very fact of being elected does not entitle the winner to automatically assume office: instead, the relevant executive agency signs a contract with them—another opportunity to weed out the "wrong" candidates.

Henceforth, ministerial agencies had broad powers to fire an elected and confirmed rector and to appoint an acting rector, often an outsider: such a temporary appointment could then postpone a new election for several years, giving the acting rector enough time to consolidate power. Nor is this the only mechanism employed to control university leaders. To give just one among numerous examples, rectors needed to have a security clearance to perform their duties, so denying such clearance—a decision that is nontransparent and cannot be appealed—automatically disqualifies a person from acting as a university head.[4]

Most strikingly, the effort to modernize universities in the 2000s included the outright abolishment of rector elections in an ever-larger group of Russian "flagship universities." Beginning in 2008, the government launched a program to create 10 federal universities and 29 national research universities under the flagship moniker. Some existing universities were named new federal universities. But most were the product of mergers of anywhere from two to half a dozen institutions. Russia's Ministry of Education provided additional funding to help both new categories of university to "modernize" and to increase their research productivity. New funding supported programs designed by each institution to boost measurable performance indicators, most notably, the number of international students, the number of internationally indexed publications, and, ultimately, the institution's standing in international university rankings.

One provision of Russia's version of a university excellence program was that rectors of federal flagship universities were now to be appointed directly by the government and, in addition, to be accountable to a new board of supervisors established at each participating institution.[5] While national research universities were not formally required to do so, many also choose to change their charters to make their rectors appointed, rather than elected.[6]

Moscow State University and Saint Petersburg State University, the two oldest and most prestigious institutions in the country, were purposefully excluded from these excellence programs. Instead, the federal government provided additional funding to both of these politically powerful universities, with their graduates in key positions in the Kremlin, to help counter their possible opposition to the program. In 2009, Moscow State and Saint Petersburg State were also given the special status of "unique research and educational complexes."[7] This brought them additional prestige and funding channeled through separate budgetary provisions negotiated directly with the top political leadership of the country, rather than with the ministries, and the promise of exemption to some extent from increasingly invasive regulations. Again, the price paid for these benefits was that rectors of these two institutions were now to be appointed and fired by President Putin himself, making the incumbent rectors nearly independent of their own faculty.

By 2012–14, the Ministry of Science and Higher Education moved to close down the most notorious diploma mills. While well intentioned, this also resulted in an intensification of government interference in the internal affairs of many universities. Numerous institutions were forcibly merged or even closed and their rectors removed, often in the face of student and faculty protests. Ironically, one of the more high-profile cases was the firing of Sergey Baburin in 2012. A rabid nationalist, he was removed as rector of the Russian State University of Trade and Economics, a former distance-learning school that in the post-Soviet era became a sprawling diploma mill with numerous branch campuses all over the country, and with tens of thousands of students. Baburin decried the ministry's "liberal extremism," seeking to present its actions as an attack on Russian patriots by liberal globalist elites. In support of Baburin, students organized sit-ins. This did not, however, prevent Baburin's removal, and the university was folded into another institution.[8]

The governance and political environment within Russian universities had changed dramatically by 2012, as universities lost their autonomy and rectors became, for all practical purposes, appointed officers fully accountable to the ministry. Tellingly, the new Law on Education No. 273-FZ adopted in 2012 avoided codifying any principles of university governance; instead, these were left to the government's discretion (Article 26). All these changes were made well before the Russian leadership openly turned in 2013 ostensibly toward a neo-nationalist posturing at home and abroad.

Academic Freedom and Civil Liberties

While the changes in university governance and the erosion of university autonomy in the 2000s are relatively easy to track, the curtailing of academic freedom is less so. When outspoken scholars are dismissed, this is rarely, if ever, done for overtly political reasons: as a rule, university officials justify such decisions as a by-product of routine, if regrettable, reduction in staff or the restructuring of academic programs. Still, the assault on academic freedom in Russia is obvious and dramatic.[9] And similar to the restructuring of university governance to gain greater control by government officials, it began long before Russia's more recent neo-nationalist turn.[10]

In the 1990s, university autonomy and more competitive elections did not necessarily mean an era of universal academic freedom. In many cases, elections did nothing more than bring to power one among the competing patronage cliques within a given institution; when triumphant, such cliques proceeded to entrench themselves in power and to marginalize their opponents. Once they consolidated control, they often continued their corrupt practices, academic (running diploma mills or degree scams) and financial. In this respect, the situation within universities echoed the dynamics of regional politics, where power tended to be captured by increasingly authoritarian local bosses.

Nevertheless, for many faculty members the period before Putin's ascendency did feel like an era of greater academic freedom, if only because it took time for some rectors to consolidate their political power within universities. Additionally, there were relatively few incentives for rectors to bother reigning in politically outspoken faculty members as long as they confined themselves to extra-academic activism and did not challenge the university rectors themselves. Finally, some faculty members could exercise their autonomy thanks to grants from international and Russian foundations that made them less financially dependent on their own universities or by moving to other institutions, in particular, those in the more pluralistic locales of Moscow and Saint Petersburg. There, a number of new universities emerged that provided institutional homes for many of the "liberal" and "pro-Western" scholars, especially in social sciences and humanities. These included both state-funded projects, such as the Russian State University for the Humanities, Smolny College, and the Higher School of Economics, as well as relatively new private institutions, such as the Moscow School of Social and Economic Sciences, the New Economic School, and the European University at Saint Petersburg.

Against this background, Russia increasingly experienced a consistent assault on the freedom of academic speech as Putin consolidated power. One of the most obvious cases was the establishment in 2009 of the so-called Commission for Combatting Attempts to Falsify History. One purpose was to foster scholarly interpretations of the Second World War that aligned with the Kremlin's official views. This presidential commission convened as early as 2009 and was then disbanded in 2012, without much of an impact.

As a next step, however, the changes to the Criminal Code of the Russian Federation Article 354.1 introduced by the 128-FZ law of May 5, 2014, made it a punishable offense to "deny the facts established by the Nuremberg Tribunal" and to spread "obviously false statements regarding the actions of the USSR in WWII." This provision was used to discourage attempts to compare the crimes committed by the Stalinist and Nazi regimes or to problematize the official interpretation of such difficult historical topics as Russia's collaboration with the Nazis, the siege of Leningrad, the prewar Soviet occupation of the Baltic countries and Western Ukraine, or the postwar occupation of Eastern Europe. Parallel to that, Federal Law 135-FZ of June 29, 2013, banned any "propaganda of non-traditional sexual relations." This made any open academic debate and teaching on LGBQT and, more broadly, gender issues extremely problematic; attempts at establishing LGBQT and gender teaching and research programs were unwelcome at many academic institutions.

While these high-profile laws and media campaigns to censor opinions and scholarly research were important in curtailing academic speech, even more significant was the increasing sense of professional vulnerability among the faculty. This also was a by-product of the effort to modernize universities in accordance with what was described as best international practice. Russian universities shifted to short-term contracts and performance-based pay, allowing university administrators wide discretion in hiring, promoting, and firing faculty members.

The replacement of elected rectors with appointed rectors was replicated in other academic administrative positions. One of the acknowledged deficiencies of the Soviet model was that universities were organized into relatively narrow mono-disciplinary departments. Merging these departments into larger multidisciplinary "institutes" was a needed reform. But this also increased the power of rectors who, under federal law, now appointed directors of departments, institutes, and schools. The result was the further reduction of faculty autonomy and freedoms, making it virtually unheard of for a university administrator at any level to step forward in defense of a faculty member who might stray from Russian government orthodoxy or criticize university management. Finally, no less stifling were the increasing bureaucratic controls and dramatically expanding volumes of paperwork and teaching loads foisted sometimes selectively on faculty.

This change in the academic environment was even more apparent for scholars in the humanities and social sciences, who might be suspected of peddling "globalist," "pro-Western," "liberal" views in classroom. Yet it affected all scholars, even those whose teaching, including engineering and natural sciences, had nothing to do with these topics. It also dramatically reduced the freedom to speak outside academia on nonacademic topics, for example, to participate in environmental or anti-corruption activism.

Some of the more notable cases of political firings of faculty members highlight the difficulty in pinpointing the exact cause. In 2014, Professor Andrey Zubov claimed he was being forced out of the Moscow State Institute of International Relations because of his stated views on Stalin's cooperation with Hitler on the eve of World War II. In 2018, Elena Panfilova, the former head of the Russian branch of Transparency International, felt forced to leave her post as the head of a corruption studies laboratory at the Higher School of Economics. According to Panfilova, the reason was her effort to involve students in anticorruption research aimed at a powerful minister.

A year later, in spring 2019, Alexander Kynev, a faculty member at the Higher School of Economics, accused the university's administration of staging the merger of two departments as a pretext for firing him and other professors who openly criticized President Putin and advocated for election transparency.[11] The university administration vehemently denied any political motives, and at least some of the professors were initially retained. In the summer of 2020, a reorganization of three departments was announced at the same university that, some faculty members claimed, was designed to purge politically suspect faculty.[12]

In yet another case, Vladimir Solovei, a prominent regime critic, announced that he was forced out of the Moscow State Institute of International Relations for political reasons, something that the university denied. The irony in this case is that Professor Solovei is a self-described Russian nationalist. This points to the ambiguity of the Kremlin's approach that seems rooted mainly in the acquisition of authoritarian control as opposed to an identifiable nationalist agenda.

All these cases are notable for the difficulty, if not impossibility, of proving beyond a doubt that the firings were politically motivated. But a pattern of systematic measures to control speech and scholarship is becoming increasingly apparent. Like in China, Russian universities are increasingly being used to police student and faculty behavior and to suppress independent activism. Students are discouraged from addressing politically sensitive topics, such as corruption or local economic problems,[13] and they are often threatened with expulsion for taking part in unauthorized political protests.

An increasing number of universities contractually ban their faculty from giving any public commentary on political and societal issues not vetted by the university's administration, or, at the very least, they demand that any such commentary be made in a private capacity (i.e., without citing the faculty member's affiliation). Even testifying as an expert in court in politically sensitive cases can lead to dismissal.[14] Some institutions, especially those involved in engineering, the natural sciences, and defense-related research, demand that their faculty clear their work with the in-house security office before submitting it for publication. The same goes for presentations at international conferences.

While these measures resemble the steps taken by many neo-nationalist regimes to muzzle universities and their faculty and students, they also fit the pattern of both generic authoritarian and past Soviet practices. Most clearly the trend toward restoring ideological control along Soviet lines expressed itself in a new measure passed in the summer of 2020 as a part of a larger package of legislative changes designed to allow Vladimir Putin to run for reelection twice more. The new law imposed on universities and schools required that their curriculum must provide "moral education" based on Russia's "traditional values," including patriotism, "respect for the defenders of the Motherland," "respect for the law," and similar principles.[15] On the face of it, this implies that students could be expelled for espousing incorrect or "nontraditional" values.

Talent Mobility and Immigration

The authoritarian tendencies of the past two decades have influenced talent mobility and academic migration. The period after 2012 saw two somewhat contradictory trends: the growing inflow of international students accompanied by the increased risks of brain drain of academics and Russian students. These trends reflect, on the one hand, Russia's aspirations to regain global influence by using higher education as a tool of soft power and, on the other hand, the growing political pressures and economic slowdown coupled with decreasing investment in higher education.

The Soviet legacy of recruiting and educating international students still shapes Russia's current efforts to attract talent from abroad. International engagement of Soviet universities was centrally planned and coordinated by the government. International students were viewed as potential agents of global Sovietization and were expected to bring Soviet influence, values, and technical expertise back to their home countries.[16] Soviet embassies abroad selected the students, and Russian universities had little or no control over the incoming student body.[17] In 1960, the Soviet Union established a special university for international students from communist countries: the Peoples' Friendship University, originally named after Patrice Lumumba, a Congolese political leader. This and other universities educated political elites in developing countries within the Soviet sphere of influence; alumni included the presidents of Honduras, Angola, Mongolia, and Romania and, at one time, much of China's political elite. By 1990, Russia boasted the third-largest number of international students in the world after only the United States and France, enrolling some 126,500 students, with 70 percent studying in Russia and the rest in other Soviet-controlled republics.[18]

After the collapse of the Soviet Union in 1991, the number of international students dropped by half. Universities gained greater autonomy and flexibility to attract and educate international students on their own.[19] Unlike Anglo-Saxon countries that increasingly viewed international students as a source of additional funding for universities, Russia continued to partially subsidize the education of most international students. And while in many countries the rise of neo-nationalism manifested itself in calls for curtailing the inflow of outsiders, including students, in Russia this was not the case. State-sponsored recruitment of foreign students dramatically expanded. When Vladimir Putin came to power in 2000, Russia hosted 72,400 international students—20 percent less than the Russian Soviet Federative Socialist Republic in 1990. By 2017, the number of international students increased to 313,100, and they accounted for 7 percent of all students at Russian universities.[20] The education of international students remained important for the "formation of the pro-Russian national elites" who will "promote Russian interests."[21]

However, beginning around 2015, Putin's government redistributed its quotas of international students to reflect its geopolitical priorities: most state-subsidized students now came from the former Soviet republics and East Asian countries. In 2015, the Kremlin announced a quota reduction for Turkey after the downing of a Russian warplane near the Syria-Turkey border. And because the intent of recruiting and enrolling international students was for them to return to their home countries, these students had only limited opportunities to stay and work in Russia.

At the same time, brain drain in Russia remained a major problem. The collapse of the Soviet Union in 1991 triggered the most significant departure of Russian academics, in particular faculty in the hard sciences and math. Moscow State University—one of the most prestigious universities in Russia—lost around 20 percent of its professors during this wave of emigration.[22] At first, emigration was motivated by ideological constraints and anti-Semitism. Many of those who left later in the 1990s left in the wake of a severe economic crisis that led to reductions in academic salaries and a decline in the prestige of academic profession.

More robust national economic growth in the early 2000s resulted in a steady decrease in emigration, including the outflow of academics. Still, more researchers left the country than came from abroad.[23] The Russian government introduced various initiatives to curb this trend, providing financial incentives for attracting researchers from abroad and supporting graduate education at foreign universities for Russian citizens, with the assumption of their return. A mega-grants program was established in 2010 that offered funding for leading scholars based abroad to establish research centers and labs at Russian universities. Most grants were awarded to academics from among the Russian diaspora of the 1990s. The initial program mimicked similar initiatives adopted by other countries worldwide and was instrumental in creating centers of research excellence at predominantly teaching universities.[24]

The mega-grants program along with the Global Competitiveness 5-100 Project (see more details in the next section) helped to balance the inflow and outflow of academics from 2012 onward. In 2015 and 2016, for the first time in decades the net migration rate of Russian academics (the difference between in-migration and out-migration rates per 1,000 researchers) was positive.[25] However, the gap in the quality of research outputs of those who left and those who arrived was one of highest in the world: "outflows" generally published in much better journals than "inflows," and their work generated more citations.[26] Even though Russia was able to curb its brain drain, the country was still losing in research productivity. In addition, a growing number of young people used the opportunity to continue their education abroad to emigrate. The outbound flow of students from Russia increased by 12 percent between 2016 and 2019.[27]

Putin's return to the presidency for his third term in 2012 was marked by the departure of several well-known academics, including the former rector of the New Economic School, Sergey Guriev, and professor at the Higher School of Economics, Sergey Aleksashenko, who provoked the Kremlin's ire.[28] The academics who left the country in the second half of the 2010s often cited a mix of economic and political considerations, including dissatisfaction with limits on freedom of speech and the weak rule of law.[29]

Current trends in talent mobility and immigration in Russia clearly indicate that the ability of universities to attract international students and faculty is shaped by state-funded initiatives and regulations. In particular, Russia draws on Soviet practices as it seeks to use higher education as soft power and increases the number of international students fully funded by the state. While universities complement these practices by attracting fee-paying international students, they concentrate predominantly on the markets that fit the state's geopolitical priorities. However, growing dissatisfaction with current political regime coupled with economic recession creates risks of increasing brain drain among academics and suppressing Russia's research output.

Universities and International Engagement

International engagement and participation in the global knowledge economy have long proved challenging for Russian universities. As mentioned previously, the state has always played a significant role in directing their international engagement. The Soviet Union limited cross-border collaborations to the countries of the Communist bloc. Research was mostly concentrated at the Academy of Sciences and specialized research institutes under strict ideological control, including limits on access to Western literature and the censorship of publications. The intensity and forms of this control varied between the disciplines, with social sciences and humanities suffering the most. Mobility was limited even at the national level; foreign visits were rare and available only after approval of the party and the security agency.

After 1991 and the end of the Cold War, universities were allowed to cultivate international connections. Individual researchers could now travel, attend conferences abroad, and publish without significant limitations. International collaboration was hindered primarily by the faculty's weak English-language skills, limited access to foreign publications, and low salaries. Global engagement after the collapse of the Soviet Union was mostly driven by foreign foundations, including the Open Society Foundations (founded by George Soros), Technical Assistance to the Commonwealth of Independent States (European Union), and the MacArthur Foundation (United States). Funding from these and other Western sources helped to establish new types of higher education institutions, especially in social sciences and humanities, and led to the organization of international collaborations that included the translation of Western academic literature into Russian.

In the early 2000s, Russia began to align its higher education system with European countries under the Bologna Process. This included the switch from the Soviet model with its five- or six-year specialist degree to the two-tier bachelor's/master's model geared toward the European credit transfer and accumulation system. The process was very controversial and provoked resistance from universities, employers, and students. Some disciplines successfully negotiated to maintain their old structure of courses and degrees, including in medicine and military studies. Other disciplines quickly adopted the new model. Vocal critics of Bologna Process in Russia often portrayed it as an example of Western interference that led to a decline in the high quality of the higher education system.

The arrival of global rankings of universities in the late 2000s came as a shock to Kremlin policy makers and university administrators. They expected Russian universities to rank much higher in the global hierarchy.[30] Rankings indicated that there were two important areas for improvement at Russian universities: first, the quantity and quality of internationally recognized publications and second, the number of international students and faculty. The low research output of Russian universities was associated with the legacy of separating research from teaching in the Soviet research and development system: universities provided primarily vocational and professional training, while most research was done in the research institutes of the Academy of Sciences, as well as military and industrial research institutes.

By the end of the 2000s, Russia ranked below China and India in the number of science papers published.[31] The Russian government then attempted to increase the research capacity and global competitiveness, and ranking, of Russian universities. This was the focus of measures designed to modernize higher education, including the establishment of national research universities and federal universities discussed previously. And it was the objective of the Global Competitiveness 5–100 Project established in 2013: the most ambitious effort thus far to support global engagement of Russian universities.

In his 2012 inaugural speech, Putin set the goal of at least five Russian universities being in the top-100 in the global rankings—hence the 5–100 title. Additional funding was provided to 15 selected universities (a further 6 universities joined the program in 2015). Funding allocated for each participating university varied from US$2 million to US$15 million, the exact amount determined by an international board that oversaw the program. For some universities, this constituted up to 20 percent of their annual budget. The 5–100 Project and other initiatives did make a significant impact on the research capacity and global standings of participating institutions, increasing both the quantity and quality of their research.[32]

At the same time, the initial goal of helping five universities to reach the top 100 by 2020 was not achieved. Why? First, the initial investment was not sufficient to compete with the world's best universities and their vastly more abundant resources. Two years after the start of the program, Russia faced a sharp devaluation of the ruble due to the drop in oil prices and international economic sanctions. Putin's increasingly autocratic government and ventures in Crimea and elsewhere also made it increasingly difficult to attract international faculty.

A second reason: beginning in 2012, Putin's government introduced several laws aimed at limiting or prohibiting the operations of NGOs operating in Russia that receive foreign funding. Although universities were not directly covered by these laws, they lost opportunities to collaborate with foreign foundations based in Russia and became extremely cautious when they received funding from abroad.

And third, beginning in about 2015, international collaborations of universities were increasingly scrutinized by Russia's security agencies. Individual faculty were required to get approval for their proposed international engagements (collaborative projects, publications, conferences) from the security officers at their universities—a practice that was previously limited to certain areas associated with defense research.

The Russian state sends conflicting messages to its universities with respect to international engagement. On the one hand, it provides additional support for them to improve their global standing and attract international faculty. On the other hand, it creates additional barriers and risks associated with international collaborations and receiving funding from abroad. In response, the successor of the 5–100 Project, the Strategic Academic Leadership Program launched in 2020, broadens the goals of the Putin government: it balances the goal of improving the global rankings of Russia's universities with the economic and social impact of universities at the national and regional level.

The Future of Russian University Autonomy?

Over the past two decades, Russian universities experienced steadily increasing political pressures. These included the de jure and de facto reduction of university autonomy, increasing vulnerability of faculty to administrative discretion, outright efforts to police academic speech and international contacts, the firings of politically outspoken faculty members, and using universities as instruments to police extra-academic activism of faculty and students. Some of these political pressures are common to neo-nationalist regimes found elsewhere. For example, similar to other autocratic leaning regimes, Russia banned George Soros's foundations and those of other "globalists" from operating in the country, as well as waged an assault on "gay propaganda" and liberal values. The government also aggressively promoted a more "patriotic" reading of history and gradually dismantled whatever university autonomy there existed.

Yet, unlike many neo-nationalist and illiberal democracies that have emerged as populist movements, Russia, like China, is in some form simply on a continuum of autocratic rule by political elites. After a period of liberalization, the government found new pathways to limit civil liberties and place controls on universities. For at least a decade, this trend coexisted uneasily with efforts to modernize Russia's universities according to "best international practices." Indeed, what is interesting about Russia's case is how the drive to make universities more transparent, effective, and international was used as a path to then impose greater controls over institutions and their faculty.

An important feature of the Russian case is that neo-nationalist rhetoric often takes the form of resurrecting or reinventing Soviet rhetoric. In particular, neo-nationalism itself in Russia is built not so much around references to pre-1917 national symbols but rather on the cult of the Soviet victory in World War II and, increasingly, of Stalin himself. To what extent this symbolic re-Sovietization also manifests itself in policies and institutional design is a good question. The reintroduction of *vospitanie* (character building) at universities is the strongest indication that this might be the case. More notable, however, are the ways in which administrative techniques and governance principles inspired by the "New Public Management" paradigm is utilized to resurrect quasi-Soviet forms of political control.

The political environment is evolving. The summer of 2019 protests in Moscow, in which many students and faculty played a prominent role, might have pushed the regime to further revise the uneasy equilibrium between paying lip service to the value of academic freedom and the reality of increased political controls. The 2020 Russian constitutional referendum, however, allowing Putin to run for president for two more six-year presidential terms, will likely mean a continuation of his higher education policies.

Other forces are at play that may further weaken Russia's universities. The global COVID-19 pandemic pushed universities to operate remotely during the spring 2020 term and closed Russia's national borders. This may negatively influence international student recruitment. The economic impact of the pandemic could slash university budgets and also lower their opportunities for international engagement, reinforcing their isolation and dependence on the state.

11

Bolsonaro's Brazilian Neo-nationalism and Universities

ELIZABETH BALBACHEVSKY
AND JOSÉ AUGUSTO GUILHON ALBUQUERQUE

IN THE WAKE of the 1929 global financial crash, Brazilian nationalism in its modern form first emerged as the country attempted to distance itself from its dependency on international financial markets and influence. Nationalism, state command of economic development, import substitution, and economic autarky have been, to a greater or lesser extent, permanent traits of Brazilian political economy ever since.

This was particularly the case from 1964 up to 1985 when Brazil experienced a long period of military dictatorship that used nationalist sentiment to co-opt and mobilize mass support for succeeding authoritarian regimes.[1] Starting in 1974, however, the regime began a slow process of political decline as Brazilians demanded greater civil liberties and more economic opportunity. The military dictatorship ended in 1985 when Tancredo Neves, an opposition leader, was elected president. The new democratic era brought a degree of stability that then led to the election of a leftist government headed by former union leader Luiz Inácio Lula da Silva (known as Lula), in 2002, and then Dilma Rousseff in 2011, both members of the Worker's Party.

Jair Bolsonaro's election in late 2018 as Brazil's president brought to power the most far-right neo-nationalist leader to govern the country since the end of the military dictatorship. It came at a time of severe economic decline, increased crime, and a desire among middle- and upper-class Brazilians for greater social order. Bolsonaro's populism is similar to Donald J. Trump's—he is the self-proclaimed "Brazilian Trump"—with the added feature that he romanticized Brazil's earlier military regimes and restrictive policies on civil liberties. This included a quest for greater control of public institutions, including universities. In Bolsonaro's version of nationalism, universities are viewed as hubs for Marxist academics and students and uncontrolled criticism of his government.

Sworn in as president in early 2019, his initial attacks on universities were largely rhetorical and random, including raiding the offices of a number of faculty deemed dangerous leftists. But an inept Bolsonaro administration partially protected the autonomy of the university sector, with its combination of federal and state-established institutions. Ministers of education came and went, often demonstrating little knowledge of how Brazil's higher education system is organized and works. In addition, public opinion, Congress, the media, and the Supreme Court successfully counteracted the most aggressive moves made by the Bolsonaro administration. With the combination of an already declining economy and the unknown impact of the COVID-19 pandemic, plus the low priority the government has given to funding higher education, there is much uncertainty about the financial health and future autonomy of Brazil's universities—circumstances not unlike those in other nations in South America and elsewhere.

This chapter provides a brief description of the historical path that led to Brazil's contemporary university system. This is followed by an analysis of higher education policies under Lula and Rousseff, and then of the character and impact of Bolsonaro's government on Brazil's network of federal and state universities. We also offer a preliminary analysis of the evolving impact of the COVID-19 pandemic.

Higher Education in Brazil: Historical Heritages

When compared to North America and Europe, Brazil is a relative latecomer in developing mass higher education. Although the first Brazilian higher education institutions date from the beginning of the nineteenth century, the first real universities were created only in the 1930s. Up to then, the institutional model for higher education was a series of professional schools, following the Napoleonic model of the *grandes écoles*.

Legislation passed in 1931 set out the organization of Brazil's emerging university system. Following the European model, the law required the adoption of a faculty chair system with a senior professor supervising junior faculty and teaching programs in the sciences, humanities, and philosophy. The initial focus was on developing bachelor's degree programs. University enrollment was restricted by a government-determined formula that limited the number of entry positions at each university each year. A bachelor's degree was conceived as a license for the practice of established professions, including teaching.[2]

Major reform came in the 1960s after a coup d'état led by the armed forces. Beginning in 1964 the new military government promoted the development of graduate education, allowing selected universities to grant professional, master's, and doctoral degrees. In 1968, the government enacted a reform that changed undergraduate training from the conventional sequential courses to the credit system, similar to the US model. This reform replaced the old chair system with the department model. It split the faculty of science into disciplinary science institutes, while preserving the faculty of humanities and philosophy, and it established full-time contracts for academics.[3]

Brazil's authoritarian government also initiated the first sustained public effort to expand academic research by establishing a dedicated fund to support research projects in Brazil's growing number of universities and institutes. The confluence of policies supporting science and graduate education created the conditions for establishing Brazil's first research universities.[4] This included the establishment of CAPES

(Foundation for Advancement of Higher Education Personnel), the federal agency in charge of funding and regulating graduate education. CAPES organized the first evaluation of the graduate programs that links financial support to performance.

The 1968 reform was implemented amid a dramatic increase in the demand for access to higher education and the establishment of new federal and state university campuses. In 1960, the total enrollment in Brazilian higher education was 93,000 students. By 1970 enrolment grew to 425,478; in 1975, it was more than 1.1 million.[5] At first, most of this enrollment occurred in federal- and state-established universities. In part to meet enrollment demand at a lower cost, and because government officials worried about the growing strength of a student opposition movement inside the public universities, the government allowed for the establishment and growth of private institutions.

By the early 1970s, private, mostly for-profit, higher education was absorbing the majority of the new enrollment demand. This created a critical historical juncture in Brazil's evolving higher education system.[6] From that moment on, Brazilian higher education experienced a path-dependent growth, where the private sector became an ever-increasing player in the higher education landscape. These were mostly low-cost teaching-only schools, staffed with hourly paid, largely low-qualified academic staff, catering to students who could not meet public university entrance requirements.[7]

From 1974 to 1985, university leaders, faculty, and students played a central role in the country's fight for democracy. As a result, the New Republic, established in 1986, enshrined a peculiar Brazilian understanding of university autonomy: university governance and management failed to include external stakeholders. Apprehensive of the intervention of military dictators, university autonomy became synonymous with sovereignty as a way to protect faculty and students from future political actors.[8] The constitution protected universities, but in turn it separated universities from the wants of their constituents and reinforced their sense of isolation from a rapidly changing Brazilian society.

In 1996, the National Congress approved Lei de Diretrizes e Bases da Educação, or LDB, amending Brazil's 1988 constitution. It extended academic autonomy to private universities and, for the first time, set minimum requirements for granting the status of "university" to a higher education institution. It further proposed a diversification in the types of first-level degrees: besides the old bachelor's degree and teacher license, the law also recognized a technological degree granted after three years of vocational training. Furthermore, the new law enshrined the notion of democratic governance—the ideal of equally considering the will of students, employees, and academics when selecting the university's rector—as a central value for higher education.[9]

Higher Education Policy under Lula da Silva and Dilma Rousseff

National union leader and founder of the Worker's Party (PT) Luis Ignacio Lula da Silva assumed the presidency in 2003. Lula and his successor, Dilma Rousseff, embraced a left-leaning populism aimed at mitigating poverty, supporting identity group politics, and providing corporatist privileges to the elite of labor unions, public service, and state-owned enterprises. In turn, the PT's higher education policies and initiatives reflected the interests of Lula's diverse political supporters.

Lula quickly pursued policies intended to expand access to higher education for the nation's lower-income majority.[10] Brazil's higher education system, and in particular its network of federal- and state-supported universities, remained largely the bastion of the nation's upper-income and elite classes. How to increase educational attainment rates and better promote socioeconomic mobility?

In 2003, the new government launched the Federal Universities Restructuring and Expansion Program (REUNI). The program conditioned university funding on meeting enrollment expansion goals and a set of performance indicators.[11] REUNI lasted until 2012 and was very successful. It and other programs supported an impressive expansion of federal universities. Enrollments in the federal sector grew from 527,000 in 2003 to 886,000 in 2012. The number of entrance positions to be filled each year by freshmen grew from 109,000 to 393,000. The program also supported the establishment of 14 new universities and more than 150 new campuses, many built in the less populated hinterlands of Brazil.

Another Lula era program, the University for All Program (Programa Universidade para Todos), established in 2004, offered tuition exemptions, partial or total, for children from low-income families in private institutions. At its peak, the program offered more than 300,000 places in the private sector and was extremely popular.[12] In 2008, the government also enlarged and upgraded the federal network of vocational secondary schools, allowing them to offer programs leading to tertiary vocational degrees. And in 2010, the federal government reformed and expanded a subsidized loan program to support students enrolled in the private sector, the Student Financing Fund (Fundo de Financiamento ao Estudante do Ensino Superior, known as FIES).[13] As a result, enrollment in private education continued to grow. Institutions in the private sector also underwent a process of consolidation as they became more profitable: at the beginning of the 2000s, most of the enrollments in private institutions were in small, family-owned institutions (read: businesses); by 2018, five gigantic for-profit companies with shares in the Brazilian stock market commanded almost 35 percent of all undergraduate enrollments in the country.[14]

Both the University for All and the FIES programs helped tackle the two biggest challenges historically faced by the private sector—the high cost of tuition and the high level of tuition insolvency. In 2016, more than 46 percent of all students enrolled in the private sector had access to some kind of scholarship. That year, FIES and University for All programs accounted for almost two-thirds of this support. As a result, by 2015, the subsidized private sector accounted for a startling 75.7 percent of Brazil's 8 million undergraduate students.[15]

Within the public network of federal and state universities, the Worker's Party sought to address the needs of underrepresented groups and solidify their political support. This included transforming public universities into "citizen universities" by forging a strategic alliance with social movements. The University Outreach Program (PROEXT), for example, promoted by the Brazilian Ministry of Education and launched in 2003, supported university cultural and political outreach activities. The PROEXT Program also implied a new conception of outreach initiatives.[16] The Lula government imposed an affirmative-action program requiring federal universities to admit a growing number of students from underrepresented minorities and low-income families. By 2012, a new law reserved half of the entrance positions in federal universities for candidates coming from the public secondary schools and specific Brazilian minorities.

Lula's government also sought greater engagement of federal universities in supporting the nation's industrial policy. A coalition made up of Brazil's major economic players, academic researchers, and the Ministry of Science, Technology, Innovation and Communication proposed a pathway for greater public- and private-sector collaboration. The result was the Innovation Law of 2004 and a series of programs and laws.[17] The ministry also funded the establishment of interdisciplinary and interinstitutional research networks to develop Brazil's economy.

Under Lula and then Dilma, in 2009 the Ministry of Education changed the content and design of the National Entrance Exam used since 1998 for determining admissions to federal universities. And in 2011, in the first year of Dilma's presidency, the Science without Borders program was established to promote greater international collaboration among academics.

The accomplishments of the Lula and Dilma governments were impressive. At the beginning of Lula's first term, Brazilian higher education enrolled 3.8 million students at the undergraduate level; as noted, this number jumped to 8.05 million by 2016. The net enrollment ratio (the percentage of Brazilians with some form of tertiary education) also grew from a bit more than 18 percent in 2003 to 36 percent. In 2003 distance education was almost unknown in the country. By 2015, almost 19 percent of all undergraduate enrollments were in distance education, even if this mode of learning was mostly offered by private institutions. As a result of the government's aggressive affirmative-action effort in the federal universities, followed by similar initiatives at the state level, the prestigious public universities became much more inclusive. In 2003, 36.2 percent of undergraduate students enrolled at federal universities were children from minority families, black or indigenous; by 2014 it was 48.2 percent.[18]

Implementing such an extensive policy agenda was made possible by Brazil's booming economy that lasted from approximately 2003 to 2009. As one minster observed, "At that time, resources were no longer a problem. We greatly expanded public investments, and people no longer felt threatened by the government's priorities."[19] However, Brazil's economy began to decline with the onset of the 2008 global financial crisis. In the first year of President Rousseff's second term, which began in 2015, it was clear that the country was facing significant economic challenges.

The expansion of Brazil's network of federal universities put stress on the government's shrinking budget. Newly created university campuses demanded significant investments, and the REUNI did not include a long-term plan to fund them. There no longer was money for new buildings. Funds were also scarce for large research projects and multicampus networks created by the Ministry of Science, Technology, Innovation and Communication. Funding for the Science without Borders program was cut. The FIES faced bankruptcy, given the loose criteria adopted for selecting beneficiaries, which resulted in rising default rates.[20] Since the design of the program assumed that students would renew their loans at the beginning of each term, hundreds of thousands of students were left burdened by large debts and without the needed financial support to finish their studies. All these problems emerged quickly. At the time of Rousseff's impeachment in 2016 as the result of charges of corruption and political infighting, federal higher education policy was in disarray.

When Michel Temer, Rousseff's vice president, became president of Brazil, his administration made no relevant changes to Brazilian higher education policies. The most significant outcome of his brief time in office was further dramatic cuts in federal expenditures. Shortly after Temer's inauguration, Congress approved a constitutional amendment that prohibited any inflation-adjusted increases in public expenditures in real terms for the next 20 years. The following 2 years were consumed mostly by the more urgent needs of the federal universities and the near bankruptcy of the FIES program. Brazil was in economic and political turmoil.

Toward a Far-Right Neo-nationalist Regime?

A divisive political climate permeated the 2018 campaign for president of Brazil. The countless noncompetitive presidential candidates appointed by center-left to center-right parties favored the emergence of an electoral de facto plebiscite around Lula and the Worker's Party government. Eventually the party picked Fernando Haddad as its candidate. Jair Bolsonaro ran as a Far-Right law and order candidate. The election had an unusually high turnout voting for multiple candidates, requiring a runoff election. Bolsonaro then won the runoff with Haddad.

Bolsonaro and his government became a global icon of Far-Right neo-nationalism. His mix of ideological, moral, and religious ideals is complicated and sometimes contradictory. As a member of the Congress for about 30 years, Bolsonaro sustained a profile as anti-system and anti-politician. He was a former low-ranking army officer, lacking the discipline and the intellectual training of the army's high command. He never had a leadership role in any political party, parliamentary bench, or social movement. However, he gained popularity by garnering a large WhatsApp and Twitter following, including a growing number of Evangelical faithful in Brazil who came to worship him as a mythical hero and political savior.

Once in office, Bolsonaro included representatives from his fragmented array of right-wing supporters in his cabinet. A series of inexperienced ministers came and went, including, as noted, ministers of education, many without significant knowledge of Brazil's universities, who focused their efforts on fighting the "cultural Marxism" of university faculty and students.[21] Bolsonaro's grand plans for the economic and social life of Brazil largely failed.

The newly formed Ministry of the Economy, which included the former cabinet Ministries of Labor, Social Security, Infrastructure, Regional Development, among others, was supposed to implement a new liberal, business-friendly policy through a wide range of sweeping reforms. When nominated, Paulo Guedes, Bolsonaro's economic "super-minister," announced plans to reform Brazil's Social Security program, revise labor and tax laws, reorganize the civil service, and privatize national industries. Most proposed reforms required constitutional amendments. To succeed, Bolsonaro knew he needed to generate support in Congress. However, Guedes's inexperience, limited familiarity with government cadres, disregard of parliamentary protocol, and short temper contributed to the failure of the entire reform bundle, with the exception of some reforms to Social Security. Bolsonaro's refusal to pursue concessions with Congress and his refusal to even meet with opposition party leaders also led to a situation where presidential initiatives led to misunderstandings and confusion between his cabinet members—including Guedes himself—and Congress.

Another "super-minister" was supposed to oversee the Ministry of Justice and Public Security, a sensitive policy area comprising several of Bolsonaro's pet projects valued by his supporters. Former federal judge Sérgio Moro, who became a popular celebrity combating corruption in the public sector, especially among politicians, was selected. During the run-up to the 2018 elections, Moro shared with Bolsonaro the lead as the country's most popular politician. Moro followed a similar fate as Guedes. He had no experience with the civil service and dealing with Congress. At the same time, Bolsonaro came to view him as a political rival. When Moro failed to support Bolsonaro's initiative to liberalize access to firearms, the president fired him.

In other areas of policy, Bolsonaro adopted a sort of "scorched-earth" policy, attempting to cut funding for public institutions and undoing the policies of past administrations, including efforts to protect Brazil's rain forests. Minister of the Environment Ricardo Salles proposed environmental deregulation and undermined agencies in charge of protecting the environment.[22]

Bolsonaro's Higher Education Policies

Higher education was also an area where Bolsonaro's government hoped to make major funding cuts, in part to attack his perceived political enemies. The appointment of Abraham Weintraub as the second minister of education in the Bolsonaro administration signaled a victory of the Far Right and religious movements. Weintraub started his administration by depicting federal universities as dens for communists and perverts. First, he and the Ministry of the Economy proposed cutting the budget of federal universities by 30 percent. Weintraub presented the measure as a punishment of federal universities for their lack of alignment with the new government. The impact of these proposed cuts would have been significant. Salaries occupy almost 90 percent of federal university budgets, and Bolsonaro's proposal would have meant layoffs and the firing of academic staff.[23] University leaders and unions protested the cuts, along with members of Congress, much of Brazil's media, and state governors. The ministry backed down and the budget was restored, but the experience further poisoned the relationship between universities and the ministry.

Additional planned funding cuts to the Ministry of Education and the Ministry of Science, Technology, Innovation and Communication also threatened scholarships and federal support of research, specifically calling for reduced reals for the humanities and the social sciences and research related to climate change in gender studies. Because of widespread opposition and lack of support in Congress, the government again was forced to back down from implementing much of the cuts.

In July 2019, the Ministry of Education made its first seemingly positive proposal, focused on Brazil's struggling economy. The Future-se program proposed a fund to support the expansion of entrepreneurial initiatives at universities in partnership with private enterprises. The program included changes in the rules regulating full-time academic contracts, allowing academics and universities to profit from the generation of intellectual property and any resulting agreement with businesses—a similar model to that found in the United States. A university could opt into the program. The hope was that resulting entrepreneurial activities would generate innovation, boost the economy, and bring in a stream of resources to federal universities.

But Future-se also proposed a change in university governance. A new quasi-governmental organization (QGO) would manage the intellectual property and relationship with the private sector, while leaving academic matters in the hands of the rector, deans, and the university's senate. The proposal was vague regarding the nature, responsibilities, and design of university QGOs. There were doubts about the real size of the fund, and the proposal did not clarify the regulatory changes a university should adopt if it decided to participate in the program. Because the ministry conceived it without consulting universities leaders, rectors, and faculty, many perceived Future-se as a move toward the privatization of universities, and even a breach of the social contract between the public universities and the government. As a result, less than one-quarter of federal universities showed interest in the program.[24]

Another area of contention between the Bolsonaro government and universities concerned university governance and the appointment of rectors. In the federal system, even if the final choice of a new rector is a prerogative of the ministry, that choice is conditioned. The minister must pick a name out of three proposed by a university faculty senate. Moreover, the LDB establishes that, in organizing the list, a university should consult its community. The usual procedure is to hold elections that include all academics, staff, and students as voters. Thus, the "vital constituency" of any rector is the university's internal stakeholders. The rectors have to consider interests and values supported by their electors even when under intense pressure from the government. To change the way rectors are chosen requires a change to Brazil's constitution, and that requires a majority vote in both houses of Congress. Bolsonaro could not garner such a majority for this initiative. When the COVID-19 pandemic arrived in Brazil, Bolsonaro's government issued a presidential decree vesting the minister of education with the power to unilaterally choose a pro-tempore rector whenever a rector's term ended. The justification was the circumstances of the pandemic.

However, the decree became null because the federal Senate considered it unconstitutional and refused to consider it.

Bolsonaro's administration repeatedly sought ways to limit academic freedom and elevated the theme of universities as bastions of sedition. During the electoral campaign, Bolsonaro's supporters requested intervention at some universities, alleging that some academics were conducting electoral propaganda against his candidacy in the classroom, which is prohibited by law. These complaints gave police an excuse to enter some campuses and to summon faculty to testify. However, these bullying measures were short lived. In less than a week, the Supreme Court prevented these intimidating practices from continuing. In the first few months, the Ministry of Education adopted a combative tone when addressing universities' internal affairs. Members of Bolsonaro's party in Congress proposed a bill addressing what they called the "dominance of the Marxist ideology" in education. It failed.

University leaders repeatedly counted on the support of a broad alliance in society to resist this and other initiatives, and in some instances the Supreme Court issued rulings in favor of the university sector. Federal agencies also played a role in blocking Bolsonaro's initiatives. Both CAPES and the federal agency for research support, the National Council for Research Support, belong to the Ministry of Science, Technology, Innovation and Communication and rely on the cooperation of the research community for their activities. These agencies have a small but well-qualified bureaucracy, and their decision-making lines rest on peer review and consulting representatives from different disciplinary areas not easily usurped by Bolsonaro's administration.

A threat of different nature, more difficult to stop, came from persistent efforts by Bolsonaro and his ministers to purge or hinder government and university researchers who work in areas such as climate change. Each time a research group published a report that countered official government discourse or raised doubts regarding the assumptions of government policy decisions, ministries would attempt to remove the head of the research unit. If this was not feasible, they attacked the research group's or agency's reputation. Usually, this was done by hinting that the group answered to vested interests linked to anti-national, globalist groups.

Collectively, government policies concerning higher education generated increasing distrust and estrangement between epistemic communities and policy makers, and severely damaged the morale of the research community. Weintraub's ministry ended poorly on June 20, 2020. His aggressive and boorish style created enemies everywhere as well as failed policies. He made no effort to solve the debt problem former students in the private sector incurred via the FIES program, he did not change any aspect of the policies affecting private sector education, he did not advance the implementation of the secondary education reform approved by Temer, he was unable to change the content and teaching style in primary education, and he failed to respond to challenges that Brazil's education system faced with the arrival of the COVID-19 pandemic.

Fighting the Pandemic

The COVID-19 pandemic hit Brazil hard. According to the World Health Organization (WHO), Brazil had the world's second-highest number of cases and deaths in the depths of the pandemic. Bolsonaro, like Donald Trump, called the virus a hoax, at least initially.

The public health system in Brazil provides universal and free-of-charge medical care through a network that includes almost all municipalities. The Ministry of Health, together with states and local governments, had significant experience in fighting epidemics and expertise in vaccine production and mass vaccinations. Because COVID-19 was detected in Brazil later than in other countries, the Bolsonaro government could have benefited from the time to prepare and mitigated the impact of the pandemic. However, the Ministry of Health failed to adopt a national strategic plan that could have included sourcing essential supplies, such as personal protective equipment, reliable tests, vital equipment for intensive care, and ventilators. Nor did it coordinate guidelines and actions to combat the pandemic with the federal government, the states, and local governments, or even adopt common objectives.

In no small measure, Bolsonaro is one of the major reasons why Brazil had among the highest rates of infection in the world. The president systematically downplayed the gravity of the situation. He claimed that COVID-19 was a mild flu and fiercely opposed social distancing measures, afraid of its impact on the country's fragile economy and, indirectly, his reputation. The similarity between the Brazilian situation and that of the United States is not accidental, as Bolsonaro openly sought to copy Trump's attitudes and decisions. And eventually, both Trump and Bolsonaro contracted the virus, but both with a seemingly mild case that only reinforced their messaging.

When the first cases of the disease were confirmed, the former minister of health Luiz Henrique Mandetta, a physician and a former conservative federal representative, sought to follow the WHO guidelines. He worked in coordination with the states and municipalities to encourage social distancing, mask use, and hygiene measures; expand the capacity of emergency hospital care; and limit social events. Not only did Bolsonaro repudiate the guidelines of the Ministry of Health and the WHO. He openly challenged state and municipal rules and deliberately encouraged mass gatherings without any protection against the spread of the virus.

Mandetta's refusal to adopt the indiscriminate use of hydroxychloroquine, an unproven therapy championed by Trump and Bolsonaro, led to his firing on April 16, 2020. The next minister, Nelson Teich, remained in charge for less than a month. On May 20, 2020, he resigned when the president commanded him to issue a rule adopting hydroxychloroquine as the primary treatment for the disease. Not until September 14, 2020, did President Jair Bolsonaro confirm the interim General Eduardo Pazuello as minister of health.

The pandemic had a significant impact on education in Brazil. Schools, colleges, and universities were not prepared to quickly transition to online instruction. Many universities suspended their teaching, initially hoping the pandemic would be short lived. Some federal universities decided to cancel their term, hoping to resume normal activities in August. For private institutions, the pandemic brought a sharp decline in enrollment and increased attrition rates, which was made worse by the pre-COVID-19-era decline in government financial aid for students.

The vast majority of faculty in public universities were almost illiterate about using information technology for courses. Before the pandemic, few fully online courses existed in the public sector; private higher education had more experience, but largely as a way to save costs and with questionable effectiveness. At the same time, a considerable number of students had poor or no internet access. The growth in the enrollment of minorities and low-income students pursued under the Lula and the Dilma administrations meant significant challenges for adopting distance learning strategies.

The Ministry of Education's response was bureaucratic. On March 18, it published an ordinance making the rules for distance learning more flexible. However, it was up to universities to decide whether they would adopt distance education. There was no offer of additional funding support from the Bolsonaro government. The result was a decentralized, uncoordinated response to university operations. Some state-owned universities were able to quickly allocate campus funds to support initiatives focused on helping students from low-income families by upgrading internet access and expanding support for instructional technologies. The pandemic appears to have changed the way academics perceive the role of instructional technologies and distance education in their teaching and learning activities that will be useful in a post-pandemic world. But the immediate-term result was chaotic with a disproportional impact on disadvantaged students.

If teaching was, in many cases, a victim of the pandemic crisis, research flourished. Researchers collaborated to tackle challenges created by the virus; new interdisciplinary teams were formed; and established teams changed their research agenda to assist local governments, including testing and trials of a Chinese-developed vaccine in the state of São Paulo. This elevated the status of public universities, at least in São Paulo. The pandemic also strengthened the connection between

Brazil's science community and its global partners. A pandemic requires a global response and collaboration to create and distribute therapies and vaccines.

But even in the successful development and initial distribution of a vaccine, politics were at play. The vaccine trials, as noted, were in the state of São Paulo, the largest state in population and economic power, with a governor who is a political rival of the president. Bolsonaro, who continued to deny the threat of the virus to public health, refused to support and repeatedly condemned the state government's vaccine efforts.

Bolsonaro's Failures—Thus Far

In the first two years of the Bolsonaro administration, his rhetoric and policies did not have a significant direct impact on Brazilian higher education. He largely failed to advance his agenda in part because of the inexperience of his ministers, including ignorance of the parliament's protocols and modes of operation. He also mostly failed to find support for his administration's initiatives in Congress. It was easy for Bolsonaro to make rhetorical populist statements that satisfied his political base, but much more challenging to pass bills and implement policy.

Are universities in Brazil leader or followers (see chapter 2)? Universities have always been, in one form or another, among the forces leading to social and political change in Brazil. Universities were a stronghold of the opposition forces fighting for the country's democratization in the 1970s and 1980s. Over a long period, universities developed supportive constituencies and alliances that have helped them cope with Bolsonaro's neo-nationalist government.

Past reforms and the pandemic have arguably deepened the universities' position as leaders. Thanks to the affirmative-action policies adopted during Lula's presidency, public universities became a central tool for promoting socioeconomic mobility. Brazilian universities also play a central role in what John N. Campbell and Ove K. Pedersen call Brazil's knowledge regime: "the organizational and institutional machinery that generates data, research, policy recommendations, and other ideas that influence public debate and policymaking."[25] They train the next generation of researchers, provide the country's more relevant social space for science and research, and represent Brazil's most significant hub in the global web of knowledge producers.

Brazil's young democracy seems resilient, thus far. Public opinion, many members of Congress, the media, and the Supreme Court successfully limited Bolsonaro's aggressive efforts to control university governance and leadership. Universities were largely protected as a constructive voice of dissent. Their supporters defended university autonomy and leaned on the Brazilian constitution to do so. At the same time, Brazil's public universities do not provide any systematic path for engaging with their regional and national external stakeholders. There are no university governing boards with representatives from Brazil's diverse society; the rector's superior, in the case of federal universities, is the minister of education. University governance and management is an area of needed reform to help Brazil's higher education community come closer the needs of society, engage with local communities, and build even greater political support.

NOTES

Chapter 1. Neo-nationalism and Universities in Historical Perspective

1. John Aubrey Douglass (2005), "How All Globalization Is Local: Countervailing Forces and Their Influence on Higher Education Markets," *Higher Education Policy* 18(4): 445–73.

2. Brendan O'Leary (1994), "On the Nature of Nationalism: An Appraisal of Ernest Gellner's Writings on Nationalism," *British Journal of Political Science* 27(2): 191–222.

3. Thomas Hylland Eriksen (2007), "Nationalism and the Internet," *Nations and Nationalism* 13(1): 1–17.

4. J. A. Armstrong (1982), *Nations before Nationalism* (Chapel Hill: University of North Carolina Press).

5. Yael Tamir (2019), *Why Nationalism* (Princeton, NJ: Princeton University Press); Alan Ryan (2020), "Whose Nationalism?," *New York Review of Books*, March 26.

6. For a historical review of the contradictions in nationalism, see Liah Greenfield (2013), *Nationalism: Five Roads to Modernity*; *The Spirit of Capitalism: Nationalism and Economic Growth*; and *Mind, Modernity, Madness: The Impact of Culture on Human Experience* (Cambridge, MA: Harvard University Press).

7. J. William Fulbright, forward in Walter Johnson and Francis J. Colligan (1965), *The Fulbright Program: A History* (Chicago: University of Chicago Press).

8. Fritz K. Ringer (1969), *The Decline of the German Mandarins: The German Academic Community, 1890-1933* (Cambridge, MA: Harvard University Press).

9. See Christine Musselin,(2004), *The Long March of French Universities* (New York: Routledge Falmer); Adrian Curaj, Luke Georghiou, Jennifer Cassingena Harper, and Eva Egron-Polak, eds. (2015), *Mergers and Alliances in Higher Education* (New York: Springer).

10. "To Friends of the Federal Government: A Plan for a Federal University" (1951), in *Letters of Benjamin Rush*, ed. L. H. Butterfield (Princeton, NJ: Princeton University Press): 1:491–95.

11. John Aubrey Douglass (2018), "The Rise of the Publics: American Democracy, the Public University Ideal, and the University of California," Center for Studies in Higher Education, University of California, Berkeley, February.

12. See David Madsen (1966), *The National University: Enduring Dream of the USA* (Detroit, MI: Wayne State University Press).

13. John Connelly and Michael Gruttner, eds. (2005), *Universities under Dictatorship* (University Park: Pennsylvania State University Press).

14. *Report of the Education Commission, 1964–66: Education & National Development* (1966) (New Delhi: Ministry of Education, Government of India).

15. See Andrés Bernasconi and Daniela Véiz Calderón (2016), "Latin American Flagship Universities from Early Notions of State Building to Seeking a Larger Role in Society," in John Aubrey Douglass, *The New Flagship University: Changing the Paradigm from Global Ranking to National Relevancy* (New York: Palgrave Macmillan): 139–52.

16. For an analysis of populism and the concept of neo-nationalism, see R. Wodak (2015), *The Politics of Fear: What Right-Wing Populist Discourses Mean* (London: Sage); Andre Gingrich and Marcus Banks, eds. (2006), *Neo-nationalism in Europe and Beyond: Perspectives from Social Anthropology* (New York: Berghahn Books); Maureen A. Eger and Sarah Valdez (2014), "Neo-nationalism in Western Europe," *European Sociological Review* 31: 115–30.

17. "League of Nationalists" (2016), *Economist*, November 19.

18. Fareed Zakaria (1997), "The Rise of Illiberal Democracy," *Foreign Affairs* November/December; see also Zoltan Simon (2014), "Orbán Says He Seeks to End Liberal Democracy in Hungary," *Bloomburg News*, July 28; A. Rocha Menocal, V. Fritz, and L. Rakner (2008), "Hybrid Regimes and the Challenges of Deepening and Sustaining Democracy in Developing Countries," *South African Journal of International Affairs*, 15(1): 29–40.

19. Lydia Gall (2014), "The End of Liberal Democracy in Hungary?," *Dispatches*, Human Rights Watch, July 29.

20. Freedom House (2019), "Freedom in the World 2019," Washington, DC.

21. Michael Minkenberg (2000), "The Renewal of the Radical Right: Between Modernity and Anti-modernity," *Government and Opposition* 35: 170–88.

Chapter 2. Neo-nationalism and Universities

1. Amnesty International (2020), "Hong Kong's National Security Law: 20 Things You Need to Know," July 17. The wording of the Hong Kong national security law asserts jurisdiction over people who are not residents of Hong Kong and have never even set foot there. This means anyone on earth, regardless of nationality or location, can technically be deemed to have violated this law and face arrest and prosecution if they are in a Chinese jurisdiction, even for transit. Accused foreign nationals who don't permanently reside in Hong Kong can be deported even before trial or verdict.

2. Amy Harmon and Henry Fountai (2017), "In Age of Trump, Scientists Show Signs of a Political Pulse," *New York Times*, February 6.

3. Marion Lloyd (2018), "Bolsonaro Poses a Serious Threat to Higher Education," *University World News*, November 2.

4. Quoted in Michael Fox (2018), "Education Is in the Crosshairs in Bolsonaro's Brazil," *Nation*, November 12.

5. Brendan O'Malley (2019) "Relentless Prosecutions of Academic for Peace Gather Pace," *University World News*, May 4.

6. Stockholm Center for Freedom (2018), "The Crackdown on Education: Free Thought under Siege in Turkey," July.

7. Cited in Scholars at Risk (2017), *Free to Think 2017*, September 26.

8. Eugene Vorotnikov (2018) "Parliament to Prevent Foreign Influence on Students," *University World News*, January 12.

9. John Connelly and Michael Gruttner, eds. (2005), *Universities under Dictatorship* (University Park: Pennsylvania State University Press).

10. Tom Phillips (2016), "China Universities Must Become Communist Party 'Strongholds,' Says Xi Jinping," *Guardian*, December 9.

11. Carl Minzner, quoted in Phillips 2016.

12. Matina Stevis-Gridneff et al. (2020), "E.U. Reaches Deal on Major Budget and Stimulus Package," *New York Times*, December 10.

13. See John Aubrey Douglass, *The New Flagship University: Changing the Paradigm from Global Ranking to National Relevancy* (London: Palgrave Macmillan).

14. "New Nationalism and Universities," conference held at the University of California, Berkeley, November 16–17, 2019, organized by the Center for Studies in Higher Education.

15. John Aubrey Douglass (2005), "All Globalization Is Local: Countervailing Forces and the Influence on Higher Education Markets," Center for Studies in Higher Education, Research & Occasional Paper Series: CSHE.1.05.

Chapter 3. The Mystery of Brexit

1. Yuval Noah Harari (2019), *21 Lessons for the 21st Century* (New York: Vintage): 133.

2. Martin Fletcher (2016), "Boris Johnson Peddled Absurd EU Myths and Our Disgraceful Press Followed His Lead," *New Statesman*, July 1.

3. Kate Lyons (2016), "The 10 Best Euro Myths—from Custard Creams to Condoms," *Guardian*, June 23.

4. Brendan O'Malley (2019a), "Second Pilot on European Universities' Alliances Launched," *University World News*, November 9.

5. Ludovic Highman (2019), "Future EU-UK Research and Higher Education Co-operation at Risk: What Is at Stake?," *Tertiary Education and Management* 25(1): 45–52.

6. Highman 2019.

7. Universities UK (2019), *No-Deal Briefing*, November 24.

8. Karen MacGregor (2019), "UK Pledges Continued Funding Support for 2020 EU Students," *University World News*, May 29.

9. Sally Weale (2017), "UK Risks Mass Exodus of EU Academics Post-Brexit, Report Finds," *Guardian*, November 14.

10. Highman 2019.

11. Universities UK (2019), *Erasmus+ Students Facing No-Deal Brexit Upheaval*, January 29.

12. British Council (2017), *40,000 People from the UK Benefited from Erasmus+ in 2015*, January 26.

13. For a summary of what Cameron sought and what he secured, see BBC (2016), "EU Reform Deal: What Cameron Wanted and What He Got," February 20.

14. Alan Travis (2016), "The Leave Campaign Made Three Key Promises—Are They Keeping Them?," *Guardian*, June 27.

15. Paul Rincon (2016), "Concern over Brexit's Impact on Science," BBC, April 20.

16. John Stone (2017), "Brexit Lies: The Demonstrably False Claims of the EU Referendum Campaign," *Independent*, December 17. Some claims of inaccuracy during the campaign were themselves inaccurate. On the day of the referendum, Ian Duncan Smith, a leading Leave campaigner, told the electorate via the *Mail* that Cameron was "colluding with the EU and lying" about Turkey not being about to join the European Union on the grounds that EU talks with Turkey were due to restart a few days after the referendum. He said the issue of "Turkey and the future of its 77 million population ought to be in voters' minds today as they enter the polling booth." In reality, anyone familiar with the state of diplomatic relations between Turkey and the European Union knew that there was little chance of any progress in the latest set of talks, and indeed in 2018 negotiations came to a complete standstill.

17. May Bulman (2019), "Brexit Referendum Result: Austerity and Welfare Cuts Main Driver behind Leave Vote, Finds Report," *Independent*, February 3.

18. David Matthews (2016), "Academics Take Stock after Brexiteer Victory over 'the Experts,'" *Times Higher Education*, July 1.

19. Tim Dodd (2019), "Brexit a 'Major Threat to University Research,'" *Australian*, November 16, reproduced with permission on Brunel University website.

20. Brendan O'Malley (2019b), "No-Deal Brexit 'Will Leave UK Science Dead for Years,'" *University World News*, October 11.

21. Rachael Pells (2017), "Number of EU Students Apply to UK Universities Falls by 7 Per Cent since Brexit, Latest Figures Reveal," *Independent*, February 2.

22. Karen MacGregor (2019), "Plunging Collaboration with Europe Threatens UK Research," *University World News*, July 6.

23. Adrian Smith and Graeme Reid (2019), *Changes and Choices: Advice on Future Frameworks for International Collaboration on Research and Innovation*, commissioned by the minister of state for universities, science, research and innovation. July.

24. O'Malley 2019b.

25. Brendan O'Malley (2019d), "New Prime Minister Raises Risk to HE of No-Deal Brexit," *University World News*, July 24.

26. Smith and Reid 2019.

27. O'Malley 2019d.

28. O'Malley 2019b.

29. Richard Adams (2020), "UK Students Lose Erasmus Membership in Brexit Deal," *Guardian*, December 24.

30. Universities UK 2019.

31. Anne Corbett (2019), "Erasmus+ Student and Staff Mobility Problems Loom for UK," *University World News*, April 15.

32. Highman 2019.

33. UK Government (2018), *The Future Relationship between the United Kingdom and the European Union*, July 12.

34. Brendan O'Malley (2020), "Ex Minister Calls for Four-Year Post Study Work Visa," *University World News*, June 19.

35. "China Overtakes UK in Number of Highly Cited Researchers" (2019), *University World News*, November 19.

36. Smith and Reid 2019.

37. Alice Gast (2018), "Universities Are Not Ivory Towers" Here's the Role They Can Play," World Economic Forum Annual Meeting, January 26.

38. T. F. Pettigrew and L. R. Tropp (2006), "A Meta-analytic Test of Intergroup Contact Theory," *Journal of Personality and Social Psychology* 90: 751–83.

39. Fiona Hunter and Hans de Wit (2016), "Brexit and the European Shape of Things to Come," *International Higher Education*, no. 87: 2–3.

Chapter 4. Trumpian Nationalism and American Universities

1. Derek Thompson (2017), "The Republican War on College," *Atlantic*, November 20; Uri Friedman (2018), "Trust Is Collapsing in America," *Atlantic*, January 21.

2. Richard Hofstadter (1962), *Anti-intellectualism in American Life* (New York: Alfred A Knopf). He contended that American Protestantism's anti-intellectual tradition valued the spirit over intellectual rigor.

3. Richard Hofstadter (1964), "The Paranoid Style in American Politics," *Harper's Magazine*, November. Hofstadter defined politically paranoid individuals as feeling persecuted, fearing conspiracy, and acting in an overaggressive yet socialized manner.

4. Daniel Bell, ed. (1963), *The Radical Right* (New York: Doubleday).

5. Isaac Asimov (1980), "A Cult of Ignorance," *Newsweek*, January 21.

6. Andrew Marantz (2018), "How Social-Media Trolls Turned U.C. Berkeley into a Free-Speech Circus," *New Yorker*, June 25.

7. Office of Public Affairs (2017), "Milo Yiannopoulos Event Cancelled after Violence Erupts," *UC Berkeley News*, February 1.

8. February 2, 2017, Twitter, https://twitter.com/realDonaldTrump/status/827112633224544256?s=20.

9. University of California, Berkeley, a historic flashpoint for the free speech debate rooted in the 1960s, has spent at least $2.5 million on security surrounding controversial speakers since February, stated Dan Mogulof, Berkeley's assistant vice chancellor for public affairs: $200,000 for Yiannopoulos in February, $600,000 for Ann Coulter (whose appearance was ultimately cancelled by the sponsoring student groups), and at least $600,000 for conservative commentator Ben Shapiro in September. Yiannopoulos's latest appearance, part of Berkeley's "Free Speech Week," will cost upward of $1 million, Mogulof estimated. See Caroline Simon (2017), "Free Speech Isn't Free: It's Costing College Campuses Millions," *Forbes*, November 20.

10. Kimberly Veklerov and Jill Tucker (2017), "Fights Break Out between Right, Left as Dozens March through UC Berkeley," *San Francisco Chronicle*, September 26, archived from the original on September 27; for a timeline of these events, see https://en.wikipedia.org/wiki/2017_Berkeley_protests.

11. Mulvaney, Mick (2017), "America First: A Budget Blueprint to Make America Great Again," Office of Management and Budget: White House, March 16.

12. Iris J Lav and Michael Leachman (2017), "The Trump Budget's Massive Cuts to State and Local Services and Programs," Center on Budget and Policy Priorities: Washington DC, June 13.

13. Adam Harris (2017), "What Trump's Proposed 2018 Budget Would Mean for Higher Ed," *Chronicle for Higher Education*, May 24.

14. "For the most part, the Trump budget will likely be a messaging document," stated Clare McCann, a senior policy analyst with New America's Education Policy program. "Congress will likely continue with business as usual." See Andrew Kreighbaum (2017), "A 'Repudiation' of Trump Budget," *Inside Higher Education*, May 2.

15. United States Citizenship and Immigration Services (2018), *Approximate Active DACA Recipients: Country of Birth as of August 31, 2018*, August 31.

16. Meghan Downey and Adam Garnick (2020), "Explaining the Supreme Court's DACA Decision," *Regulatory Review*, July 7.

17. American Council on Education (2018), "Statement by ACE President Ted Mitchell on Reports of Chinese Student Visa Restrictions" (Washington, DC: ACE), May 30.

18. See the NAFSA International Student Economic Value Tool, accessed November 23, 2020, https://www.nafsa.org/policy-and-advocacy/policy-resources/nafsa-international-student-economic-value-tool-v2.

19. Ellie Bothwell (2018), "Insuring against Drop in Chinese Students: U of Illinois at Urbana-Champaign is paying $424,000 to Protect Itself in Case of a Falloff," *Times Higher Education*, November 29.

20. Council of Graduate Schools (2019), Graduate Enrollment and Degrees 2008–2018 (Washington, DC: CGS), October.

21. Elizabeth Redden (2018), "Did Trump Call Most Chinese Students Spies?," *Inside Higher Education*, August 9.

22. Elizabeth Redden (2018), "Chinese Students: Security Threat or Stereotype Threat?," *Inside Higher Education*, August 9.

23. US Senate Permanent Subcommittee on Investigations, Committee on Homeland Security and Governmental Affairs (2018), *Threats to the U.S. Research Enterprise: China's Talent Recruitment Plans*, November 18.

24. "NIH Reveals Its Formula for Tracking Foreign Influences" (2019), *Science* 366(6461): 19–20.

25. "NIH Reveals Its Formula for Tracking Foreign Influences" 2019.

26. US Senate Committee on Homeland Security and Government Affairs (2019), *China's Impact on the US Education System*, staff report, February 22.

27. National Association of Scholars (2019), "Confucius Institutes in the US That Are Closing," June.

28. Brendan O'Malley (2019), "Universities Failed to Report $1.3 Bn in Foreign Funding," *University World News*, December 13.

29. US Senate Permanent Subcommittee on Investigations 2018.

30. Larry Diamond and Orville Schell (2019), *China's Influence & American Interests: Promoting Constructive Vigilance* (Stanford, CA: Hoover Institution Press).

31. Lawrence Bacow to Secretary of State Mike Pompeo and Acting Secretary of Homeland Security Kevin McAleenan, July 16, 2019.

32. Jennifer Ruth and Yu Xiao (2019), "Academic Freedom and China: Every Instructor Walks on Thin Ice," *Academe*, Fall. Some academics objected. "I am tired of journalists accusing China scholars of caving to the CCP," Rory Truex, an assistant professor of political science and international affairs at Princeton University, tweeted. Citing Margaret Roberts (author of *Censored: Distraction and Diversion inside China's Great Firewall* and a few others), Truex dared, "Tell me the field is craven." And yet, as the discussion unfolded on Twitter and then during a panel a month later at the Center for Strategic and International Studies in Washington, DC, it became clear that American universities and colleges do have a problem with self-censorship. The problem, however, lies less with academics than with administrators and university officials who either explicitly cater to the Chinese Communist Party (for funding and student recruitment reasons) or preemptively discourage events and projects out of broad fear of offense or ignorance.

33. Scholars at Risk (2019), *Obstacles to Excellence: Academic Freedom & China's Quest for World Class Universities*, Freedom Monitoring Project.

34. Human Rights Watch (2019), "China: Government Threats to Academic Freedom Abroad: New 12-Point Code of Conduct to Help Educational Institutions Respond," March 21.

35. Union of Concerned Scientists (2019), *The State of Science in the Trump Era: Damage Done, Lessons Learned, and a Path to Progress*, January.

36. Brennan Center for Justice (2019) *Proposals for Reform*, vol. 2, *National Task Force on Rule of Law & Democracy*, October 3.

37. White House Press Conference (2017), "Statement by President Trump on the Paris Climate Accord," June 1.

38. For example, the Trump administration has relaxed US rules requiring oil and gas firms to reduce leaks of methane, a potent greenhouse gas, at land-based wells and pipelines.

39. Union of Concerned Scientists 2019.

40. American Association of University Professors (2019), *National Security, the Assault on Science, and Academic Freedom: National Security Report*, October 17.

41. "Donald Trump's Attacks on Science" (2019), *Guardian*, October 6.

42. Sinan Aral and Dean Eckles (2019), "Protecting Elections from Social Media Manipulation," *Science* 365, no. 6456, August 30. It should be noted that the Department of Energy did recently establish the Office of Cybersecurity, Energy Security,

and Emergency Response, but it largely focused on protection the nation's electrical grid.

43. Steven Ross Johnson (2019), "Gun Violence Research at a Standstill due to Lack of Federal Funding," *Modern Healthcare*, April 13.

44. US National Academy of Sciences (2020), "Statement to Restore Science-Based Policy in Government," June.

45. Scott Jaschik (2016), "Trump's Emerging Higher Education Platform," *Inside Higher Education*, May 13.

46. Ian Tuttle (2016), "Yes, Trump University Was a Massive Scam," *National Review*, February 26.

47. Andrew Kreighbaum (2019), "Trump Signs Broad Executive Order," *Inside Higher Education*, March 22. The executive order directs federal agencies to ensure colleges are following requirements already in place. And it doesn't spell out how enforcement of the order would work. It directs 12 federal grant-making agencies to coordinate with the Office of Management and Budget to certify that colleges receiving federal research funds comply with existing federal law and regulations involving free academic inquiry. Although the administration expects public institutions to uphold the First Amendment, the order says private colleges are expected to comply with their "stated institutional policies" on freedom of speech. The free-speech directive doesn't apply to federal student aid programs.

48. Ambitious conservative state lawmakers also took up the argument that universities and colleges, on the whole, are intolerant to conservative views, passing laws designed to require institutions to teach conservative political principles. See Gene Nichol (2019), "Political Interference with Academic Freedom and Free Speech at Public Universities," *Academe*, Fall. Nichol notes that "a growing array of states, including my own, have enacted versions of a national advocacy group's Campus Free Speech Law. North Carolina's is called the Restore/Preserve Campus Free Speech Act. Among its notable features, the statute empowers governing boards to regulate 'administrative and institutional neutrality with regard to political or social issues'—not exactly tight and precise free-expression language. Even more alarming, President Donald Trump now seems anxious to jump on board with such efforts, as evidenced by his recent statements and executive action on campus free speech."

Chapter 5. Turbulent Times

1. Hannah Arendt (1967), "Truth and Politics," *New Yorker*, February 25. Quoted from https://idanlandau.files.wordpress.com/2014/12/arendt-truth-and -politics.pdf.

2. Hartmut Rosa (2013), *Acceleration and Alienation: Towards a Critical Theory of Late-Modern Temporality* (Frankfurt: Suhrkamp).

3. Eduardo Porter and Karl Russell (2018), "Migrants on the Rise around the World, and Myths about Them Are Shaping Attitudes," *New York Times*, June 20, https://www.nytimes.com/interactive/2018/06/20/business/economy/immigration -economic-impact.html.

4. George Soros (2019), "Europe, Please Wake Up," *Project Syndicate*, February 11, https://www.project-syndicate.org/commentary/political-party-systems-undermining-european-union-by-george-soros-2019-02.

5. Carsten Könneker (2019), "Was die Forschung zwitschern könnte," *Der Tagesspiegel*, March 17: 5.

6. Dominique Moïsi (2010), *The Geopolitics of Emotion: How Cultures of Fear, Humiliation, and Hope Are Reshaping the World* (New York: Anchor): 52.

7. Felix Ackermann (2019), "Herr Grzesiek und mein Großvater," *Merkur* 836, January 3.

8. Steven Levitsky and Daniel Ziblatt (2018), *How Democracies Die: What History Tells Us about Our Future* (New York: Crown).

9. Hans Müller-Steinhagen (2015), Twitter, October 15, https://twitter.com/tudresden_de/status/654619876233977856; DPA (2015), "TU-Rektor sieht Imageschaden durch Pegida für Dresdner Wissenschaft," *Dresdner neueste Nachrichten*, September 9, http://www.dnn.de/Dresden/Lokales/TU-Rektor-sieht-Imageschaden-durch-Pegida-fuer-Dresdner-Wissenschaft.

10. ."Dresdens Wissenschaft leidet unter Pegida" (2015), *Die Zeit*, August 15, https://www.zeit.de/politik/deutschland/2015-08/pediga-dresden-sachsen-wirtschaft-leidet.

11. TU Dresden (2018), "Zahlen und Fakten," https://tu-dresden.de/tu-dresden/profil/zahlen-und-fakten.

12. Jutta Allmendinger (2017), "Um Vertrauen werben—der 'March for Science' lebt fort," in *Die Werte der Wissenschaft: Reden und Gedanken zum "March for Science" in Deutschland*, ed. Reiner Korbmann: 13.

13. American Academy (2019), "German President Delivers the 2019 Fritz Stern Lecture," https://www.americanacademy.de/german-president-steinmeier-delivers-the-2019-fritz-stern-lecture/.

14. Wissenschaft im Dialog (2018), Wissenschaftsbarometer 2018, https://www.bosch-stiftung.de/sites/default/files/publications/pdf/2018-09/Broschuere_Wissenschaftsbarometer_2018.pdf.

15. Könneker 2019: 5.

16. Central European University (2013), *CEU Brochure*, https://www.ceu.edu/sites/default/files/attachment/article/10297/ceu20brochure2c20july202013.pdf.

17. Michael Ignatieff (2018), "Academic Freedom and the Future of Europe," Centre for Global Higher Education Working Paper Series, No. 40, July 2018 (London: University College London Institute of Education).

18. Keno Verseck (2018), "Verwirrspiel um die Soros-Uni," *Spiegel Online*, March 24. http://www.spiegel.de/lebenundlernen/uni/ungarn-verwirrspiel-um-soros-uni-darf-ceu-doch-in-budapest-bleiben-a-1259183.html.

19. CEU (2019), press release, February 11, https://www.ceu.edu/article/2019-02-11/ceu-faculty-awarded-hungarian-civil-legion-honor.

20. Joseph Croitoru (2019), "Die letzte Insel der Freiheit," *Frankfurter Allgemeine Zeitung*, no. 49 (February 27): N4.

21. Maya Oppenheim (2018), "Hungarian Prime Minister Victor Orban Bans Gender Studies Programmes," *Independent*, October 24, https://www.independent

.co.uk/news/world/europe/hungary-bans-gender-studies-programmes-viktor
-orban-central-european-university-budapest-a8599796.html.

22. Martina Scherf (2019), "Kämpferin," *Süddeutsche Zeitung*, January 29, 42.

23. Levitsky and Ziblatt 2018.

24. NCP Poland (2018), press release, http://en.kpk.gov.pl/gowin-the
-government-has-adopted-the-university-reform-project-spending-on-science
-will-increase-by-pln-3-7-billion-in-2019/.

25. NCP Poland 2018.

26. Mateusz Laszczkowski (2019), "Anthropology? What 'Anthropology'?,"
Allegralab, January 24, http://allegralaboratory.net/anthropology-what
-anthropology/.

27. Antonio Loprieno (2019), "How Political Should Universities Be?," *DUZ
Wissenschaft & Management*, July.

28. Yehuda Elkana (2015), "The University of the 21st Century: An Aspect of
Globalization," in *The Globalization of Knowledge in History*, edited by Jürgen Renn
(Berlin: Max Planck Research Library for the History and Development of
Knowledge); see also John Aubrey Douglass (2016), *The New Flagship University:
Changing the Paradigm from Rankings to National Relevancy* (New York:
Palgrave-Macmillan).

29. Emmanuel Macron (2017), Sorbonne speech, http://international.blogs
.ouest-france.fr/archive/2017/09/29/macron-sorbonne-verbatim-europe-18583
.html.

30. Von Jens Schmitz (2018), "Land will Universitäten am Oberrhein zu
Europäischer Universität entwickeln," *Badische Zeitung*, March 6.

31. Ellen Hazelkorn (2016), "Contemporary Debates Part 2: Initiatives and
Governance and Organizational Structures," in *The Civic University: The Policy
Leadership Challenges*, ed. John Goddard et al. (Cheltenham: Edward Elgar): 65–94.

32. Andrée Sursock (2018), *Higher Education and Its Communities: A Transatlantic View on Openness, Democracy and Engagement* (Brussels: European University
Association).

33. See Thomas Brunotte (2018), "Gestiftete Autonomie: Welchen Beitrag
leistet das Stiftungs-Modell zur Autonomie von Universitäten?," in *Opuscula*
(Berlin: Maecenata Institut): 110; Wilhelm Krull (2002), "Entscheidung für den
Wandel," in *Vom Staatsbetrieb zur Stiftung: Moderne Hochschulen für Deutschland*, ed.
Thomas Oppermann (Göttingen: Wallstein): 73–82.

34. Sursock 2018: 21–22.

35. Leopoldina Nationale Akademie der Wissenshaften (2014), *Die Synthetische
Biologie in der öffentlichen Meinungsbildung: Überlegungen im Kontext der wissen-
shaftsbasierten Beratung von Politik und Öffentlichkeit* (Halle: Saale): 77 and 82.

36. Friederike Hendriks, Dorothe Kienhues, and Rainer Bromme (2016), "Trust
in Science and the Science of Trust," in *Trust and Communication in a Digitized
World*, ed. Bernd Blöbaum (Berlin: Springer): 143–59.

37. Stefan Wegner (2018), "Das große Public Misunderstanding," Volkswagen
Stiftung, *Impulse Ausgabe*, July 18.

38. Hightech Forum (2017), Fachforum Partizipation und Transparenz des Hightech Forums, Partizipatives Agenda-Setting—Gesellschaft an Forschung und Innovation beteiligen, Berlin.

Chapter 6. Neo-nationalism in the European Union and Universities

Epigraph. Quoted in C. Pazzansese (2019), "At Commencement, German Chancellor Urges Them 'to Embrace New Beginnings,'" *Harvard Gazette*, May 30.

1. M. C. van der Wende (2009), "European Responses to Global Competitiveness in Higher Education," in *Globalization's Muse: Universities and Higher Education Systems in a Changing World*, ed. John Aubrey Douglass, Jud King, and Irwin Feller (Berkeley, CA: Berkeley Public Policy Press, Institute of Governmental Studies): 317–40.

2. "Europe and Right-Wing Nationalism: A Country-by-Country Guide" (2019), BBC, November 13.

3. R. Eatwell and M. Goodwin (2018), *National Populism: The Revolt against Liberal Democracy* (London: Penguin UK); C. Mudde (2019), *The Far Right Today* (Hoboken, NJ: John Wiley & Sons).

4. F. Bieber (2018), "Is Nationalism on the Rise? Assessing Global Trends," *Ethnopolitics*, 17(5): 519–40.

5. European Commission (2018), *Standard Eurobarometer 90* (Brussels: European Union).

6. Center for Politics and Communication (2019), *ERC Europinions: Data Collection around the 2019 EP Elections Finished*, November.

7. J. Stone (2017), "More Europeans Than Ever Say They Feel like Citizens of the EU," *Independent*, August 2.

8. Bieber 2018.

9. President Macron attempted to clearly distinguish patriotism and nationalism in his speech at the 100th anniversary of the end of World War I. A. Pasick (2018), "Macron Confronts Trump and Putin: 'Nationalism Is a Betrayal of Patriotism,'" *Quartz*, November 11.

10. Germany held the rotating EU presidency for the second half of 2020.

11. European Council (2020), *Conclusions of the Special Meeting of the European Council*, July.

12. "EU's 'Moment of Truth' as Leaders Seek COVID Funding Deal" (2020), BBC.

13. Eurobarometer (2019), *Spring 2019 Standard Eurobarometer: Europeans Upbeat about the State of the European Union—Best Results in 5 Years*, August.

14. Eurobarometer (2020), *EU Citizens Want More Competences for the EU to Deal with Crises like COVID-19*. May.

15. I. Krastev and M. Leonard (2020), *Europe's Pandemic Politics: How the Virus Has Changed the Public's Worldview*, European Council for Foreign Relations.

16. E. Bothwell (2019), "Overseas Student Numbers in UK up, but EU Numbers Fall," *Times Higher Education*, February 28.

17. B. O'Malley (2020), "Most EU Students 'Will Not Study in UK' after Fees Decision," *University World News*, July 1.

18. A. Cuddy (2018), "European Parliament Votes to Trigger Article 7 Sanctions Procedure against Hungary," *Euronews*, September 12; D. R. Cameron (2018), "EU Deploys Article 7 against Poland & Hungary for Democratic Backsliding," Yale Macmillan Center, September 17.

19. European Union (2012), Consolidated Version of the Treaty on European Union, *Official Journal of the European Union C 326*, October 26.

20. However, accession negotiations have stalled since 2016.

21. D. Matthews (2019), "Netherlands Universities 'Must Improve' Foreign Students' Dutch," *Times Higher Education*, September 17.

22. This was partially reversed in a 2017 referendum intended to ease the naturalization of third-generation immigrants.

23. A. Corbett and C. Gordon (2020), "Is Erasmus Participation under Threat in Brexit Britain?," *University World News*, July 11.

24. See OECD (2018), "Education at a Glance 2018" (Paris: OECD), table B6.1.

25. Associate of Universities of the Netherlands (VSNU) (2019), "Facts and Figures," https://www.vsnu.nl/en_GB/facts-and-figures.html.

26. M. C. van der Wende (2017a), "Opening Up: Higher Education Systems in Global Perspective," ESRC/HEFCE Centre for Global Higher Education Working Paper.

27. Laid down in Article 3(2) of the Treaty on European Union (TEU); Article 21 of the Treaty on the Functioning of the European Union (TFEU); Titles IV and V TFEU; Article 45 of the Charter of Fundamental Rights of the European Union.

28. EHEA (2020), "European Higher Education Area and Bologna Process," EHEA, http://www.ehea.info/.

29. J. Huisman and M. C. van der Wende (2004), "The EU and Bologna: Are Supra and International Initiatives Threatening Domestic Agendas?," *European Journal of Education* 39(3): 349–59.

30. VSNU (2020a), *The Netherlands Appeals to International Talent*, https://vsnu .nl/en_GB/nederland-is-aantrekkelijk-voor-internationaal-talent.html.

31. VSNU (2020b), *International Rankings Universities*, https://www.vsnu.nl/en _GB/f_c_rankings.html.

32. VSNU (2018), *Internationalisation Agenda*, https://vsnu.nl /internationalisation-agenda.

33. Study Portals (2020), *Tuition Fees at Universities in Europe in 2019—Overview and Comparison*, Study Portals: Masters.

34. Another 20,000 are expected from outside the EU-EEA, but these do not count toward the government's budget, as they usually pay full-cost fees.

35. M. Janse (2018), "Taartverdeling universiteiten kan eerlijker," NRC Next, January 24, https://www.nrc.nl/nieuws/2018/01/23/taartverdeling-universiteiten -kan-eerlijker-a1589464 (emphasis original).

36. S. Custer (2019), "Copenhagen Rector Laments Impact of International Student Cuts," *Times Higher Education*, January 29.

37. J. Morgan (2019a), "Dutch Populists Seek Reports of 'Left Indoctrination' on Campuses," *Times Higher Education*, April 1.

38. J. Morgan (2019b), "Dutch Election Victor's University Attack Has Roots in PhD Thesis," *Times Higher Education*, March 28.

39. For incoming and outgoing student mobility in the Netherlands, see "Dutch Degree Students Abroad" (2020a), *Nuffic*, https://www.nuffic.nl/en/subjects /countries-of-origin/.

40. TU Delta (2011), "Verbied het werven van Duitse studenten" [Prohibit recruiting German students], Journalistic Platform TU Delta.

41. J. Pieters (2019), "Amsterdam University Drops Bachelor's Degree in Dutch," *NL Times*, March 1, https://www.universityworldnews.com/post.php ?story=20190301125347590.

42. B. W. Ansell (2010), *From the Ballot to the Blackboard: The Redistributive Political Economy of Education* (Cambridge: Cambridge University Press).

43. Magna Charta Universitatum (2018a), "Read the Magna Charta Universita-tum," Observatory Magna Charta Universitatum.

44. Magna Charta Universitatum (2018b), "History," Observatory Magna Charta Universitatum.

45. Magna Charta Universitatum (2018c), "Observations," Observatory Magna Charta Universitatum.

46. Magna Charta Universitatum (2018d), "Speeches at the XXX Anniversary of the Magna Charta Universitatum," Observatory Magna Charta Universitatum, http://www.magna-charta.org/observatory-events/magna-charta-anniversaries /2018-xxx-anniversary/speeches.

47. EUA (n.d.a), "Universities & Values," accessed on December 9, 2020, https://eua.eu/issues/25:universities-values.html

48. EUA (n.d.b), "University Autonomy in Europe," accessed on December 9, 2020, https://www.university-autonomy.eu/.

49. EUA (n.d.c), "Autonomy & Governance," accessed on December 9, 2020, https://eua.eu/issues/4:autonomy-and-governance.html.

50. T. Estermann (2017), "Why University Autonomy Matters More Than Ever," *European University Association*, April 7.

51. M. Gardner (2018), "Rectors' Bodies of 10 Nations Sign 'Vienna Declaration,'" *University World News*, December 24.

52. European Union (2000), Charter of Fundamental Rights of the European Union, December 18, C 364/1, http://www.europarl.europa.eu/charter/pdf/text_en .pdf.

53. European Parliament (2018), *Defence of Academic Freedom in the EU's External Action*, European Union.

54. Aurora (2019), "Parliament Wants European SAR Scheme," *Aurora Universities Network*, January 1.

55. A. McKie (2019), "German Deal Could Allow CEU to Stay in Hungary," *Times Higher Education*, March 18.

56. P. Basken (2019), "Ignatieff Condemns West for Failure to Protect CEU," *Times Higher Education*, June 13.

57. M. Ignatieff (2019), "Speech by M. Ignatieff at the 43rd Anniversary of Maastricht University," *Observant*, January 30.

58. J. A. Douglass, ed. (2016), *The New Flagship University: Changing the Paradigm from Global Ranking to National Relevancy* (New York City: Springer).

59. C. Ziguras (2016), "The Five Stages of Brexit Grief for Universities," *University World News*, October 14.

60. Vught, Wende, and Westerheijden 2002. "

61. Wende 2009.

62. M. C. van der Wende (2007), "Internationalisation of Higher Education in the OECD Countries: Challenges and Opportunities for the Coming Decade," *Journal on Studies in International Education* 11(3/4): 274–90.

63. D. van Damme and M. C. van der Wende (2018), "Global Higher Education Governance," in *Handbook on the Politics of Higher Education*, ed. B. Cantwell, H. Coates, and R. King (Northampton: Edward Elgar): 91–114.

64. M. C. van der Wende (2011), "The Role of Higher Education Institutions in Globalization" (keynote address at the "New Horizons for the International University," Bonn, Deutscher Akademischer Austauschdienst); M. C. van der Wende (2017b), "Internationalisation Futures in Light of Anti-globalisation Sentiments," in *A Mosaic of Cultures*, EAIE Conference Conversation Starter: 29–37.

65. Council of the European Union (2016), "Council Resolution on A New Skills Agenda for an Inclusive and Competitive Europe," European Union, December 15.

66. A. Corbett and C. Gordon (2018), "Brexit and Higher Education and Research," in *The Routledge Handbook of the Politics of Brexit* (London: Routledge): 103–17.

67. VSNU 2019.

68. A Claeys-Kulik and T. Jørgensen (2018), "Universities' Strategies and Approaches towards Diversity, Equity and Inclusion: Examples from across Europe," *European University Association*, May.

69. EUA (2018), "Refugees Welcome Map," *European University Association*, http://refugeeswelcomemap.eua.be/Editor/Visualizer/Index/48.

70. DAAD (2018), https://www.daad.de/der-daad/fluechtlinge/en/.

71. Eurydice (2019), "Integrating Asylum Seekers and Refugees into Higher Education in Europe: National Policies and Measures," European Union.

72. Universities of Sanctuary (2020), "Homepage," https://universities.cityofsanctuary.org/.

73. M. Malgina and S. A. Skjerven (2019), "Towards Global Recognition of Refugees' Qualification," *University World News*, January 11.

74. G. Stubbs (2017), "Oxford and Cambridge Universities Accused of 'Social Apartheid' over Failure to Offer Places to Black Students," *Independent*, October 20.

75. UPP Foundation (2019), "UPP Foundation Civic University Commission: About the Commission," May 1; see also J. Morgan (2019), "Call for £500 Million Fund to Boost UK Universities' Civic Role," *Times Higher Education*, February 12.

76. G. Swerling (2019), "Oxford University Agrees to Let in Disadvantaged Students with Lower Grades," *Telegraph*, May 21; it should be noted that this statement seems to overlook the fact that early modern Oxford included many endowed benefices for "disadvantaged" students.

77. V. Mallet (2019), "Macron to Propose Abolition of Elite Ena Government School," *Financial Times*, April 20, https://www.ft.com/content/4d67c1e2-6065-11e9-b285-3acd5d43599ee; J. Morgan (2019), "Could Macron's Move against His Alma Mater Make France's HE System Fairer?," *Times Higher Education*, September 19.

78. D. Sammon (2019), "New Report Finds Overwhelming Support among Europeans for Open Society Values," Open Society Foundation, February 19, https://www.opensocietyfoundations.org/newsroom/new-report-finds-overwhelming-support-among-europeans-open-society-values.

79. N. Ferguson (2019), "Don't Tear Down Trumpman's Wall: It's like an Episode of South Park, but History's on the President's Side," *Sunday Times*, January 13, https://www.thetimes.co.uk/article/i-m-not-yet-writing-off-trump-s-mexican-wail-lvqzk6msh.

80. A. Gorman (2019), "The New Academies for Europe's Far Right," *New Statesman*, May 25, https://www.universityworldnews.com/post.php?story=20190524144451472.

81. ALLEA (2019), "Trust in Science and Changing Landscapes of Communication," Berlin: All European Academies Discussion Paper #3, January, https://www.allea.org/wp-content/uploads/2019/01/ALLEA_Trust_in_Science_and_Changing_Landscapes_of_Communication-1.pdf.

82. C. Stolke (2019), "Brexit Won't Hold Back Science," *Times Higher Education*, February 18, https://www.timeshighereducation.com/blog/brexit-wont-hold-back-science.

Chapter 7. Turkish Academics in the Era of Erdoğan

1. "Turkey Jails Academic after Raids over Gezi Park Protests" (2018), *Middle East Eye*, November 18.

2. Christopher de Bellaigue (2013), "Turkey: 'Surreal, Menacing . . . Pompous,'" *New York Review of Books*, December 19.

3. Fatma Nevra Seggie and Veysel Gokbel (2015), "Academic Freedom in Turkey: From Past to Present" (Washington, DC: SETA / Foundation for Political, Economic and Social Research): 20–22.

4. European Commission (2019), "Chapter of the Acquis," European Neighbourhood Policy and Enlargement Negotiations, Conditions for Membership, last updated April 17, https://ec.europa.eu/neighbourhood-enlargement/policy/conditions-membership/chapters-of-the-acquis_en.

5. Patrick Kingsley (2016), "We See Him as One of Us: Why Many Turks Still Back Authoritarian Erdogan," *Guardian*, July 20.

6. Brendan O'Malley (2008), "Turkey: Headscarf Ban to Be Lifted but Jail Sentence a Blow," *University World News*, February 3; Jonathan Head (2010), "Quiet End to Turkey's College Headscarf Ban," BBC, December 31.

7. "Turkey Ergenekon Case: Ex-Army Chief Basbug Gets Life" (2013), BBC, August 5.

8. A. Kadir Yildirim (2014), "The Slow Death of Turkish Higher Education," Aljazeera.com, July 10.

9. Yildirim 2014.

10. Brendan O'Malley (2016), "Lecturers Detained, Threatened for Opposing Military Action," *University World News*, January 15.

11. US Embassy and Consulates in Turkey (2006), statement by Ambassador John Bass on free expression, January 16, https://tr.usembassy.gov/amb_bass_011616/.

12. O'Malley 2016; and Brendan O'Malley and Michael Gardner (2016), "Growing Global Opposition to Breach of Academic Freedom," *University World News*, January 21.

13. Frontline Defenders (2019), "Request for Retrial of an Academic for Peace Turned Down by an Istanbul Court," *Judicial Harassment against the Members of Academics for Peace*, Dublin, Ireland, November 8.

14. Stockholm Center for Freedom (2019), *Turkey's Constitutional Court Rules Academics' Rights Violated in Peace Petition Case*, Stockholm, Sweden, July 26.

15. W. Robert Pearson (2016), "What Caused the Turkish Coup Attempt?," *Politico*, July 16. Pearson is a former US ambassador to Turkey and a scholar at the Middle East Institute, a Washington think tank.

16. "Turkey Officially Designates Gulen Religious Group as Terrorists" (2016), Reuters, May 31.

17. Amnesty International (n.d.), *Turkey 2017/18*, accessed December 10, 2020, https://www.amnesty.org/en/countries/europe-and-central-asia/turkey/report-turkey/.

18. "Turkey Coup Attempt: More Than 130 Media Outlets Shut" (2019), BBC, July 28.

19. House of Commons Foreign Affairs Select Committee (2017), *The UK's Relations with Turkey*, 10th report of session 2016–2017, March 21.

20. Education and Science Workers Union (2017), *Report on the Effect of the State of Emergency and Decree-Laws on Education Members*, July 14 (Ankara, Turkey); Stockholm Center for Freedom (2018), *The Crackdown on Education in Turkey: Free Thought under Siege in Turkey*, July (Stockholm, Sweden): 15, 23, 43; and Scholars at Risk Academic Freedom Monitoring Project (2018), *Free to Think 2018* (New York): 31, 33.

21. Council of Higher Education (YÖK) (2016), press release, July 19; and "How the State of Emergency Affected Universities: Distribution of Academics Dismissed by Decree-Laws by University" (2017), *Cumhuriyet*, July 11. Both are cited in Stockholm Center for Freedom 2018: 24; "23,427 Academics Affected by State of Emergency in Turkey" (2017), *Turkish Minute*, July 11. Across all sectors only 30,000 cases out of 118,660 appeals were reviewed, and of those only 1,900 resulted in favorable outcomes for the appellants. Scholars at Risk 2018: 33.

22. Overall, the purge involved around 1,700 detentions or warrants issued to academics involved in the Academics for Peace petition and the physical detention of more than 1,250 of them. By the end of September 2019, more than 800 signatories of the petition had been tried or their trials were ongoing, and more than 200 had been sentenced. Of these 146 of were sentenced to 15 months in prison, and the rest for between 15 months and three years.

23. Correspondence with the Brendan O'Malley, August 9, 2019.

24. Scholars at Risk 2018, Incident Report for September 11.

25. Candan Badem (2017), "The Quest to Quell Opposition Leads to 'Academo-cide,'" *University World News*, February 11.

26. Scholars at Risk 2018, Incident Report for July 11: 28, 31, 32.

27. Human Rights Watch (2019), "Turkey: Baseless Charges over Landmark 2013 Protests," March 25, https://www.hrw.org/news/2019/03/25/turkey-baseless-charges-over-landmark-2013-protests.

28. "Turkey Academic Jailed after Raids on Professors and Activists" (2018), Al Jazeera, November 19.

29. Amnesty International (2019), "Turkey: Outlandish Charges against Osman Kavala and 15 Others Must Be Dropped," February 20.

30. Decree 676, Article 85, cited in *Yeni Safak* [New dawn], https://www.yenisafak.com/en/15-july-coup-attempt-in-turkey/decree-law-no-676---education-ohal-khk-en-detail. University leaders have also colluded in pressuring targeted academics. SCF cites the case of Cenk Yiğiter, who was dismissed from his post at Ankara University's School of Law. He then took and passed the national university exam and was placed at the same university in the radio-TV-cinema department of the communications faculty. But the university's rector and senate issued a custom-made regulation to deny him enrollment. Stockholm Center for Freedom 2018.

31. Decree 676, Article 85, cited in New Dawn.

32. Scholars at Risk 2018: 33; Stockholm Center for Freedom 2018.

33. Mustafa Akyol (2014), "Turkey Pulse, What You Should Know about Turkey's AKP-Gulen Conflict," *Al Monitor*, January 3, https://web.archive.org/web/20150424173852/http://www.al-monitor.com/pulse/originals/2014/01/akp-gulen-conflict-guide.html; Kadri Gursel (2013), "Crackdown Shatters AKP 'Anti-corruption' Taboo," *Al Monitor*, Turkey Pulse, December 19.

34. M. Hakan Yavuz and Ahmet Erdi Ozturk (2019), "Turkish Secularism and Islam under the Reign of Erdogan," *Southeast Europe and Black Sea Studies* 19: 1–9.

35. Berk Esen and Sebnem Gumuscu (2016), "Rising Competitive Authoritari-anism in Turkey," *Third World Quarterly* 37(9): 1581–606.

36. Scholars at Risk 2018: 34.

37. Vezir Aktras, Marco Nilsson, and Klas Borell (2019), "Social Scientists under Threat: Resistance and Self-Censorship in Turkish Academia," *British Journal of Educational Studies* 67(2), https://www.tandfonline.com/doi/full/10.1080/00071005.2018.1502872.

Chapter 8. Nationalism Revived

1. Yangyang Cheng (2019), "Protesting in the Name of Science: The Legacy of China's May Fourth Movement," *SupChina*, April 24.

2. Chris Buckley and Amy Qin (2019), "Xi Praises a Student Protest in China: From 100 Years Ago," *New York Times*, April 29: A6.

3. Merle Goldman and Rudolf Wagner (1987), "China: Intellectuals at Bay," *New York Review of Books*, March 26.

4. Ruth Hayhoe (1996), *China's Universities, 1895–1995: A Century of Cultural Conflict* (New York: Garland).

5. Douglas Stiffler (2005), "Resistance to the Sovietization of Higher Education in China," in *Universities under Dictatorship*, ed. John Connelly and Michael Gruttner (University Park: Pennsylvania State University Press): 213–44.

6. John King Fairbanks and Merle Goldman (2006), *China: A New History* (Boston: Belknap).

7. Yidi Wu (2017), "Blooming, Contending, and Staying Silent: Student Activism and Campus Politics in China, 1957" (PhD diss., University of California Humanities Research Institute, University of California at Irvine), https://escholarship.org/uc/item/4xk023h8.

8. Hayhoe 1996.

9. Wu 2017.

10. Violet Law (2016), "His Students Beat Him to Death during the Cultural Revolution: The School Called It Suicide," *Los Angeles Times*, October 24.

11. Hayhoe 1996.

12. Xin Meng and Robert Gregory (2007), "Exploring the Impact of Interrupted Education on Earnings: The Educational Cost of the Chinese Cultural Revolution," Institute of Labor Economics Discussion Paper (Bonn, Germany: Institute of Labor Economics), https://ideas.repec.org/p/iza/izadps/dp2548.html.

13. Rowena Xiaoqing He (2017), "The 1989 Tiananmen Movement and Its Aftermath," *Oxford Research Encyclopedia of Asian History* (Oxford: Oxford University Press), https://oxfordre.com/asianhistory/view/10.1093/acrefore/9780190277727.001.0001/acrefore-9780190277727-e-157?rskey=pbvrMi&result=1.

14. He 2017.

15. Hayhoe 1996.

16. Dennis Overbye (2006), "China Pursues Major Role in Particle Physics," *New York Times*, December 5: F1.

17. Hayhoe 1996.

18. Organisation for Economic Co-operation and Development (2000a), "University Autonomy in China: History, Present Situation, and Perspective," in *Current Issues in Chinese Higher Education* (Paris: OECD).

19. Hao Xin (2012), "With Eye to Innovation, China Revamps Its Universities," *Science*, August 10: 634.

20. Jeff Tollefson (2018), "China Declared World's Largest Producer of Scientific Articles," *Nature*, January 23.

21. Karin Fischer (2012), "Bucking Cultural Norms, Asia Tries Liberal Arts," *Chronicle of Higher Education*, February 5.

22. Yangyang Chen (2017), "The Future of Particle Physics Will Live and Die in China," *Foreign Policy*, November 2.

23. Chris Buckley (2017), "Liu Xiaobo, Chinese Dissident Who Won Nobel While Jailed, Dies at 61," *New York Times*, July 13: A1.

24. Karin Fischer (2014a), "Email Suggests Embattled Chinese Scholar Was Fired for Political Views," *Chronicle of Higher Education*, January 3.

25. Bethany Allen-Ebrahimian and Zach Dorfman (2019), "China Has Been Running Global Influence Campaigns for Years," *Atlantic*, March 14.

26. Martin Patience (2013), "What Does Xi Jinping's China Dream Mean?," BBC News, June 6.

27. Isabel Hilton (2018), "Making China Great Again: Xi Jinping's Troubled Nationalist Revival," *New Statesman*, October 10.

28. Communist Party of China (2013), *Communique on the Current State of the Ideological Sphere*, trans. and pub. ChinaFile, November 8.

29. Lara Farrar (2013), "China Bans 7 Topics in University Classrooms," *Chronicle of Higher Education*, May 20.

30. Emilie Tran (2017), "China: Zero Tolerance for Academic Freedom," *Conversation*, October 17.

31. Christian Shepherd (2019), "Disappearing Textbook Highlights Debate in China over Academic Freedom," Reuters, February 1.

32. Tom Phillips (2017), "Cambridge University Press Censorship 'Exposes Xi Jinping's Authoritarian Shift,'" *Guardian*, August 20.

33. Elizabeth Redden (2019), "Brill Severs Ties with Chinese Publisher," *Inside Higher Ed*, April 29.

34. Elizabeth Redden (2017), "Publisher Complies with Chinese Censorship," *Inside Higher Ed*, November 2.

35. Editorial (2017), "China Quarterly Debate a Matter of Principle," *Global Times*, August 20.

36. Didi Teng (2018), "Beijing Disbands Student Marxist Group for Backing Workers' Rights," *Times* (London), December 31.

37. Eduardo Baptista, Yong Xiong, and Ben Westcott (2019), "Six Marxist Students Vanish in China in the Lead Up to Labor Day," CNN, May 1.

38. Zheping Huang (2019), "China's Top App Teaches Xi Jinping Propaganda," *Inkstone*, February 14.

39. Nick Taber (2018), "How Xi Jinping Is Shaping China's Universities," *Diplomat*, August 10.

40. Christian Shepherd (2018), "In China, Universities Seek to Plant 'Xi Thought' in Minds of Students," *Reuters*, June 21.

41. Jun Mai (2016), "Xi Calls for More Thought Control on China's Campuses," *South China Morning Post*, December 10.

42. Yojana Sharma (2018), "Beijing Signals Tighter Control over Dissenting Scholars," *University World News*, November 1.

43. Mai 2016.

44. Xi Wang, Han Jie, Wong Siu-san, and Lau Siu-fung (2019), "Chinese Universities Ordered to Spy on Staff, Students in Ideological Crackdown," *Radio Free Asia*, April 8.

45. Taber 2018.

46. Taber 2018.

47. Yojana Sharma (2017), "Universities Told to Credit Propaganda as Publication," *University World News*, September 26.

48. Gao Feng, Wong Siu-san, and Wen Yuqing (2017), "China Warns Officials to Behave Online as Two Universities Fire Lecturers," *Radio Free Asia*, August 4.

49. Wong Siu-san, Lau Siu-Fung, and Jia Ao (2018), "Chinese Lecturer Fired for Raising Presidential Term-Limit in Class," *Radio Free Asia*, May 21.

50. Joyce Huang (2019), "Students Snitch on Teachers as China Pushes Ideology on Campus," *Voice of America*, June 29.

51. Aris Teon (2018), "Xiamen University Professor Dismissed after Posting Comments Calling China an 'Inferior Nation,'" *Greater China Journal*, September 3.

52. Wen Yuqing and Qiao Long (2019), "University in China's Chongqing Demotes Professor over Comments Made in Class," *Radio Free Asia*, March 29.

53. Editorial (2018), "A Professor Dared Tell the Truth in China—and Was Fired," *Washington Post*, August 23.

54. Annie Wu (2018), "(Another) Chinese Professor Punished for His Speech," *Epoch Times*, October 16.

55. Elizabeth Redden (2018), "Not Feeling Safe in China," *Inside Higher Ed*, July 23.

56. Gerry Mullany (2018), "A Chinese Activist Was Challenging Xi on Live TV: The Police Came to Stop Him," *New York Times*, August 2.

57. Gao Fang (2019), "Nanjing Scholar Guo Quan Is Detained Again," *Radio Free Asia*, April 19.

58. James Millward (2019), "'Reeducating' Xinjiang's Muslims," *New York Review of Books*, February 7.

59. Uyghur Human Rights Project (2019), *Detained and Disappeared: Intellectuals Under Assault in the Uyghur Homeland* (Washington, DC: Uyghur American Association).

60. Chris Buckley and Austin Ramzy (2018), "Star Scholar Disappears as Crackdown Engulfs Western China," *New York Times*, August 10: A9.

61. Shohret Hoshur (2018), "Prominent Uyghur Intellectual Given Two-Year Suspended Death Sentence for 'Separatism,'" *Radio Free Europe*, September 28.

62. Edward Wong (2014), "China Sentences Uighur Scholar to Life," *New York Times*, September 23: A6.

63. Chris Buckley (2019), "A Chinese Law Professor Criticized Xi: Now He's Been Suspended," *New York Times*, March 26: A9.

64. Chris Buckley (2019).

65. Open letter to Tsinghua University (n.d.), accessed May 1, 2019, http:// chinaheritage.net/journal/an-open-letter-to-tsinghua-university-signed-and -sealed/.

66. Xia Yeliang, interview with the author, April 2019.

67. James Millward, interview with the author, April 2019.

68. Organisation for Economic Co-operation and Development (2000b), "Academic Freedom and Academic Duty in Chinese Universities," in *Current Issues in Chinese Higher Education* (Paris: OECD).

69. Human Rights Watch (2019), *China: Government Threats to Academic Freedom Abroad* (New York: Human Rights Watch).

70. Sheena Chestnut Greitens and Rory Truex (2018) "Repressive Experiences among China Scholars: New Evidence from Survey Data," *China Quarterly*, August: 1–27.

71. Robin Matross Helms, Lucia Brajkovic, and Brice Struthers (2017), *Mapping Internationalization on U.S. Campuses* (Washington, DC: American Council on Education).

72. Karin Fischer (2014b), "After Wellesley's Debate, a Push for Scrutiny of Overseas Ties," *Chronicle of Higher Education*, September 29.

73. Javier C. Hernandez (2018), "Cornell Cuts Ties with Chinese School after Crackdown on Students," *New York Times*, October 29: A21.

74. Fischer 2014b.

75. Isabella Steger (2019), "Harvard President Read a Uyghur Poem to Students at Peking University," *Quartz*, March 20.

76. Task Force on American Innovation (2019), *Second Place America? Increasing Challenges to U.S. Scientific Leadership* (Washington, DC: Task Force on American Innovation).

77. Emily Feng (2018), "China Closes a Fifth of Foreign University Partnerships," *Financial Times*, July 17.

78. Emily Feng (2017), "Beijing Vies for Greater Control of Foreign Universities in China," *Financial Times*, November 18.

79. Institute of International Education (2019), *Open Doors* (New York: Institute of International Education).

80. Karin Fischer (2015), "A Chinese Mother's American Dream," *Chronicle of Higher Education*, July 6.

81. Karoline Kan (2016), "Shanghai's Move to Curb International Programs in Schools Worries Parents," *New York Times*, December 29.

82. Nicole Hao (2018), "China Said to Issue Secret Order Barring Senior Officials' Children from Studying in US," *Epoch Times*, October 3.

83. Karin Fischer (2019), "For American Colleges, China Could Be the New Travel Ban—but Worse," *Chronicle of Higher Education*, January 3.

84. Grace Karram Stephenson (2018), "Future Still Uncertain for Saudi Students in Canada," *University World News*, November 9.

85. James Millward, interview with the author, April 2019.

86. Matt Schrader (2017), "Surprise Findings: Chinese Youth Are Getting Less Nationalistic, Not More," *Foreign Policy*, February 7.

87. Simon Denyer and Congcong Zhang (2017), "A Chinese Student Praised the 'Fresh Air of Freedom' at a U.S. College: Then Came the Backlash," *Washington Post*, May 23.

88. Gerry Shih and Emily Rauhala (2019), "Angry over Campus Speech by Uighur Activist, Chinese Students in Canada Contact Their Consulate, Film Presentation," *Washington Post*, February 14.

89. Anastya Lloyd-Damnjanovic (2018), *A Preliminary Study of PRC Political Influence and Interference Activities in American Higher Education* (Washington, DC: Woodrow Wilson International Center for Scholars).

90. Bethany Allen-Ebrahimian (2018), "China's Long Arm Reaches into American Campuses," *Foreign Policy*, March 7.

91. Sophie Richardson, interview with the author, April 2019.

92. Lloyd-Damnjanovic 2018.

93. Hoover Institution Working Group on Chinese Influence Activities in the United States (2018), *Chinese Influence and American Interests: Promoting Constructive Vigilance* (Palo Alto, CA: Hoover Institution Press).

94. Peter Schmidt (2014), "AAUP Rebukes Colleges for Chinese Institutes and Censures Northeastern Ill.," *Chronicle of Higher Education*, June 15.

95. US Senate Permanent Subcommittee on Investigations (2019) *China's Impact on the U.S. Educational System* (Washington, DC: US Government Printing Office).

96. Mary E. Gallagher (2019), "Are Confucius Institutes Good for American Universities?," *ChinaFile*, April 4.

97. Government Accountability Office (2019), *Agreements Establishing Confucius Institutes at U.S. Universities Are Similar, but Institute Operations Vary* (Washington, DC: US Government Printing Office).

98. Hoover Institution Working Group 2018.

99. US Senate Permanent Subcommittee on Investigations 2019.

100. Ryan Woo and Ben Blanchard (2019), "China Aims to 'Optimize' Spread of Controversial Confucius Institutes," Reuters, February 23.

101. Coco Liu and Tashny Sukumaran (2017), "Belt and Road: How China Is Exporting Education and Influence to Malaysia and other Asean Countries," *South China Morning Post*, July 30.

102. Institute of International Education (2017), *Project Atlas* (New York: Institute of International Education).

103. Anton Crace (2019), "Australia: Belt and Road Disruption Warning," *PIE News*, March 2.

104. Ehsan Mahsood (2019), "How China Is Redrawing the Map of World Science," *Nature*, May 1.

105. Mahsood 2019.

106. Yojana Sharma (2015), "University Collaboration Takes the Silk Road Route," *University World News*, June 12.

107. Yangyang Chang, interview with the author, April 2019.

108. Joe McDonald (2017), "China's Xi Calls for More Technology Development," Associated Press, October 17.

109. Futao Hong (2017), "Double World-Class Project Has More Ambitious Aims," *University World News*, September 29.

110. Times Higher Education (2019), *2019 World University Rankings* (London: Times Higher Education).

111. Task Force on American Innovation 2019.

112. Larry Diamond and Orville Schell (2019), *China's Influence & American Interests: Promoting Constructive Vigilance* (Stanford, CA: Hoover Institution Press).

113. Karin Fischer (2016), "The Spy Who Wasn't," *Chronicle of Higher Education*, January 10.

114. Lindsay Ellis (2018), "Political Tensions With China Put Pressure on Universities' Research Commitments," *Chronicle of Higher Education*, November 15.

115. Jane Perlez (2019), "FBI Bars Some China Scholars from Visiting U.S. over Spying Fears," *New York Times*, April 14: A9.

116. Robert Daly, interview with the author, April 2019.

117. Beijing Overseas Study Service Association and Chinese Overseas Study Service Alliance (2020), *Chinese Agency Survey Results* (Beijing: BOSSA-COSSA).

118. Robert Daly, interview with the author, April 2019.

Chapter 9. Balancing Nationalism and Globalism

1. Hong Kong is home to a majority ethnic Chinese population, which comprises 93 percentage of the population, and a very low birthrate, at 1.2 children born per woman. Singapore is home to a more ethnically diverse population, with a majority 74 percent ethnic Chinese population and minority Malay and Indian populations comprising 13 and 7 percent, respectively. Like Hong Kong, Singapore is experiencing a low birth rate, which has dropped to only 1.14 in 2019.

2. Examples from European nations include Catalonia, the Basque territories, Wales, Brittany, and Friesland, which all exert strong resistance to a central national authority based on distinct linguistic and cultural identity that inspires movements for more political autonomy. B. C. H. Fong (2017), "One Country, Two Nationalisms: Center-Periphery Relations between Mainland China and Hong Kong, 1997–2016," *Modern China*, 43: 523.

3. Dennis Normile (2019), "Hong Kong Student Protesters Demand More Support from Their Universities," *Science Magazine*, October 29.

4. Phil C. W. Chan (2019a), "Why Hong Kong Protesters Are Forcing University Leaders To Pick a Side—Academic Freedom Is at Stake," *South China Morning Post*, November 6.

5. Amnesty International (2020), *"Hong Kong's National Security Law: 20 Things You Need to Know,"* July 17.

6. Yiu-chung Wong (2004), *One Country, Two Systems in Crisis: Hong Kong's Transformation* (Hong Kong: Lexington Books).

7. Basic Law, Article 137 reads, "Educational institutions of all kinds may retain their autonomy and enjoy academic freedom. They may continue to recruit staff and use teaching materials from outside the Hong Kong Special Administrative Region. Schools run by religious organizations may continue to provide religious education, including courses in religion."

8. "Huge Turnout by Protesters Keeps Heat on Hong Kong's Leader" (2019), *New York Times*, June 16, https://www.nytimes.com/2019/06/16/world/asia/hong-kong-protests.html.

9. H. Chan (2019b), "The Writing on the Wall: Understanding the Messages Left by Protesters during the Storming of the Hong Kong Legislature," *Hong Kong Free Press*, July 4, https://www.hongkongfp.com/2019/07/04/writing-wall-understanding-messages-left-protesters-storming-hong-kong-legislature/.

10. M. Ives (2019), "Mob Beats Antigovernment Protesters in Hong Kong," *New York Times*, July 21, https://www.nytimes.com/2019/07/21/world/asia/hong-kong -protest-police.html?module=inline.

11. Yojana Sharma (2019), "Students' Defy University Warnings with Classes' Boycott," *University World News*, September 3.

12. Lily Kuo (2019), "Hong Kong' Students Boycott Classes as Chinese Media Warns 'End Is Coming,'" *Guardian*, September 2.

13. HKU Staff and Students (2019), joint declaration, October 22.

14. Normile 2019.

15. CUHK Vice Chancellor and President Professor Rocky S. Tuan's Open Letter (2019), Communications and Public Relations Office, Chinese University of Hong Kong, October 18, https://www.cpr.cuhk.edu.hk/en/press_detail.php?id=3140&t =cuhk-vice-chancellor-and-president-professor-rocky-s-tuan-s-open-letter&s=.

16. Chan 2019a.

17. D. Y. K. Tsang (2007), *The 2007–2008 Policy Address: The New Direction for Hong Kong* (Hong Kong: Government Printer), https://www.policyaddress.gov.hk /07-08/eng/docs/policy.pdf.

18. K. Carrico (2018), "Academic Freedom in Hong Kong since 2015: Between Two Systems," *Hong Kong Watch*, https://www.hongkongwatch.org/all-posts/2018 /1/22/academic-freedom-report.

19. Carrico 2018.

20. E. Tong (2018), "Lawmaker Cheng Chung-tai's Poly U Teaching Contract Not Renewed after Flag-Turning Conviction," *Hong Kong Free Press*, January 13, https://www.hongkongfp.com/2018/01/13/lawmaker-cheng-chung-tais-poly-u -teaching-contract-not-renewed-flag-turning-conviction/.

21. J. Chan and D. Kerr (2016), "Academic Freedom, Political Interference and Public Accountability: The Hong Kong Experience," *AAUP Journal of Academic Freedom* 7: 1.

22. P. Mathieson, interview with author Bryan Penprase, August 1, 2019.

23. J. Lam (2018), "Retired at 60: Why Some of Hong Kong's Most Renowned Scholars Find They Are No Longer Wanted at University," *South China Morning Post*, September 27, https://www.scmp.com/news/hong-kong/society/article /2165864/retired-60-why-some-hong-kongs-most-renowned-scholars-find.

24. The two highest-ranked universities in Hong Kong, the University of Hong Kong and Hong Kong University of Science and Technology, are currently ranked 36 and 41 in 2019 by the *Times Higher Education*. These rankings remain impressive but reflect a small decline for HKU's rankings from before the 2014 Occupy protests (HKU was ranked 21 back in 2011). Times Higher Education, World University Rankings, https://www.timeshighereducation.com/world-university-rankings, accessed July 24, 2019.

25. C. H. Teo (2000), "Education towards the 21st Century" (address at the Alumni International Singapore Lecture, Singapore's Universities of Tomorrow, Singapore); K. Ho Mok (2008), "Singapore's Global Education Hub Ambitions: University Governance Change and Transnational Higher Education," *International Journal of Educational Management* 22(6): 527–46.

26. W. Y. W. Lo (2014), "Think Global, Think Local: The Changing Landscape of Higher Education and the Role of Quality Assurance in Singapore," *Policy and Society* 33: 264.

27. L. Basillote et al. (2016), "Singapore's Higher Education Cluster," Harvard Business School white paper, https://www.isc.hbs.edu/resources/courses/moc -course-at-harvard/Documents/pdf/student-projects/Singapore%20Higher %20Education%202016.pdf.

28. QS World University Rankings (2019), "QS Top Universities," https://www .topuniversities.com/university-rankings/world-university-rankings/2019.

29. A. Nowrasteh (2018), "Singapore's Immigration System: Past Present and Future," Cato Working Paper No. 53, https://object.cato.org/sites/cato.org/files /pubs/pdf/cato-working-paper-53-update.pdf.

30. M. Mathews and J. Zhang (2016), "Sentiments on Immigrant Integration and the Role of Immigrant Associations," IPS Exchange Series, no. 7, Lee Kuan Yew School of Public Policy, NUS.

31. Lo 2014: 264.

32. L. Perera (2019), "Scholarships and Other Forms of Financial Aid Given to Foreign Students," https://www.moe.gov.sg/news/parliamentary-replies /scholarships-and-other-forms-of-financial-aid-given-to-foreign-students.

33. J. Chia and C. Kang (2014), "Where Are My Country(wo)men? The Lack of Singaporean Academics in Singapore's Universities," *Kyoto Review of Southeast Asia*, no. 15, https://kyotoreview.org/yav/where-are-my-countrywomen-the-lack-of -singaporean-academics-in-singapores-universities/#return-note-6204-5.

34. P. E. Fong and L. Lim (2017), "Singapore's Fling with Global Stars Sidelines Local Talent," *Times Higher Education*, August 24, https://www .timeshighereducation.com/opinion/singapores-fling-global-stars-sidelines-local -talent.

35. J. J. Woo (2017), "Educating the Developmental State: Policy Integration and Mechanism Redesign in Singapore's SkillsFuture Scheme," *Journal of Asian Public Policy* 11(3): 267–84.

36. N. W. Gleason (2018), *Higher Education in the Era of the Fourth Industrial Revolution* (London: Palgrave Macmillan).

37. Z. L. Liang (2015), "Singapore Budget 2015: Every Singaporean above 25 to Get $500 for a Start under Skills Future," *Straights Times*, February 23, https:// www.straitstimes.com/singapore/singapore-budget-2015-every-singaporean -above-25-to-get-500-for-a-start-under-skillsfuture.

38. L. Lim (2018), "How Singapore's Obsession with University Rankings Only Serves to Hurt It," *South China Morning Post*, December 21, https://www.scmp.com /week-asia/opinion/article/2178967/how-singapores-obsession-university -rankings-only-serves-hurt-it.

39. E. Bothwell (2019), "Singapore Legal Challenge 'Will Chill Academic Freedom," *Times Higher Education*, January 23, https://www.timeshighereducation .com/news/singapore-legal-challenge-will-chill-academic-freedom.

40. S. Yap (2019), "Opaque Policies, Fixation with KPIs, Rankings: Why Arts and Humanities Academics Quit NUS, NTU," originally published in *Today*,

reposted at Majapahit Panorama and https://medium.com/the-majapahit
-panorama/opaque-policies-fixation-with-kpis-rankings-why-arts-and
-humanities-academics-quit-nus-ntu-b8ddoee98141.

41. Yip Jia Qi (2019), "College Cuts Week 7 LAB on Dialogue and Dissent in Singapore," *Octant*, September 14.

42. P. Salovey (2019), "Statement Regarding the Cancellation of an Offering at Yale-NUS," *Yale News*, September 14.

43. P. Lewis (2019), "Report on Cancellation of LAB Module on Dialog and Dissent," September 28, https://news.yale.edu/sites/default/files/files/Pericles -Lewis-Yale-NUS-report.pdf.

44. Shibani Mahtani (2019), "At Yale's Venture in Singapore, a Canceled Course on Dissent Prompts Censorship Claims," *Washington Post*, September 27.

45. T. P. Tijn and K. Han (2019), "Singapore's 'Fake News' Bill: The FAQ," *New Naratif*, https://newnaratif.com/research/singapores-fake-news-bill-the-faq/share /xuna/cfcd208495d565ef66e7dff9f98764da/.

46. J. Seow (2018), "170 Academics Sign Open Letter Expressing Concern about Academic Freedom in Singapore," *Straits Times*, April 13, https://www.straitstimes .com/politics/170-academics-sign-open-letter-expressing-concern-about -academic-freedom-in-singapore.

47. E. Bothwell (2019), "Singapore's 'Fake News' Law 'Threatens Academic Freedom Worldwide,'" *Times Higher Education*, April 23, https://www .timeshighereducation.com/news/singapore-fake-news-law-threatens-academic -freedom-worldwide.

48. "Facebook Says 'Deeply Concerned' about Singapore's Order to Block Page" (2020), Reuters Internet News, February 18.

49. P. Yang (2014), "Authenticity and Foreign Talent in Singapore: The Relative and Negative Logic of National Identity," *SOJOURN: Journal of Social Issues in Southeast Asia*, no. 2: 408.

50. Amnesty International 2020.

Chapter 10. The Role of Universities in Putin's Russia

1. Lionel Barber, Henry Foy, and Alex Barker (2019), "Vladimir Putin Says Liberalism Has 'Become Obsolete,'" *Financial Times*, June 27, https://www.ft.com /content/670039ec-98f3-11e9-9573-ee5cbb98ed36.

2. For an overview of contemporary Russian nationalism, see Charles Clover (2016), *Black Wind, White Snow: The Rise of Russia's New Nationalism* (New Haven, CT: Yale University Press); Marlene Laruelle (2018), *Russian Nationalism: Imaginaries, Doctrines and Political Battlefields* (London: Routledge).

3. P. Anatoly Oleksiyenko, Qiang Zha, Igor Chirikov, and Jun Li (2018), *International Status Anxiety and Higher Education: Soviet Legacies in China and Russia*, CERC Studies in Comparative Education Series (New York: Springer).

4. Irina Rostova (2019), "Otstavka po sekretu: Eks-rektor Viatskogo gosuni- versiteta oprotestoval v sude uvol'nenie iz-za gostainy," *Kommersant Nizhnii Novgorod*, November 10, https://www.kommersant.ru/doc/1272112.

5. See the Law 10-FZ of February 10, 2009.

6. Strong incentives for that were provided by the Law on Autonomous Institutions No. 174-FZ of November 3, 2006.

7. Law 259-FZ of November 10, 2009.

8. "Sergeiia Baburina uvolili s posta rektora RGTEU" (2012), BBC Russian Service, December 25, https://www.bbc.com/russian/russia/2012/12/121225 _trade_economics_university_court; Sergei Baburin (2012), "Liberal'nyi ekstremizm Livanova dlia nas nepriemlem," *Russkaia narodnaia liniia*, December 25, http://ruskline.ru/news_rl/2012/12/25/sergej_baburin_liberalnyj_ekstremizm _livanova_dlya_nas_nepriemlem/.

9. For a broad overview, see Dmitry Dubrovskiy (2017), "Escape from Freedom: The Russian Academic Community and the Problem of Academic Rights and Freedoms," *Interdisciplinary Political Studies* 31: 171–99.

10. Evgeniy Senshin (2019), "V takikh usloviiakh ni odna nauka normal'no sushchestvovat ne mozhet," *Znak*, June 25.

11. Senshin 2019.

12. Anna Vasil'eva and Ivan Tiazhlov (2020), "Vyshku zamenili uvol'neniami: 'Kommersant' vyiasnial, naskol'ko svobodnym universitetom ostaetsia VShE," *Kommersant*, September 1, https://www.kommersant.ru/doc/4474299.

13. "Studenta SFU otchislili za kritiku kraevoi vlasti v diplomnoi rabote" (2019), *Krasnews*, June 24, https://krasnews.com/news/13852/.

14. "Professor iz Peterburga raskritikoval sdelannuiu ego vuzom ekspertizu: Ego uvolili," BBC Russian Service, December 4, https://www.bbc.com/russian /features-46429215.

15. Ksenia Kolesnikova (2020), "Gosduma priniala prezidentskii zakon o vospitanii v shkolakh i vuzakh," *Rossiiskaia gazeta*, July 22, https://rg.ru/2020/07 /22/gosduma-priniala-zakon-o-vospitanii-obuchaiushchihsia.html.

16. Alex Kuraev (2014), "Internationalization of Higher Education in Russia: Collapse or Perpetuation of the Soviet System? A Historical and Conceptual Study" (PhD diss., Boston College, Boston, MA).

17. Sergey Malinovskiy and Maia Chankseliani (2018), "International Student Recruitment in Russia: Heavy-Handed Approach and Soft-Power Come-back," in *International Status Anxiety and Higher Education: Soviet Legacy in China and Russia*, ed. Anatoly Oleksiyenko, Qiang Zha, Igor Chirikov, and Jun Li, CERC Studies in Comparative Education Series (New York: Springer): 281–307.

18. Alexander Arefiev (2018), *Obuchenie inostranny'kh grazhdan v vy'sshikh uchebny'kh zavedeniiakh Rossii'skoi' Federatsii: Statisticheskii' sbornik*, 15th ed. (Moscow: Ministerstvo obrazovaniia i nauki Rossii'skoi' Federatsii, Centr sotciologicheskikh issledovanii').

19. Malinovskiy and Chankseliani 2018; Kuraev 2014.

20. Arefiev 2018.

21. Alexander Chernykh and Elena Kiseleva (2015), "Rossiya narashchivaet import studentov," *Kommersant*, April 24, http://www.kommersant.ru/doc /2715149.

22. Yuriy Ammosov (2003), "Kaliforniia stavit na nas." *Expert*, September 1, https://expert.ru/expert/2003/32/32ex-nauka_31866/.

23. Alexander Subbotin and Samin Aref (2020), "Brain Drain and Brain Gain in Russia: Analyzing International Migration of Researchers by Discipline Using Scopus Bibliometric Data 1996–2020" (arXiv preprint), arXiv:2008.03129.

24. Sergey Riazantsev and Elena Pis'mennaia (2013), "E'migratciia ucheny'kh iz Rossii: 'Tsirkuliatsiia' ili 'utechka' umov," *Sotciologicheskie issledovaniia* 4: 24–35.

25. Subbotin and Aref 2020.

26. Organisation for Economic Co-operation and Development (2017), *OECD Science, Technology and Industry Scoreboard 2017: The Digital Transformation* (Paris: OECD), https://doi.org/10.1787/9789264268821-en; Subbotin and Aref 2020.

27. UNESCO (2019), "Global Flow of Tertiary-Level Students," http://uis .unesco.org/en/uis-student-flow.

28. Oleg Sukhov (2013), "Economist and Kremlin Critic Aleksashenko Moves to Washington," *Moscow Times*, October 29, https://www.themoscowtimes.com/2013 /10/29/economist-and-kremlin-critic-aleksashenko-moves-to-washington-a29038.

29. John Herbst and Sergei Erofeev (2019), *The Putin Exodus: The New Russian Brain Drain* (Washington, DC: Atlantic Council, February 21.

30. Isak Froumin and Alexander Povalko (2014), "Top Down Push for Excellence," in *How World-Class Universities Affect Global Higher Education*, ed. Ying Cheng, Qi Wang, and Nian Cai Liu (Rotterdam: Sense): 47–63; Igor Chirikov (2018), "The Sputnik Syndrome: How Russian Universities Make Sense of Global Competition in Higher Education," in *International Status Anxiety and Higher Education: Soviet Legacy in China and Russia*, ed. Anatoly Oleksiyenko, Qiang Zha, Igor Chirikov, and Jun Li, CERC Studies in Comparative Education Series (New York: Springer): 259–80.

31. National Science Board (2014), *Science and Engineering Indicators* (Arlington, VA).

32. Oleg Poldin, Nataliya Matveeva, Ivan Sterligov, and Maria Yudkevich (2017), "Publication Activities of Russian Universities: The Effects of Project 5-100," *Educational Studies Moscow* 2: 59.

Chapter 11. Bolsonaro's Brazilian Neo-nationalism and Universities

1. Francisco C. Weffort (1989), *O populismo na política Brasileira* (Rio de Janeiro: Paz e Terra).

2. Clarissa Eckert Baeta Neves (2017), "Higher Education Systems and Institutions, Brazil," in *Encyclopedia of International Higher Education Systems and Institutions*, ed. Jung Cheol Shin and Pedro Teixeira (Dordrecht: Springer Netherlands): 1–11, https://doi.org/10.1007/978-94-017-9553-1_401-1; Simon Schwartzman (1991), *A Space for Science: The Development of the Scientific Community in Brazil*, 1st ed. (University Park: Pennsylvania State University Press).

3. Lucia Klein (1992), "Política e políticas de ensino superior no Brasil: 1970–1990," Documentos de Trabalho NUPES 2/91, São Paulo, http://nupps.usp.br /downloads/docs/dt9202.pdf; Eunice Ribeiro Durham (1998), "Uma política para o

ensino superior Brasileiro: Diagnóstico e proposta," *Documentos de Trabalho NUPES* 1: 98.

4. Elizabeth Balbachevsky (2013), "Academic Research and Advanced Training: Building Up Research Universities in Brazil," in *Latin's America's New Knowledge Economy: Higher Education, Government and International Collaboration*, ed. Jorge Balan (Washington, DC: Institute of International Education): 113–33; Elizabeth Balbachevsky and Simon Schwartzman (2010), "The Graduate Foundations of Research in Brazil," *Higher Education Forum*, 7: 85–101.

5. Simon Schwartzman 1991.

6. James Mahoney (2006), "Analyzing Path Dependence: Lessons from the Social Sciences," in *Understanding Change* (New York: Springer): 129–39.

7. Helena Sampaio (2000), *Ensino superior no Brasil: O setor privado*, 1st ed. (São Paulo: Hucitec/Fapesp).

8. Andrés Bernasconi (2016), "Autonomía y formas de gobierno universitario," in *Asuntos de gobierno universitario* (Bogotá: Editorial Pontificia Universidad Javeriana): 130–43.

9. Neves 2017.

10. Stephen Kosack (2012), *The Education of Nations: How the Political Organization of the Poor, Not Democracy, Led Governments to Invest in Mass Education*, 1st ed. (Oxford: Oxford University Press). A vital constituency corresponds to "citizens on whom the government depends for power" (36).

11. Dietmar Braun (2003), "Lasting Tensions in Research Policy-Making—a Delegation Problem," *Science and Public Policy* 30(5): 309–21.

12. Helena Sampaio (2011), "O setor privado de ensino superior no Brasil: Continuidades e transformações," *Revista Ensino Superior Unicamp* 4: 28–43.

13. Carlos Benedito Martins (2013), "Reconfiguring Higher Education in Brazil: The Participation of Private Institutions," *Análise Social* 48(208): 622–58.

14. HOPER/Infográficos" (n.d.), accessed July 23, 2020, https://www.hoper .com.br/infograficos.

15. Neves 2017.

16. Zenilde Nunes Batista (2019), "Políticas para a extensão universitária e sua implementação na UFG: 2006 a 2016" (PhD diss., Federal University of São Carlos, São Carlos, SP, Brazil).

17. Bárbara Regina Vieira Lopes (2019), "Do pioneirismo desacompanhado ao consenso multipartidário: O que os bastidores da negociação da 'lei de inovação' (2002–2004), na transição PSDB-PT, revelavam sobre o jogo político em voga no setor de C&T&I?" (PhD diss., University of São Paulo, São Paulo).

18. FONAPRACE/ANDIFES (2016), "*IV pesquisa do perfil sócio-econômico e cultural dos estudantes de graduação das instituições federais de ensino superior—2014*," http:// www.andifes.org.br/wp-content/uploads/2017/11/Pesquisa-de-Perfil-dos-Graduanso -das-IFES_2014.pdf.

19. Lopes 2019.

20. Júnior Almeida, Vicente de Paula, and Pedro Antônio Estrella Pedrosa (2018), "Fundo de Financiamento Estudantil (FIES): Vicissitudes e desafios,"

Radar—Tecnologia, Producao e Comercio Exterior, Institute of Applied Economic Research.

21. Ronaldo de Almeida (2019), "Bolsonaro presidente: Conservadorismo, evangelismo e a crise Brasileira," *Novos Estudos CEBRA* 38(1): 185–213.

22. André Scantimburgo (2018), "O desmonte da agenda ambiental no governo Bolsonaro," *Perspectivas: Revista de Ciências Sociais* 52: 103–17.

23. Maria Helena de Magalhães Castro and Soraya Smaili (2019), "Os cortes no Ministério da Educação television," *Entre aspas*, https://globosatplay.globo.com/globonews/entre-aspas/.

24. "Maioria das universidades federais rejeita o Future-se, plano do MEC" (2019), *Exame*, September 26, https://exame.com/brasil/maioria-das-universidades-federais-rejeita-o-future-se-plano-do-mec/.

25. John N. Campbell and Ove K Pedersen (2014), *The National Origins of Policy Ideas: Knowledge Regimes in the United States, France, Germany and Denmark*, 1st ed. (Princeton, NJ: Princeton University Press).

José Augusto Guilhon Albuquerque holds a doctorate in sociology from the Université Catholique de Louvain and a habilitation in political science from the University of São Paulo, Brazil, where he is professor of political science, retired. He is currently a Senior Research Fellow with the USP's Research Center for International Relations. He held visiting professorships at Georgetown University, Université Catholique de Louvain, Universidad Central de Venezuela, and the Rio Branco Chair at Chatham House. His research focuses on Brazilian domestic and foreign politics. At the University of São Paulo, he founded the Department of Political Science and served as chief of staff of the rector. He also served as chief of staff of the state of São Paulo Department of Planning and as special advisor to the federal minister of planning, to the Speaker of the state of São Paulo Assembly, and to the governor of the state of São Paulo. He published and edited numerous books and several dozen scholarly articles in English, Spanish, French, German, and Portuguese. He has been awarded the Marcus Garvey Research Award (Organization of American States), the National Order of Scientific Honor (Brazilian government), National Order of Defense (Brazilian government), the Order of Ipiranga (state of São Paulo), and the Order of Rio Branco (Brazilian Foreign Ministry).

Elizabeth Balbachevsky is associate professor at the Department of Political Science at the University of São Paulo, Brazil, and director, Center for Public Policy Research at the Institute for the Advanced of Studies (NUPPs/IEA-USP). Since 2013, she is also an invited lecturer at the Erasmus Mundus Master's in Research and Innovation in Higher Education (MARIHE) at the Tampere University (TUNI), Finland. She was the Brazilian Ministry of Education's general coordinator for policies supporting higher education internationalization between 2016 and 2017, a Fulbright New Century Scholar for 2005-6, an Erasmus Mundus Scholar at the European Master's in Higher Education Programme (2009). She is also the editor for Latin America of the new Springer's Encyclopedia of International Higher Education Systems and Institutions.

Thomas Brunotte is CEO of the Hochschullehrerbund (German association of professors of applied sciences). Until December 2020 he served as an executive assistant to the secretary-general of the Volkswagen Foundation and from 2008 to 2015 as a program manager for various funding initiatives. After finishing a *Studium generale* at the Leibniz Kolleg in Tübingen, Brunotte studied philosophy in Munich, Oxford, Paris, and Göttingen. He finished his doctoral thesis on Aristotle's metaphysics and philosophy of nature in 2009. In 2018 he completed an extra-occupational MBA program, education and science management, at the University of Oldenburg with a thesis on the autonomy of universities are governed by independent foundations (Maecenata Institut, Berlin, Opusculum 110).

Igor Chirikov is senior researcher and the director of the Student Experience in the Research University (SERU) Consortium at the Center for Studies in Higher Education, University of California, Berkeley. His research involves student experience and learning outcomes, international comparative higher education (focusing on Russia and China), and organizational change in higher education. His papers have been published in *Science Advances*, *PNAS*, *Studies in Higher Education*, *Assessment and Evaluation in Higher Education*, *Post-Soviet Affairs*, and other journals. His most recent coedited book *International Status Anxiety and Higher Education: Soviet Legacy in China and Russia* (Springer, 2018) explores how the Soviet model of higher education and global competition impacts higher education systems in China and Russia.

John Aubrey Douglass is senior research fellow and research professor in public policy and higher education at the Center for Studies in Higher Education (CSHE) at the University of California, Berkeley. His research focuses on globalization and higher education, the role of universities in economic development and socioeconomic mobility, and the history of higher education. He is the author of *The New Flagship University: Changing the Paradigm from Global Ranking to National Relevancy* (Palgrave Macmillan, 2016) and the follow-up book *Envisioning the Asian New Flagship University* (Berkeley Public Policy Press, 2017), *The Conditions for Admissions* (Stanford University Press, 2007), *The California Idea and American Higher Education* (Stanford University Press, 2000), and with Jud King and Irwin Feller (eds.) *Globalization's Muse: Universities and Higher Education Systems in a Changing World* (Public Policy Press, 2009). Among the research projects he founded is the Student Experience in the Research University (SERU) Consortium—a group of major research universities in the United States and internationally that conduct survey research on undergraduates and graduate students. He is also the founding editor of the Center's Research and Occasional Paper Series (ROPS).

Igor Fedyukin is director of the Center for Russian Imperial History at the National Research University Higher School of Economics in Moscow. He received his PhD in history from the University North Carolina at Chapel Hill and was a Diderot Fellow and a directeur d'études associés at Fondation Maison de science de l'homme in Paris, a visiting fellow at the Woodrow Wilson International Center for Scholars (Washington, DC), and a Prokhorov Foundation Fellow at the University of Sheffield. His works have appeared in *Theory and Society*, *Slavic Review*, *Russian Review*, *Kritika*, *Journal of Social History*, and *Journal of Interdisciplinary History*, among others, and his monograph *The Enterprisers: The Politics of School in Early Modern Russia* was published by Oxford University Press in 2019. In 2012–13 he was the vice minister of education and science of the Russian Federation.

Karin Fischer is a journalist who focuses on higher education and a research associate with the Center for Studies in Higher Education at the University of California, Berkeley. Her primary area of focus is international education, including American colleges' activities overseas, study abroad, the globalization of the college experience, and international student recruitment, acculturation, and employability. She also writes about higher education public policy in the States and about the relationship between colleges and the economy. Her work has appeared in the *New York Times*, the *Chronicle of Higher Education*, *Washington Monthly*, and *University World News*. A graduate of Smith College, she received the East-West Center's Jefferson Fellowship for reporting in Asia and the International Reporting Project fellowship for work on education and gender, also in Asia. Her work has been honored by the Education Writers Association, the National Press Foundation, and the Poynter Institute.

Wilhelm Krull is the founding director of The New Institute and was secretary-general of the Volkswagen Foundation from 1996 to 2019. After studies in German, philosophy, education, and political science, he held an appointment as a DAAD lecturer at the University of Oxford as well as leading positions at the Wissenschaftsrat (German Council of Science and Humanities) and at the headquarters of the Max-Planck-Gesellschaft (Max Planck Society). Besides his professional activities in science policy as well as in the promotion and funding of research, he was and still is a member of numerous national, foreign, and international committees. At present he is the chairman of the board of the Foundation Georg-August-Universität Göttingen, a member of the Scientific Advisory Commission of the state of Lower Saxony and of the Board of Regents of several Max Planck Institutes. His latest book, *Die vermessene Universität* (Passagen, 2017), deals with the impact of ratings and rankings on the development of European universities.

Brendan O'Malley is chairman of Higher Education Web Publishing, publisher and managing editor of *University World News*. As a consultant for international organizations including UNESCO he has specialized for many years in research into political and military violence against education students, staff, and institutions. He was author of the first two global studies on this issue, *Education under Attack* (UNESCO, 2007) and *Education under Attack 2010* (UNESCO), and lead author of the third such study, *Education under Attack 2014* (GCPEA). He has addressed many international conferences on both this issue and international relations related to UK and US foreign policy and the eastern Mediterranean. He is author of *The Cyprus Conspiracy: America, Espionage and the Turkish Invasion* (IB Taurus, 1999), which was shortlisted for the Orwell Prize and was a Guardian Book of the Year. He is a member of the nonpartisan all-party Parliamentary Group Friends of Cyprus, which seeks a peaceful settlement of the Cyprus problem.

Bryan E. Penprase is dean of faculty at Soka University of America, where he is developing new initiatives in global liberal arts, as well as a new interdisciplinary life sciences concentration, and has been working on a variety of topics in global higher education and STEM education both as an academic leader and as a researcher in astrophysics. Prior to coming to Soka University of America, he was a founding faculty member of the Yale-National University of Singapore, where he served as the inaugural director of the Yale-NUS Centre for Teaching and Learning. In 2012–13 he served at Yale University as an American Council on Education (ACE) Fellow, where he was one of the authors of the blueprint for the Yale-NUS College curriculum and advised Yale president Peter Salovey on topics ranging from online learning, math education at Yale, and Teaching and Learning Centers. Dr. Penprase was a professor for 20 years at Pomona College, where he served as chair of physics and astronomy and worked on several projects related to online learning and international liberal arts. Dr. Penprase received his BS in physics and an MS in applied physics from Stanford University and a PhD from the University of Chicago in astronomy and astrophysics, with a postdoctoral fellowship at Caltech, before beginning his career as a professor and academic leader.

Marijk van der Wende is Distinguished Faculty Professor of Higher Education at Utrecht University's Faculty of Law, Economics and Governance. Her research focuses on the impact of globalization and internationalization on higher education systems, institutions, curricula, and teaching and learning arrangements. She is also affiliate faculty and research associate at the Center for Studies in Higher Education (CSHE) at the University of California, Berkeley; guest professor at Shanghai Jiao Tong University; and member of the International Advisory Board of its Graduate School of Education. She is a member of the Academy of Europe and has been a chair and member of numerous national and international advisory committees and editorial boards. Previously she has held full professorial positions at Center for Higher Education Policy Studies (CHEPS), University of Twente; Vrije Universiteit Amsterdam; and visiting scholar at Harvard University (Fairbank Center for Chinese Studies and Graduate School of Education), Shanghai Jiao Tong University (Center for World-Class Universities and Graduate School of Education), University of California, Berkeley (CSHE), and Boston College (Centre for International Higher Education). She served as dean of graduate studies at Utrecht University, founding dean of Amsterdam University College, president of the program on Institutional Management in Higher Education (IMHE) of the Organisation for Economic Co-operation and Development (OECD), member of the Higher Education Authority Ireland, the Scientific Board of the Dutch Military Academy, and a range of other boards and advisory bodies.

Dalai Lama, 83, 189, 190, 194

defense. *See* military and defense

Deferred Action for Childhood Arrivals (DACA), 27, 62, 76–77

demographic changes, as characteristic of neo-nationalism, vii, 17–18

demonstrations and protests: and China, xiv, 29, 34, 40, 160, 165, 190–91; in France, 39; in Hong Kong, xiii, xiv, 24, 29–30, 34, 203, 205–8, 209, 218; in Hungary, 134, 163; in Russia, 237; in Turkey, 141, 143–44, 147–48, 155–56, 158; in US, 27, 40, 63, 69–72, 89–90

Deng Xiaoping, 166–69, 205

Denmark, 118, 124–25, 128–29

detentions: in Brazil, 251; in China, xiii, 32, 162, 164, 166, 169, 173, 180; in Hong Kong, 205–8, 209; increase in, viii, 23; and spectrum of neo-nationalism, 31–32; in Turkey, xiii, 28, 124, 133, 141, 148, 149–50, 152–56

Dirks, Nicholas, 70

Document No. 9, 29, 171–73

Double World-Class Project, 197–98

Duke University, 168, 187, 212

economic development: and China, 163, 197; as leadership variable, 35, 37, 38; role of universities in, 5, 65–66; and US, 65–66

economic pressures: as accelerator of neo-nationalism, vii, 17–18, 93–94; in Europe, 93–94; as leadership variable, 40; and left-wing neo-nationalism, 20; and rise of nationalism, 2, 3–4, 41; and rise of Trump, 61–62; in Turkey, 142–43, 159

educated citizenry, 4, 6, 35, 37, 38

education policy: in Brazil, 27–28, 241–47, 249–56; in China, early, 162–66; in China, under Deng, 166–69; in China, under Xi, 29, 32–33, 83–84, 171–82, 186–87, 197–98; in China and soft power, 192–96; in Germany, 107, 112–13; in Hong Kong, 203–4, 205, 208–10, 217–19; in Hungary, 28, 33, 98, 101–4, 107, 124; and nation building, 2, 4, 9, 11–12; in Poland, 105–8; in Russia, 28–29, 222–33, 235–36; in Singapore, 210–15, 218–19; in Turkey, 28, 133, 148, 152–59; in UK, 7, 51–55, 57; in US, 27, 62–65, 72–76, 89–90

elitism, 10, 15, 23, 40, 93–94, 242

emotional factors, 96–97, 100–101

environmental policy: in Brazil, 248; and China, 197; and Trump, 65, 74, 85–87. *See also* climate change

Erasmus+ program: and academic freedom, 135; and Brexit, 43, 44, 48–49, 55, 56–58; and COVID-19, 125; and EU identity, 138; and public attitudes, 123, 130; and refugees, 137; role of, 47, 126–27; and Switzerland, 125

Erdoğan, Recep Tayyip: consolidation of power, 28, 30, 141–43, 146–51, 157–59; education policy, 28, 147, 152–59; and Gezi Park protests, 141, 143–44, 147–48, 155–56, 158; and Putin, 220

espionage, 63, 78, 79, 80–83, 189, 190, 198–200

ethnosymbolism, 2–3

Eucor–The European Campus, 109

Europe: European identity, 49, 108, 119–20, 124, 138; leaders *vs.* followers in, 135–40; network of universities in, 109–11; rise of nationalism in, ix, 92–98, 108–17. *See also* European Union

European Federation of Academies of Sciences and Humanities (ALLEA), 139

European Higher Education Area (EHEA), 25, 47–48, 109, 117, 123

European Innovation Council, 55

European Qualifications Passport for Refugees, 137

European Research Area (ERA), 117, 123

European Research Council (ERC), 53, 54

European Union: Article 7, 124; Article 13, 134; attitudes toward, 44, 45, 46, 49, 118–23, 124, 139; and Central European University, 33, 103, 124, 133, 134–35; and COVID-19, 122–23; elections, 119, 121–22, 138; and Russia, 220–21; and Turkish firings, 133. *See also* Brexit; Erasmus+ program; Horizon 2020

European Universities Initiative, 47

European University Alliance 4EU, 109

European University Association (EUA), 133–34, 137

expertise, disdain for, xiv, 44, 45, 59, 63–65. *See also* anti-intellectualism; science, denial of

137; and Hungary, 85, 95, 101, 124; and Netherlands, 130–31; and Singapore, 204, 213; skills-based, 56, 130; and Switzerland, 125; and Trump, 27, 61, 62, 63, 76–79, 90; and Turkey, 157; and UK, ix, 45, 47, 50, 56, 94, 121; and US, ix, 27, 61, 62, 63, 65, 68, 76–79, 90. *See also* refugee crisis

income and revenue: from branch campuses, 82; and COVID-19, 25, 90; from international students, 7, 48, 55, 57, 78–79, 137, 185, 189; in Russia, 222

India, 16, 22

Indonesia, 41, 195

institutional autonomy. *See* autonomy, institutional

institutional forbearance, 97–98

intellectual property: espionage, 63, 78, 79, 80–83, 189, 190, 198–200; management in Brazil, 249–50; and spectrum of neo-nationalism, 31

international collaboration: advantages of, 47–48, 110; and Brexit, viii, 44, 45, 47–48, 53, 111, 139; as case study factor, xi; and China, 182–87, 196–99; and COVID-19, xi, xv–xvi, 25, 36, 91, 125, 140, 254–55; and espionage, 199–200; European network proposal, 109–11; and Germany, 111; and illiberal democracies, 20–21; as leadership variable, 36, 38; in Netherlands, 130; and rankings, 7; and Russia, 233–36; and Singapore, 204; and spectrum of neo-nationalism, 31

International Covenant on Civil and Political Rights, 154

international faculty: in China, 179; in Germany, 99–100; as leadership variable, 36; and local engagement, 59–60; in Netherlands, 126; in Russia, 236; in Singapore, 211–12, 218–19; in Turkey, 157; in UK, 48, 55–56; in US, 64, 78–79, 199–200. *See also* talent mobility

International Human Rights Network of Academies and Scholarly Societies, 150

international students: in Australia, 7, 30, 195–96; as case study factor, xi; from China, 30, 78–79, 84, 167, 168, 185, 187–92, 199–200, 203, 208, 209, 212–13, 217; in China, ix, 7, 195–96, 200; and COVID-19, 57–58, 64, 200, 238; in Denmark, 118,

124–25, 128–29; financial aid for, 7, 128–29, 209, 211–12, 213, 231, 232; from Germany, 129–30; in Germany, 99–100; in Hong Kong, 203, 208, 209, 217; in Japan, 7; as leadership variable, xiv–xv, 36; and local engagement, 59–60; in Netherlands, 118, 124–30; and rankings, 235; revenue from, 7, 48, 55, 57, 78–79, 137, 185, 189; from Russia, 230, 233; in Russia, ix, 224, 230–32, 233, 238; from Saudi Arabia, 189; in Singapore, 204, 211–13, 218–19; in South Korea, 7; and spectrum of neo-nationalism, 31; in Switzerland, 125; from Turkey, 231; in Turkey, 157; from UK, 130; in UK, viii, ix, xiii, 7, 43, 48–49, 55, 56–58, 123–24, 125–26; in US, ix, 30, 64, 78–79, 185, 187, 199–200. *See also* talent mobility

Ireland, 137

Islam: and Erdoğan, 142, 148, 158; Islamism as threat in Turkey, 144, 146; Muslim ban in US, ix–x, 76, 77. *See also* Uighurs

jailing. *See* detentions

Japan, 7, 195

Johnson, Boris, 44, 45, 46, 52, 53, 55, 56–57, 58

Journal of Chinese Political Science, 172

judiciary, control of, 34, 104–5, 152

Kavala, Osman, 155–56

key performance indicators (KPIs), 214–15

knowledge production. *See* learning and knowledge production

Krupa, Matthias, 110

Kurds, 141, 142, 143, 144, 145, 149–51, 152

Lam, Carrie, 206

land grants and land-grant universities, 5, 14, 66

Laos, 195

leaders *vs.* followers: in Brazil, 255–56; in Europe, 135–40; in Hong Kong, 203; overview of, xiv–xvi, 34–42; as query, viii, xii; in Turkey, 159; variables in, xiv–xv, 35–38

learning and knowledge production, xi, 4–6, 15, 16

Le Pen, Marine, 18

LexisNexis, 172

LGBT studies, 104, 107, 227, 237
Lin Jianhua, 175
loans, student, 73, 89, 244, 246, 252
Lovász, László, 104
Lula da Silva, Luiz Inácio, 239, 243–45

Macron, Emmanuel, 94–95, 109, 138, 267n9
Magna Charta Universitatum, 132–33
Malaysia, 195, 196
management controls. *See* autonomy, institutional
Mao Zedong, 4, 163–64, 173
Marie Sklodowska-Curie Actions, 53
May, Theresa, 52
McCarthyism, 67–68
McMaster University, 190–91, 192
media: and Berkeley protests, 69, 70–71; and Brexit, 44, 46, 49–50; bypassing of, 17; in Europe, 96; increase in control of, 17, 31, 34; in Singapore, 216–17, 219; in Turkey, 144. *See also* fake news; social media
Merkel, Angela, 117, 122, 137
Mexico, 16
military and defense: in China, 163; role of universities in, xiv, 5, 7; and Trump, 85–86; in Turkey, 144–45, 146, 147, 151–52; in US, 61, 66, 68, 85–86
Moro, Sérgio, 248
Morrill Land-Grant College Act of 1862, 5, 13–14
Moscow State University, 224–25
movement, freedom of, 47, 119–21, 123, 124, 126–27, 139
Müller-Steinhagen, Hans, 99–100
Muslim travel ban, ix–x, 76, 77
mutual toleration, 97–98

Nanyang Technical University, 212, 213, 214, 215
Napoleon, 11–12
NASA (National Aeronautics and Space Administration), 68, 85
National Institutes of Health (NIH), 27, 62, 73, 74, 75, 76, 81, 87
nationalism: as concept, 1–4; diversity of forms, 1–4; and national identity, 2; and nation building, 2, 4–8; *vs.* neo-nationalism, 17; peripheral nationalism, 203. *See also* neo-nationalism

nationalist-leaning governments, 26–27, 31–34, 41
National Security Law (Hong Kong), 24, 203–4, 218, 258n1
National University of Singapore, 197, 212, 213, 214–16
nation building: in Brazil, 16; in China, 15–16, 161–62, 166–69; in France, 11–12; in Germany, 3, 9–11; historical examples, 8–16; and nationalism, 2, 4–8; postcolonial nations, 16; and public education, 2; role of universities in, viii–ix, 4–9, 23; by US, 5, 12–14
nativism, 18, 22, 61, 65, 67
neoliberalism, 105, 107, 220, 223
neo-nationalism: accelerators of, vii, 17–18, 93–94; characteristics of, vii, 17; conceptual model, 22–25, 31–34; defined, vii; diversity of causes, 23; diversity of forms, ix, 41; as fluid, x, xii, 41; *vs.* nationalism, 17; political determinist effect, 23–25; spectrum of, 25–32, 41; as term, 118. *See also* nationalism
Netherlands, 26, 94, 118–19, 124–31
New York University, 168, 187
985 Project, 198

Observatory Magna Charta, 132–33
Occupy protests, 209
One Belt One Road. *See* Belt and Road Initiative
online learning, xi, 25, 245, 253–54
Open Society Foundation (OSF), 102, 156, 234, 237
Orbán, Viktor: education policy, 28, 33, 98, 101–4, 107, 124; on illiberal democracy, 19; on immigration, 95; and Putin, 220

Paris Agreement, 74, 86
partisan bias, 95
passports, xiii, 28, 153, 155
Patriotic Education Campaign, 165–66
PEGIDA, 99–100
Peking University: control of, 173, 175, 186; firings, 169, 179, 181, 184; founding of, 15; and Hundred Flowers Campaign, 163–64; rankings, 198; and Xi Jinping Thought, 174
peripheral nationalism, 203